GETTING TO
DAYTON

GETTING TO DAYTON

The Making of America's Bosnia Policy

IVO H. DAALDER

BROOKINGS INSTITUTION PRESS
Washington, D.C.

Library of Congress Cataloging-in-Publication data
Daalder, Ivo H.
    Getting to Dayton : the making of America's Bosnia policy / Ivo H.
Daalder.
        p. cm.
    Includes bibliographical references and index.
    ISBN 0-8157-1692-3 (alk. paper) — ISBN 0-8157-1691-5 (pbk. : alk.
paper)
    1. United States—Foreign relations—Bosnia and Hercegovina. 2.
Bosnia and Hercegovina—Foreign relations—United States. 3. United
States—Foreign relations—1993—Decision making—Case studies. 4.
Dayton Peace Accords (1995) 5. Yugoslav War, 1991–1995—Bosnia and
Hercegovina. 6. Yugoslav War, 1991–1995—Peace. I. Title.
    E183.8.B67 D33 2000   99-050468
    949.703—dc21   CIP

                    9 8 7 6 5 4 3 2 1

The paper used in this publication meets minimum requirements of the
American National Standard for Information Sciences—Permanence of
Paper for Printed Library Materials: ANSI Z39.48-1984.

Typeset in Sabon

Composition by Cynthia Stock
Silver Spring, Maryland

Maps by Parrot Graphics
Stillwater, Minnesota

Printed by R. R. Donnelley and Sons
Harrisonburg, Virginia

ℬ THE BROOKINGS INSTITUTION

The Brookings Institution is an independent organization devoted to nonpartisan research, education, and publication in economics, government, foreign policy, and the social sciences generally. Its principal purposes are to aid in the development of sound public policies and to promote public understanding of issues of national importance.

The Institution was founded on December 8, 1927, to merge the activities of the Institute for Government Research, founded in 1916, the Institute of Economics, founded in 1922, and the Robert Brookings Graduate School of Economics and Government, founded in 1924.

The general administration of the Institution is the responsibility of a Board of Trustees charged with safeguarding the independence of the staff and fostering the most favorable conditions for scientific research and publication. The immediate direction of the policies, program, and staff is vested in the president, assisted by an advisory committee of the officers and staff.

In publishing a study, the Institution presents it as a competent treatment of a subject worthy of public consideration. The interpretations or conclusions in such publications are those of the author or authors and do not necessarily reflect the views of the other staff members, officers, or trustees of the Brookings Institution.

To Marc and Michael

Foreword

THE WARS THAT RESULTED from the breakup of Yugoslavia occupied a central place in American foreign policy during the 1990s. Of these, none was more heart wrenching and challenging to American and allied policymakers than the three-and-a-half years of war in Bosnia. For much of that period, American policy was characterized by an extreme reluctance to get too deeply involved. The Bush and Clinton administrations alike feared getting drawn into what many senior officials viewed as a likely quagmire. Yet, by 1995, it was no longer possible to ignore developments on the ground. The humanitarian toll—from the bombing of Dubrovnik and Vukovar in 1991 to the ethnic slaughter in Bosnia that culminated in the horrifying massacre in Srebrenica in 1995—had become too large; the impact of the Balkan conflict on NATO's credibility and even its continued viability had become too great. Developments in the former Yugoslavia threatened stability throughout southeastern Europe. U.S. disengagement was no longer a viable option. The only remaining question was how, not whether, the United States would get involved.

Ivo H. Daalder's book recounts how the Clinton administration came to abandon a policy of containment in favor of engagement. This is not an effort to reexamine what happened on the ground in Bosnia or how the international community sought to mitigate, ameliorate, and ultimately overcome a humanitarian nightmare. Others, including other Brookings scholars, have already done so admirably. Rather, Daalder's focus is the policy debate and process in Washington, and how events in Bosnia affected the internal deliberations among the top officials in the Clinton administration. The battles he describes take place in the White House situation room, not in the mountains, valleys, and villages of Bosnia. It is a quintessential Washington tale of how people in power maneuver to get their way by exploiting opportunities, meeting challenges, and forging policy consensus. This is a book about Washington at work at a time when Bosnia was at war.

Daalder is uniquely placed to recount these developments. For much of the period he describes, Daalder served on the staff of the National Security Council (NSC), where his responsibility included helping to coordinate U.S. policy during the implementation of the Dayton Peace Accords. This experience is supplemented by interviews with many of the important players during this critical period. Those interviewed on a not-for-attribution basis include (titles indicate positions held in 1995): Peter Bass (executive assistant to Anthony Lake), Thomas Donilon (chief of staff to Warren Christopher), John Feeley (director for European affairs, NSC), Peter Galbraith (U.S. ambassador to Croatia), Robert Gallucci (special adviser to the president and secretary of state for Bosnian peace implementation), Philip Goldberg (Bosnia desk officer, Department of State), General George Joulwan (Supreme Allied Commander Europe), Anthony Lake (assistant to the president for national security affairs), Douglas Lute (Bosnia branch chief, European Affairs Division, J-5, Joint Chiefs of Staff), John Menzies (U.S. ambassador to Bosnia-Herzegovina), Major General William Nash (commander, First Armored Division, U.S. Army), James O'Brien (adviser to the U.S. ambassador to the United Nations), James Pardew (director, Balkan Task Force, Department of Defense), James Rubin (communications director to the U.S. ambassador to the United Nations), David Scheffer (senior adviser to the U.S. ambassador to the United Nations), General John Shalikashvili (chairman of the Joint Chiefs of Staff), Walter Slocombe (undersecretary of policy, Department of Defense), Alexander Vershbow (senior director for European affairs, NSC), and others who did not wish to be identified.

Daalder is grateful for the significant assistance many of his students, colleagues, and friends have provided in support of his research and writing. Valuable research assistance was provided by Laura Hall, Russell Harrison, Micah Zenko, and, especially, Michael Fooks, who helped draft a version of chapter two. Karla Nieting provided indispensable assistance not only with research, but also in editing the manuscript for clarity and concision and in writing the chronology. Daalder would also like to thank Susan Jackson, Mohammed Sulaiman, and Bridget Alway for their verification of the manuscript. Robert Art, Derek Chollet, Hans Daalder, Mac Destler, Jim Goldgeier, Richard Haass, Jane Sharp, and Leon Sigal read the entire manuscript, some more than once, and provided invaluable comments. The staff at the National Security Council reviewed the entire manuscript and cleared it for publication without requiring any changes.

At the Brookings Institution Press, Nancy Morrison copyedited the manuscript, while Carlotta Ribar proofread and Mary Mortensen indexed the pages.

Much of this book was researched and written when Daalder was associated with the University of Maryland's Center for International and Security Studies. His research benefited greatly from an International Affairs Fellowship by the Council on Foreign Relations, enabling him to join the NSC staff. Additional financial support was provided by a grant from the Foreign Ministry of Sweden when Daalder was still associated with the University of Maryland. The German Marshall Fund of the United States and the John M. Olin Foundation also provided important support for the book once Daalder joined us here at Brookings.

The views expressed here are those of the author and should not be ascribed to any of the persons whose assistance is acknowledged above, or to the trustees, officers, or other staff members of the Brookings Institution.

MICHAEL H. ARMACOST
President

Washington, D.C.
December 1999

Contents

Chronology of Key Events

Date	Events Elsewhere	Events in Washington
1994 **December** 7		President Bill Clinton agrees in principle to supply 20,000–25,000 U.S. troops to assist in possible withdrawal of UN Protection Force (UNPROFOR) from Bosnia
1995 **January** —	UN, NATO agree UN Security Council must ask for and NATO Council must approve a NATO withdrawal of UNPROFOR	
1	Four-month cease-fire goes into effect	
4		Senator Robert Dole introduces bill to lift arms embargo if Bosnia asks or when cease-fire expires
February —	UN asks NATO to plan for possible UNPROFOR withdrawal	Administration begins Bosnia policy review, focuses negotiating efforts on Serbian president Slobodan Milosevic

Date	Events Elsewhere	Events in Washington
14	The Contact Group of the United States, key European allies, and Russia agrees to revise sanctions if Milosevic recognizes Bosnian and Croatian borders, accepts peace plan, and ends aid to Serb rebels	
20	Milosevic refuses to recognize Bosnian or Croatian borders	
March		
12	Croatian president Franjo Tudjman agrees to continued UN presence in Croatia	
16		National Security Council (NSC) paper offers post-UNPROFOR withdrawal options; principals agree status quo is best option
April		
30	Cease-fire expires; fighting quickly erupts in Bosnia	
May		
7	Sarajevo shelling kills eleven; UN resists retaliation	National Security Adviser Anthony Lake orders another policy review focused on post-UNPROFOR
12	UN Secretary General orders "fundamental review" of UNPROFOR	
15		Administration proposes suspending some sanctions in return for Serb recognition of Bosnia, closure of Serb-Bosnian border
16	Contact Group offers modified sanctions proposal to Milosevic	
19		Principals discuss UNPROFOR options, NATO's OPLAN 40104

Date	Events Elsewhere	Events in Washington
22	Serbs seize artillery in Sarajevo weapons exclusion zone	
23		Principals agree if UNPROFOR withdraws, United States will lift arms embargo, arm and train Bosnians, but not conduct air strikes
24	NATO launches limited air strikes	
25	Serbs threaten peacekeepers, shell Tuzla, killing seventy-one	
26	NATO attacks ammunition sites; UN peacekeepers taken hostage	
27	UN Security Council fails to back more NATO air strikes	Clinton and French president Jacques Chirac discuss creation of a Rapid Reaction Force (RRF)
28		Principals agree on air strikes suspension; discuss OPLAN 40104, help for UNPROFOR withdrawal and/or redeployment
29		Clinton agrees United States will help redeploy allied forces if necessary and if Congress agrees
29–30	Contact Group meets in The Hague, approves RRF proposal	
31		Clinton's speech explains commitment to help UN troops in Bosnia
June		
2		Clinton briefed on and approves OPLAN 40104 outline
3	NATO approves RRF proposal	Clinton says United States will send ground troops only if UN withdrawal requires aid, emergency extraction is necessary, or there is peace

Date	Events Elsewhere	Events in Washington
8		U.S. House of representatives approves amendment to lift arms embargo if Bosnian government asks
9	UN says UNPROFOR will return to "traditional peace-keeping principles"; Carl Bildt becomes Balkans negotiator	U.S. Senate draft resolution says United States should lift arms embargo and use troops to help UNPROFOR withdraw
14	NATO considers but does not endorse OPLAN 40104	
16	UNSC endorses RRF creation; Group of Seven meets in Halifax	Clinton says United States will lift arms embargo if UNPROFOR goes, offers support for RRF
20		Clinton approves OPLAN 40104 preparations
21		Clinton, advisers discuss RRF, long-term strategy; memo by U.S. Ambassador to the United Nations Madeleine Albright memo argues for U.S. lead on air strikes
24		NSC staff meets to develop endgame strategy
July		
—	RRF deploys to Bosnia	Secretary of State Warren Christopher sends "night note" to Clinton urging new diplo-matic initiative, caution on OPLAN 40104
6–16	Assault on Srebrenica kills almost 8,000	
13	Chirac demands action or admit defeat, proposes taking stand in Gorazde	Administration considers near- and medium-term strategy
14	British call for conference in London	Principals discuss Chirac pro-posal; Clinton tells Great Britain of U.S. support for air campaign
16	Assault on Zepa begins	Chairman of the Joint Chiefs of Staff, General John Shalikashvili, tells allies air strikes necessary

Date	*Events Elsewhere*	*Events in Washington*
17		Principals meet to discuss endgame strategy
18		Administration decides air power needed; Chirac agrees after call from Clinton
21	London conference agreement to defend Gorazde with air campaign	
22	Tudjman and Bosnian President Alija Izetbegovic agree to defend Bihac	Clinton supports Croat-Bosnian agreement
23	Croatian forces enter Bosnia	
25	NATO approves London conference plan	
26		Senate votes to end arms embargo
August		
1	NATO approves planning for deterring attacks on safe areas	House votes to end arms embargo
2	NATO says it will use air power to protect remaining safe areas	
4	Croatia's Operation Storm to liberate Krajina begins	
7		Clinton, advisers review long-term strategy papers
8		Clinton agrees to endgame strategy
9		Lake leaves for Europe
10	NATO/UN agree on circumstances for air strikes and targets	Senators Dole and Helms introduce bill to give Bosnia military aid, create coalition to provide arms
11		Clinton vetoes bill to end arms embargo
14		Lake concludes European trip; Assistant Secretary of State Richard Holbrooke becomes lead Balkan negotiator

Date	Events Elsewhere	Events in Washington
19	Three U.S. negotiators killed in accident in Mount Igman near Sarajevo	
25–26	Patriarch Paper makes Milosevic chief Serb negotiator	
27		Holbrooke declares there will be consequences if peace initiative stalls
28	Serbs shell Sarajevo marketplace	
30	NATO's Operation Deliberate Force begins	
September		
1	NATO suspends air strikes	
2	NATO gives Serbs forty-eight hours to comply with demands	
5	NATO bombing resumes	
8	Bosnian, Croatian, Yugoslav foreign ministers sign basic principles agreement on Bosnia	
9	Croatian forces enter Bosnia	
13		Holbrooke arrives in Belgrade
14	Operation Deliberate Force suspended	
19	Croatian offensive ends	Holbrooke announces Tudjman and Izetbegovic will not attack Banja Luka
20	NATO/UN declare Serbs in compliance with heavy weapons withdrawal from Sarajevo	
25		Clinton, principals discuss Holbrooke's progress, agree next step is "proximity talks"
26	Bosnian, Croatian, Yugoslav ministers meeting in New York agree to "Further Agreed Principles" for Bosnian peace	

Date	Events Elsewhere	Events in Washington
October		
5	Cease-fire is announced	
10	Cease-fire goes into effect	
11	NATO approves Implementation Force (IFOR) operation plan	
17		Clinton gives IFOR one-year deadline
23	Clinton and Russian President Boris Yeltsin agree on Russia's role in IFOR	
25–27		Principals meet to determine IFOR mission, mandate
November		
1	Dayton proximity talks begin	
21	Dayton Accords initialed	
December		
14	Dayton Accords signed	
29–30	IFOR enters Bosnia	

Note: Dates are from Office of the Historian, *The United States and the Breakup of Yugoslavia, 1980–1995* (Bureau of Public Affairs, Department of State, 1996); "Key Meetings/Event Chronology" (White House Background Briefing Paper, August 1995); and interview with a senior administration official, March 1, 1999, relying on contemporaneous notes.

Introduction

THE VIOLENCE SPAWNED by the breakup of Yugoslavia posed the first major
post–cold war test for the United States and its European allies. It is a test
they failed miserably, as did the international organizations they used to
respond to the violence. Yugoslavia was allowed to disintegrate into five
separate entities, all but one of which emerged violently. Conflict was
brief and relatively minor in Slovenia in June 1991, partly because its
desire for independence from Yugoslavia was supported by an ethnically
homogeneous population and because so few Serbs lived there. War did
break out in Croatia and then in Bosnia, killing and maiming hundreds of
thousands of people and displacing millions. While Macedonia escaped
violence, its path to independence was tortured as a result of Greece's
refusal to accept the legitimacy of "Macedonia" as the new country's name.
Finally, though it was not until 1998 that war erupted in what remained
of Yugoslavia (Serbia and Montenegro), the explosion in Kosovo was long
expected and no less bloody.

From the onset of violence in early 1991, the major Western powers
appealed to European institutions and the United Nations to deal with the
problem created by the disintegration of this multi-ethnic state in the heart
of southern Europe. Lulled by the supposed peace that a post–cold war
Europe represented, these regional and global institutions sought to prove
their relevance and credibility in the new world order. The Conference
(later Organization) on Security and Cooperation in Europe was the first
to fail—thwarted by its requirement for unanimous agreement among all
its members to take the action needed to prevent or halt the violence that

I

flared. The European Community eagerly entered the fray, first negotiating an agreement to end the violence in Slovenia but then demonstrating its inability to formulate a coherent response in Croatia. The United Nations secured a fragile peace in Croatia and deployed more than 10,000 peacekeepers under its auspices to supervise the truce. However, the UN refused to act preventively in Bosnia, which soon erupted in a violent convulsion of its own. Many more thousands of UN peacekeepers were sent to Bosnia to try to mitigate the worst humanitarian consequences of the war. They, in turn, were supported by NATO, which had pledged to conduct air strikes in defense of the peacekeepers as well as six isolated "safe areas" inhabited by a debilitated Muslim population. The conflict between the United Nations and NATO over when and to what extent to use force effectively nullified NATO's possible deterrent effect and threatened the credibility of history's most successful and strongest military alliance.

The collective failure of these regional and international institutions to deal with Yugoslavia's disintegration was due to many factors, including institutional incompetence and overconfidence. But at bottom, it was a failure of the major powers, which used the institutions in an attempt to obfuscate their own unwillingness to employ the right combination of diplomacy and force to end the fighting. In the end, it was a failure of the United States, first in deferring to the Europeans while failing to back them up, and then in trying to intervene with half-measures designed more to limit risks than to have an impact on the ground.

Numerous explanations for these collective, European, and U.S. failures have been provided by others in detailed analyses of the tepid international responses to the breakup of Yugoslavia.[1] The purpose here is not to retrace this well-trodden ground. Rather, the focus is on the U.S. decision in the summer of 1995 to break the deadlock that had prevented collective action by taking responsibility for halting the worst violence spawned by the breakup of Yugoslavia, namely the war in Bosnia. After four years of standing on the sidelines, watching as many thousands died

---

1. Among the many excellent analyses, consult especially Steven L. Burg and Paul S. Shoup, *The War in Bosnia-Herzegovina: Ethnic Conflict and International Intervention* (Armonk, N.Y.: M. E. Sharpe, 1999); Mark Danner's series of articles in the *New York Review of Books* that appeared in 1997–98; James Gow, *Triumph of the Lack of Will: International Diplomacy and the Yugoslav War* (Columbia University Press, 1997); Laura Silber and Allan Little, *Yugoslavia: Death of a Nation* (New York: TV Books, distributed by Penguin USA, 1996); and Susan L. Woodward, *Balkan Tragedy: Chaos and Dissolution after the Cold War* (Brookings, 1995).

and millions were displaced, why did Washington reverse course? Why in August 1995 and not earlier? And why decide to engage as Washington ultimately did—combining a push for a negotiated settlement that would concede the Bosnian Serbs more than they would have gotten under earlier peace proposals with a military track aimed at establishing a military balance that would for the first time provide the Bosnian Muslims with a capacity to defend themselves?

What follows is an attempt to answer these questions, to recount how the policy shift—and its ultimate success—came about. It is a story that until now has not been fully told.[2] It aims to shed light on the process by which the policy was made, the calculations underlying it, and its subsequent implementation. The focus is on Washington: on the corridors of power where memos are written and read; meetings are convened; deals are cut; decisions are made and ignored; bureaucratic games are played; and egos are confirmed and broken. The concern is not with Bosnia, the rights and wrongs of particular sides in the war or its possible resolution, or with the allies or NATO and their contribution to ending the war. The aim is, instead, more limited: to tell the tale of how U.S. policy on Bosnia shifted suddenly and dramatically, and ultimately achieved what none who had valiantly tried had been able to accomplish before. It is, above all, a story of people—public servants—working against great odds to do what they believed to be the right thing.

The story of the making of America's Bosnia policy is told in four parts. Chapter 1 sets the stage for the shift in U.S. policy by recounting how Western policy toward Bosnia had evolved until 1995, including Europe's lead in the initial Western response and the Clinton administration's early promises to become more engaged in Bosnia than the Bush administration. Chapter 2 reviews how the contradictions in U.S. and western policy toward Bosnia became too evident to be ignored and how the pressure for change became irresistible. This second chapter focuses on the failure of the UN mission after repeated attacks by the Bosnian Serbs on UN-declared safe areas; the absence of a credible NATO response; the prospect of deploying U.S. and other NATO forces to assist the UN in withdrawing

---

2. One of the main participants in this story, Richard Holbrooke, has written extensively on his role, recounting the shuttle diplomacy he led from mid-August until October 1995 as well as the actual negotiations at Dayton in November. See Richard Holbrooke, *To End a War* (Random House, 1998). However, there is much about the U.S. decision to change course, especially regarding policy formulation in Washington, that is not included in Holbrooke's detailed account of his crucial negotiating role.

its forces to more tenable positions (if not depart from Bosnia completely); and the U.S. and NATO response to the Bosnian Serb takeover of the eastern enclaves—including the unspeakable horrors in and around Srebrenica. Chapter 3 turns to the policy review conducted in the middle of 1995, primarily by the National Security Council (NSC) staff, and the development of the "endgame strategy," the strategy paper that would form the basis of U.S. policy from August 1995 onward. Chapter 4 examines how we got to the peace agreement ending Europe's most bloody war since World War II that was negotiated during twenty-one tiring and trying days at a U.S. air force base in Dayton, Ohio. Instead of repeating the detailed account in Richard Holbrooke's masterful narrative of the negotiations, the focus here is on the key decisions—made in Washington—that would have a profound impact on the implementation of the peace agreement.

The final chapter attempts to draw lessons for U.S. foreign policy. A detailed examination of how America's Bosnia policy was made yields important lessons for those making and analyzing policy alike—including the critical role of the national security adviser and his staff in molding the decisionmaking process, if not implementation. The ultimate success of the policy shift on Bosnia that resulted from this process also has important implications for U.S. policy toward Bosnia, the use of force, and Europe more broadly. Having secured an end to the war in Bosnia, the United States will remain involved there for many years to come. The question is not whether it will stay, but what to do while there. Bosnia also has consequences for how the Clinton administration and others viewed the relationship between force and diplomacy, confirming for many the belief that the carefully wielded threat of force can support diplomatic efforts. Finally, the resolution of the Bosnia issue has opened the way for the administration's ambitious policy of achieving a Europe that is undivided, peaceful, and democratic. Once the war ended, progress was rapid on many fronts. New members have joined old in a transformed NATO now dedicated to extending stability and security throughout Europe. And allied NATO troops were deployed far beyond their territory in an effort to safeguard and enforce a precarious peace in other parts of the continent. As the twentieth century comes to an end, the dream of a Europe both whole and free that emerged in the wake of the cold war finally seemed to have come within reach.

CHAPTER ONE

"The Problem from Hell"

WHEN THE CLINTON ADMINISTRATION came to office in January 1993, it inherited a U.S.—indeed Western—Bosnia policy that was in complete disarray. The previous year had been witness to the most brutal war in Europe since 1945. It was a war marked by concentration camps, massive expulsions of Muslims and Croats from their homes in a self-described Serb campaign of "ethnic cleansing," widespread incidents of rape, and the unrelenting shelling of cities, including the capital, Sarajevo—together accounting for the deaths of tens of thousands of people, mostly civilians, and well over a million refugees. The Western response to these atrocities had been to condemn Serb actions and impose a total economic embargo on Serbia and Montenegro to force an end to their involvement in the Bosnian war, to deploy a UN peacekeeping force to protect humanitarian relief supplies being transported to affected communities, and to scurry around to find a diplomatic solution acceptable to the warring sides.

By the time the new administration took office, these international efforts were producing limited results. The embargo succeeded in devastating the economies of Serbia and Montenegro, although not in ending Belgrade's support for Bosnian and Croatian Serbs. A United Nations Protection Force (UNPROFOR) of nearly 9,000 troops was deployed in February 1993 to protect the relief effort, which reached millions of people and prevented an even worse humanitarian disaster. And the diplomatic effort had produced an intricate plan, dividing Bosnia into ten ethnic majority provinces. Conspicuously lacking, however, was U.S. engagement in—let alone leadership of—the international effort in Bosnia. Having rejected the use of U.S. (and NATO) military muscle for any purpose in Bosnia, the Bush administration had effectively deferred the design and implementation of Western policy to the Europeans.[1] The Europeans, in turn, had eagerly seized the policy reins—even declaring at the outset that this was "the hour of Europe"[2]—only soon to realize that the break-up of Yugoslavia represented too large a challenge for them to resolve on their own.[3]

Presidential candidate Bill Clinton had campaigned vociferously in support of greater U.S. engagement in Bosnia. As the first press reports of Bosnian concentration camps appeared in late July,[4] the Clinton campaign released a statement in support of air strikes to deter attacks against relief agencies and urged appropriate U.S. military support to the effort.[5] Weeks later, candidate Clinton went further, suggesting the need to lift the arms embargo against the Bosnian Muslims, an embargo that had been instituted against Yugoslavia as a whole prior to its formal political disintegra-

1. For an overview of the Bush administration's policy toward the former Yugoslavia, including Bosnia, see James A. Baker III, *The Politics of Diplomacy: Revolution, War, and Peace, 1989–1992* (G. P. Putnam's Sons, 1995), pp. 634–51; Mark Danner, "The U.S. and the Yugoslav Catastrophe," *New York Review of Books*, vol. 44 (November 20, 1997), pp. 56–64; Mark Danner, "America and the Bosnia Genocide," *New York Review of Books*, vol. 44 (December 4, 1997), pp. 55–65; David C. Gompert, "The United States and Yugoslavia's Wars," in Richard H. Ullman, *The World and Yugoslavia's Wars* (New York: Council on Foreign Relations Press, 1996), pp. 122–44; and Warren Zimmermann, *Origins of a Catastrophe: Yugoslavia and Its Destroyers—America's Last Ambassador Tells What Happened and Why* (Times Books, 1996).

2. Cited in Alan Riding, "Europeans Send High-Level Team," *New York Times*, June 29, 1991, p. 4.

3. For an overview of these efforts, consult especially Henry Wijnaendts, *L'Engrenage; Chroniques Yougoslaves, Juillet 1991–Août 1992* (Paris: Denoël, 1993); James Steinberg, "Yugoslavia," in Lori Fisler Damrosch, ed., *Enforcing Restraint: Collective Intervention in Internal Conflicts* (New York: Council on Foreign Relations Press, 1993), pp. 27–76; James E. Goodby, "Peacekeeping in the New Europe," *The Washington Quarterly*, vol. 15 (Spring 1992); Marc Weller, "The International Response to the Dissolution of the Socialist Federal Republic of Yugoslavia," *The American Journal of International Law*, vol. 86 (1992); and John Newhouse, "The Diplomatic Round: Dodging the Problem," *The New Yorker*, vol. 68 (August 24, 1992), pp. 60–71.

4. See Roy Gutman, "Prisoners of Serbia's War; Tales of Hunger, Torture at Camp in North Bosnia," *Newsday*, July 19, 1992, p. 7.

5. "Statement by Governor Bill Clinton on the Crisis in Bosnia," July 26, 1992; and E. J. Dionne Jr. and others, "Clinton Turns Sights to Foreign Policy," *Washington Post*, July 29, 1992, p. A1.

tion.[6] Operating in a campaign atmosphere free of the responsibilities of governing, Clinton and his foreign policy advisers had urged a course that would up the ante of U.S. involvement in the Balkans once the new administration took office.

Once in power, however, the Clinton administration failed to back its forceful campaign rhetoric with concrete action. Like his predecessor, President Clinton proved unwilling either to put Bosnia center stage in his foreign policy or to commit the type of military capabilities that would be necessary to bring the conflict to a halt. That left the administration with the option of trying to persuade its allies—notably Great Britain and France, which had substantial numbers of troops on the ground to protect the humanitarian effort—to endorse forceful military action. As was to be expected, the allies consistently rejected any effort that would either escalate the fighting (as lifting the arms embargo surely would) or increase the risk to their troops (as one-sided air strikes threatened to do). Instead, the allies predicated their endorsement of the use of force—notably air power—on the United States accepting equivalent risks by deploying American forces alongside European troops. This, the Clinton administration consistently refused.

For two years the Clinton administration tried various ways to escape the dilemma created by this situation. In the process, relations with key allied countries significantly deteriorated. By late 1994, differences over how to respond to a Bosnian Serb assault on the UN-declared "safe area" around the northwestern Bosnian city of Bihac reached crisis proportions. While the United States insisted that the defense of this area required large-scale air strikes, London and Paris warned that they would pull out their troops from Bosnia altogether if Washington insisted on bombing Serb forces. In the face of a transatlantic crisis on a par with the one the Atlantic alliance had last witnessed over the Suez Canal in 1956 and fearing that NATO itself could be torn asunder by disagreement over Bosnia, the administration switched course. It opted for a policy of containment, designed to ensure that developments inside Bosnia would not spread beyond that unfortunate country's borders. Like its predecessor, moreover, the Clinton administration once again acceded to allied policy preferences. The push for bombing was shelved, the preferred European diplomatic framework of working through Belgrade to get a resolution of the conflict

6. See Michael Kelly, "Surrender and Blame," *The New Yorker*, vol. 70 (December 19, 1994), p. 47.

in Bosnia was endorsed, and the de facto (though not de jure) partition of Bosnia between Bosnian Muslims and Croats on the one hand and Bosnian Serbs on the other was accepted as a reality. To those in the administration who had fought consistently for a more activist policy (including the use of significant force), acceptance of European policy preferences represented a bitter defeat, leaving some (such as Madeleine K. Albright, U.S. ambassador to the United Nations) dejected and others (including National Security Adviser W. Anthony [Tony] Lake) contemplating resignation. In the end, they stayed on, only to lead the effort to forge a new U.S. policy direction—one that ultimately would end the war. That success, however, would be built on more than two bitter years of failure.

Presidential Review Directive

One of President Clinton's first official acts was to ask his national security team to review U.S. policy toward the Balkans. This, the first in a series of presidential review directives (PRDs) directing a reassessment of U.S. foreign policy, called for "a comprehensive, wall-to-wall approach" toward evaluating the situation in Bosnia.[7] Reflecting previous campaign rhetoric, PRD-1 asked a series of probing questions of the State and Defense Departments and the Central Intelligence Agency in order to stimulate serious consideration of more activist U.S. policy options, including those that had long been rejected by the Bush administration. Among the options to be considered were:

—Using air power to enforce the "no-fly zone" over Bosnia that the UN had declared in October 1992;

—Engaging in air strikes against Serb artillery positions and airfields;

—Altering the UN arms embargo to allow the Bosnian Muslims to obtain more weapons;

—Establishing UN peacekeeping operations in Macedonia and Kosovo to prevent the further spread of conflict in the region; and

—Creating an international war crimes commission to investigate reports of atrocities.[8]

Clinton's senior foreign policy advisers formally met for the first time as the Principals Committee (PC) on January 28, 1993, to review the ini-

---

7. John M. Goshko and Don Oberdorfer, "U.S. to Study Wider Options on Balkans," *Washington Post*, January 28, 1993, p. A16.

8. Ibid.

tial results of the presidential review. Attending this and subsequent PC meetings were National Security Adviser Anthony Lake, who chaired the meetings, Secretary of State Warren Christopher, Secretary of Defense Les Aspin, U.S. Ambassador to the United Nations Madeleine Albright, Director of Central Intelligence R. James Woolsey, and Chairman of the Joint Chiefs of Staff General Colin Powell, the only holdover from the previous administration. As was to become a pattern for PC meetings on Bosnia in the months to come, many issues were raised, discussed, and debated during this first meeting, but little was decided.[9] Upon emerging from the meeting, Secretary Christopher told reporters that "a very wide range of options" was under consideration, suggesting no decisions were near.[10]

At the end of the third PC meeting on Bosnia on February 5, Lake invited President Clinton and Vice President Al Gore to join their senior advisers. Clinton made clear that the United States had to lead. "If the United States doesn't act in situations like this, nothing will happen." As if to underscore the point, Clinton stressed that a "failure to do so would be to give up American leadership."[11] To provide that leadership, Clinton agreed that the United States would:

—Support efforts to find a political solution by working closely with key allies, particularly with Russia, and appointing a special U.S. envoy to participate in negotiations;

—Reject imposing a settlement that was not voluntarily accepted by all parties;

—Contribute directly to humanitarian relief efforts by taking additional measures to facilitate the delivery of aid (such as air-dropping food from U.S. military transport aircraft);

—Enforce the no-fly zone as an effort to forestall further bloodshed;

—Tighten sanctions on Serbia, repeat the Bush administration warning against disruptive action in Kosovo, and strengthen the international presence in Macedonia to discourage the further spread of conflict; and

9. A somewhat disbelieving Colin Powell, who as President Reagan's last national security adviser had chaired his share of similar meetings, later commented that "discussions continued to meander like graduate-student bull sessions or the think-tank seminars in which many of my new colleagues had spent the last twelve years while their party was out of power." Colin L. Powell, with Joseph E. Persico, *My American Journey* (Random House, 1995), p. 576.

10. Don Oberdorfer, "U.S. Reviews Deteriorating Situation in the Balkans," *Washington Post*, January 29, 1993, p. A19.

11. Cited in Elizabeth Drew, *On the Edge: The Clinton Presidency* (Simon and Schuster, 1994), p. 146.

—Offer U.S. troops to help implement and enforce a peace agreement that was acceptable to all parties. [12]

The results of the policy review, which were made public by Secretary Christopher on February 10, were notable in two respects.[13] First, there was a noticeable mismatch between the rhetoric of the policy announcement and its content. Christopher's rhetoric was strong: "Bold tyrants and fearful minorities are watching to see whether 'ethnic cleansing' is a policy the world will tolerate. . . . [Our] answer must be a resounding no." [14] Yet there was no mention of the kind of military measures the Clinton campaign had championed just months earlier. To the consternation of some but the contentment of others (notably the European allies, who greeted the new policy with a heavy sigh of relief),[15] neither air strikes nor the lifting of the arms embargo was mentioned. Instead, Christopher emphasized the limits of America's engagement: under no circumstances short of a comprehensive peace settlement that was voluntarily accepted by all the parties would U.S. ground troops be deployed to Bosnia.

Second, although the administration did not say so openly, the new policy conveyed a notable reluctance to support the diplomatic approach then on the table. Known as the Vance-Owen Peace Plan—after the UN and EU mediators, Cyrus Vance and David Owen—this plan sought to balance the competing desires for ethnic autonomy and Bosnia's territorial unity by dividing Bosnia on a geographic and ethnic basis into ten semi-autonomous districts.[16] In the days leading up to Christopher's announcement, the new administration had been highly critical of the plan,

---

12. "New Steps toward Conflict Resolution in the Former Yugoslavia," Opening statement by the secretary of state at a news conference, February 10, 1993. Reprinted in *Dispatch*, vol. 4 (February 15, 1993), p. 81.

13. See also Mark Danner, "Clinton, the UN and the Bosnian Disaster," *New York Review of Books*, vol. 44 (December 18, 1997), p. 68.

14. "New Steps toward Conflict Resolution." In his memoirs, Christopher admitted, "this rhetoric proved to be well ahead of our policy." Warren Christopher, *In the Stream of History: Shaping Foreign Policy in the New Era* (Stanford University Press, 1998), p. 345.

15. John Darnton, "Europe Welcomes U.S. Policy, Especially the Arms," *New York Times*, February 12, 1993, p. A10.

16. For a detailed description of the plan, see David Owen, *Balkan Odyssey* (Harcourt, Brace and Company, 1995) pp. 89–149. See also James Gow, *Triumph of the Lack of Will: International Diplomacy and the Yugoslav War* (Columbia University Press, 1997), pp. 232–48 and 307–15; and Steven L. Burg and Paul S. Shoup, *The War in Bosnia-Herzegovina: Ethnic Conflict and International Intervention* (Armonk, N.Y.: M. E. Sharpe, 1999), pp. 189–262.

believing it to be both a reward for ethnic cleansing and largely unenforceable. Indeed, on the very day the administration entered office, the State Department spokesman remarked that the incoming secretary of state had "expressed doubts about whether it can realistically be achieved, whether they can, in fact, find an agreement."[17] This sentiment was reinforced in early February when Christopher met with Vance and Owen in New York. While appreciative of the two negotiators' efforts, Christopher noted his particular concern over the "feasibility, practicality, and enforceability" of the plan.[18] Even President Clinton weighed in, describing the plan as "flawed" and making clear that the United States would not pressure the Muslims into accepting an agreement they would be unwilling to live by on their own.[19]

Yet despite this evident lack of enthusiasm for the Vance-Owen plan and notwithstanding considerable doubts about its enforceability, the Clinton administration was reluctant to oppose it altogether. In part, this reflected the fact that the European Union foreign ministers had put the administration in a bind by unequivocally backing it on February 1. In making this announcement, which was arrived at without any prior consultation with Washington, the EU underscored that U.S. rejection of the diplomatic approach would place responsibility for the failure of the peace talks squarely on Washington.[20] Thus instead of sponsoring new talks between the parties or formulating a new version of the peace plan, the administration decided to throw its weight behind the peace process. Reginald Bartholomew, a senior and seasoned diplomat, was assigned to assist Vance and Owen in modifying the proposal to better address Muslim concerns. For now, at least, Vance-Owen was the only game in town.

Lift and Strike

Throughout February and March 1993, all international efforts focused on getting Bosnian President Alija Izetbegovic to sign on to the Vance-

17. See Elaine Sciolino, "Christopher Leery of Bosnia Accord," *New York Times,* January 22, 1993, p. A1.

18. Elaine Sciolino, "U.S. Declines to Back Peace Plan as the Balkan Talks Shift to UN," *New York Times,* February 2, 1993, p. A9.

19. Gwen Ifill, "Clinton and Mulroney Fault Balkan Peace Plan," *New York Times,* February 6, 1993, p. 3; and Thomas Friedman, "U.S. Will Not Push Muslims to Accept Bosnia Peace Plan," *New York Times,* February 4, 1993, p. A1.

20. John Newhouse, "No Exit, No Entrance," *The New Yorker,* vol. 69 (June 23, 1993), p. 46.

Owen plan. The strategy was to get the Bosnian Muslims and Croats on board, and then pressure the Bosnian Serbs, with the hope that the Serbs' growing international isolation would force them into accepting the plan. By mid-March however, it was clear that this strategy would not work without additional forms of pressure. Whereas the Muslims appeared to be ready to accept Vance-Owen as a result of U.S. pressure, the Serbs continued to stonewall any peace effort and remained intent on achieving their objectives through the use of force. On March 18, the Bosnian Serbs launched an assault on the predominantly Muslim enclave of Srebrenica; the resulting carnage was shown on televisions around the globe courtesy of CNN. As the events taking place in Srebrenica came into focus and negotiations dragged on, there was growing concern in the United States that the opportunity for reaching a political agreement was slipping away. For many in the administration—especially Al Gore, Tony Lake, and Madeleine Albright—something new was needed if they hoped to bring the Serbs to the table.

On March 25, Lake called a Principals Committee meeting to discuss the situation in Srebrenica and urge his colleagues to come up with new ideas.[21] The Muslims and Croats had just that day signed the Vance-Owen plan. Lake was looking for ways to end the Serb offensive and persuade the Bosnian Serbs—who were headquartered just outside of Sarajevo in the ski resort of Pale, site of the 1984 Olympic ski competitions—to sign the peace agreement. Two options quickly emerged. One was to increase military pressure against the Bosnian Serbs—by lifting the arms embargo, by using U.S. and NATO air strikes, or by a combination of both. The other was to try to get a cease-fire in place and to offer some form of protection for Muslim enclaves, like Srebrenica, that were under Bosnian Serb assault.

Neither option was without its problems. The cease-fire option, strongly favored by Aspin and the rest of the Pentagon, offered a way to get Bosnia out of the headlines and the issue off the president's desk, but at the cost of accepting what Clinton had opposed during the campaign and what most in the administration would view as a moral calamity at best and a strategic defeat at worst. The option to increase military pressure also was problematic. For one, the allies had rejected any entreaties to use force, which would increase the risk to their own troops that were deployed in Bosnia

21. This and subsequent meetings are described in detail in Drew, *On the Edge*, pp. 148–56. See also Newhouse, "No Exit, No Entrance," pp. 46–50.

as part of the UN operation protecting humanitarian relief efforts. Since Clinton rejected a unilateral U.S. military intervention for fear that Bosnia would then become an American responsibility, the allied position was crucial. For another, there were questions about the effectiveness of each option. It was possible that lifting the arms embargo would provoke a massive Serb offensive that might devastate the Muslims before they had a chance to rearm. Meanwhile, the military and intelligence assessments of what air power alone could achieve were far from optimistic. There would be few lucrative targets after the initial bombing run. And while the air force (including its chief of staff) believed that air power alone could bring the Bosnian Serbs to their knees, others in the U.S. military (including Joint Chiefs of Staff chair General Powell and NATO supreme commander General John Shalikashvili, who would soon succeed Powell) strongly argued that substantial ground forces would be necessary to exploit the opening provided by air strikes.[22]

Throughout April, the principals met several times with and without the president to discuss the pros and cons of these options, but nothing was decided.[23] The administration was divided internally, with Gore and Albright strongly favoring air strikes against the Bosnian Serbs (and Albright arguing the United States should do so unilaterally if necessary); Aspin supporting at most limited protection of the Muslim enclaves; and Lake and Christopher championing a lifting of the arms embargo against the Bosnian government and limited air strikes during the transition period.[24] In the absence of a consensus among his advisers—or even majority support for a single option—Clinton deferred a final decision on what to do. As one high-level official noted, the delay was a "bad sign" and the end-

---

22. See Drew, *On the Edge*, pp. 149, 154; Daniel Williams, "White House Defers Action on Balkans for Several Days," *Washington Post*, April 21, 1993, p. A26; Elaine Sciolino, "U.S. Military Split on Using Air Power against the Serbs," *New York Times*, April 29, 1993, pp. A1, A6; and Carroll Doherty, "Voices of Restraint Grow Louder amid Cries for Military Action," *Congressional Quarterly*, May 1, 1993, p. 1094.

23. Several multilateral steps were taken in an attempt to obtain Bosnian Serb cooperation, including NATO's decision on April 12 to begin enforcing the no-fly zone; the designation of Srebrenica as a "safe area" by the UN Security Council, a status that would later be extended to five other Muslim enclaves; and approval by the Security Council of a sanctions package that threatened to isolate Belgrade completely if the Pale Serbs had not signed the Vance-Owen plan by April 26.

24. Drew, *On the Edge*, pp. 149–55. For Albright's views, see also Michael R. Gordon, "12 in State Dept. Ask Military Move against the Serbs," *New York Times*, April 23, 1993, pp. A1, A12.

less meetings had little to do with policymaking. "It was group therapy—an existential debate over what is the role of America, etc."[25]

At the same time, pressure mounted on the administration to do something. By the middle of April, the Serb assault threatened to topple Srebrenica. Influential members in Congress, such as Senator Joseph Biden (D-Del.), were becoming more vocal, calling for direct military action against the Serbs.[26] And on April 23, a letter to Secretary Christopher signed by several State Department Balkan specialists calling on the administration to intervene militarily was leaked to the *New York Times*.[27] The administration responded with heightened rhetoric, and a policy shift appeared imminent. Already in a televised interview in late March, Clinton had hinted at the possibility of lifting the arms embargo if the Bosnian Serbs did not sign on to Vance-Owen, a position reinforced by Clinton and other administration officials in the days that followed.[28] As the situation in Srebrenica deteriorated, the president's rhetoric went further. At a press conference on April 16, Clinton noted that "At this point, I would not rule out any option except the option I have never ruled in, which was the question of American ground troops." When asked whether the time had come to convince the Europeans to lift the arms embargo and conduct air strikes, Clinton responded, "I think the time has come for the United States and Europe to look very honestly at where we are and what our options are and what the consequences of various courses of action will be. And I think we have to consider things which at least previously have been unacceptable."[29]

It would take another two weeks for Clinton to make up his mind, even though lengthy principals' meetings over the weekend of April 17–18 had narrowed the options to two. The first, "lift and strike," was to lift the arms embargo and threaten air strikes if the Bosnian Serbs tried to take

---

25. Quoted in Drew, *On the Edge*, p. 150.

26. Elaine Sciolino, "In Congress, Urgent Calls for Action against Serbs," *New York Times*, April 20, 1993, p. A9.

27. Gordon, "12 in State Dept. Ask Military Move against the Serbs."

28. See Steven A. Holmes, "U.S. Presses Serbs by Hinting at End of Arms Embargo on Bosnia," *New York Times*, March 26, 1993, p. A13; and John Goshko and Daniel Williams, "U.S. to Urge Serbs to Sign Bosnia Pact; Clinton Promises 'Full-Court Press,'" *Washington Post*, March 27, 1993, p. A13.

29. "Remarks by the President and [Japanese] Prime Minister [Kiichi] Miyazawa in Joint Press Availability" (White House, Office of the Press Secretary, April 16, 1993).

advantage of their fleeting military superiority. The second option consisted of a cease-fire and protection of Muslim enclaves.[30] The president finally committed to making a decision on May 1, when he met with his chief advisers for five hours. All options (except U.S. ground troops) were once again debated. In the end, Clinton opted for lift and strike, the option that by then had the support of all his senior advisers with the exception of Aspin, who continued to favor a cease-fire and protection of Muslim enclaves. Even Powell supported lift and strike, believing that once armed and trained, Muslim forces on the ground would improve the effectiveness of air power.

The president and his foreign policy team opted for lift and strike notwithstanding indications from the Europeans suggesting that they would resist any proposal to lift the arms embargo.[31] They surmised that with the public outrage accompanying the assault on Srebrenica and the refusal by the Bosnian Serbs to accept Vance-Owen before the UN-mandated deadline of April 26, attitudes among the allies might change enough to permit a more aggressive policy. But everyone knew it would be a hard sell. The president assigned Christopher the unenviable task of talking to the allies, telling him, "You've been a great lawyer and advocate all these years—now you've really got your work cut out for you."[32]

Christopher departed the night of May 1 for London, Paris, Moscow, Brussels, Bonn, and Rome. His assignment was to sound out allied support for lift and strike, but he was not to negotiate over the policy or pressure them into going along. As Christopher recalls, "we decided not to frame the president's plan as a fait accompli. My instructions were to take a more conciliatory approach, laying the proposal before our allies, describing it as the only complete option on the table, and asking for their support."[33] Thus at each stop, Christopher began his presentation by providing an overview of how the administration had arrived at its decision, including the options that had been considered (a large-scale air campaign, lifting the arms embargo, air strikes in defense of Muslim enclaves, and lift and strike). He would note that there were "no good options" for dealing with Bosnia, but that lift and strike was the "least worst" among

---

30. Drew, *On the Edge*, p. 151.
31. See Roger Cohen, "U.S. and Allies Differ on Arms for Bosnia Muslims," *New York Times*, April 22, 1993, p. A15; and William Drozdiak, "European Allies Hurry Up and Wait on Action in Bosnia," *Washington Post*, April 27, 1993, p. A12.
32. Quoted in Drew, *On the Edge*, p. 156.
33. Christopher, *In the Stream of History*, p. 346.

them.[34] The tone of the secretary of state's presentation reflected the long internal discussions and bore the unmistakable imprint of General Powell, notably in denigrating the effectiveness of air power and other limited forms of military force. Christopher stressed that lift and strike could not change the course of the war; its aim was the more limited one of convincing the Serbs to sign Vance-Owen.[35]

Christopher's presentation was hardly convincing. The Bosnian Serbs had taken much of the wind out of Christopher's sails by announcing just as his plane landed in London that they would sign the Vance-Owen plan on the condition that the Bosnian Serb parliament and people would agree. Although everyone realized that this announcement was a tactical ploy (as became clear when the plan was in effect rejected in a referendum on May 15–16), it provided the allies an excuse to hold off supporting, if not rejecting, the U.S. proposal.[36] Christopher's nuanced, lawyerly presentation constituted a highly unusual way for a U.S. secretary of state to make a major policy presentation. Normally, these presentations, while couched in the language of consultation, are direct and to the point: "American policy is X, and we thank you for your support." Christopher's self-described "conciliatory approach"—consisting of talking points that, at least in Whitehall, started with the phrase, "I am here in a listening mode"— differed so completely from the prevailing norm that the allies could not believe that the administration was serious.[37] Indeed, London and Paris were as distraught over the fact that the Clinton administration was not really willing to take the promised lead of the West's Bosnia policy as they were over Washington's decision to propose a course of action they had explicitly and repeatedly rejected.[38]

34. Interview with a senior administration official, October 21, 1997.

35. Interview with a senior administration official, October 21, 1997. See also Drew, *On the Edge*, pp. 155–57; and Newhouse, "No Exit, No Entrance," p. 49.

36. On the impact of the Bosnian Serb announcement, see Sidney Blumenthal, "Lonesome Hawk," *New Yorker*, vol. 69 (May 31, 1993), p. 39.

37. Quotation in Martin Walker, *The President We Deserve: His Rise, Falls, and Comebacks* (Crown Publishers, 1996), p. 265.

38. In Brussels, NATO Secretary General Manfred Wörner, a forceful advocate of NATO military intervention in Bosnia, had arisen from his sickbed to lend his strong support to Christopher. Wörner suggested that Christopher go first and make his pitch for lift and strike to the NATO ambassadors and that he would then back him up before anyone else had a chance to say something. Christopher rejected the suggestion, saying, "I prefer to have my bilateral meetings first." Cited in Walker, *The President We Deserve*, p. 265. See also William Safire, "Who's Got Clout?" *New York Times Magazine*, June 20, 1993, p. 34.

Of course, the allies were right. Washington was not ready to push the issue to its logical conclusion for fear that Bosnia would then become America's problem. As one top policymaker confided, "The basic strategy was, This thing is a no-winner, it's going to be a quagmire. Let's not make it our quagmire. That's what lift the arms embargo, and the limited air strikes, was about."[39] Moreover, even while Christopher was traveling around Europe, it became clear that the president himself had reservations. One reason was Clinton's fear that pushing the issue now would undermine his support for the reform policies of Russian president Boris Yeltsin, who warned Clinton privately that he could not countenance military action against the Serbs so long as the peace process was still ongoing.[40] Another reason was Clinton's sense that lift and strike might not do the job and might in fact risk a new American quagmire. A key moment came after a White House photo-op with U.S. troops returning from Somalia. Clinton pulled Aspin and Powell aside to tell them about a book he had been reading by Robert D. Kaplan called *Balkan Ghosts: A Journey through History*, which detailed the region's history of violent ethnic conflict. Aspin was astonished. "Holy shit! He's going south on lift and strike," he thought. After returning to the Pentagon, Aspin called Lake and Undersecretary of State for Political Affairs Peter Tarnoff to warn them. "Guys, he's going south on this policy. His heart isn't in it. . . . We have a serious problem here. We're out there pushing a policy that the President's not comfortable with."[41] Clinton's apparent second thoughts may also have been influenced by a *Wall Street Journal* article on "How to Think about Bosnia," by Arthur Schlesinger Jr., published on May 3. In it, Schlesinger warned the president that, like Lyndon Johnson and Vietnam, intervention in the Balkans could undermine his domestic policy.[42]

Upon returning to Washington, Christopher immediately went to the White House to brief the president on his trip. He was blunt about what it would take to rescue the lift and strike policy, reporting that the allies "will only be persuaded by the raw power approach. . . . That is, we have to tell them that we have firmly decided to go ahead with our preferred

39. Quoted in Drew, *On the Edge*, p. 155.
40. Walker, *The President We Deserve*, p. 267. At the time, U.S.-Russia relations topped the administration's foreign policy agenda and there was widespread agreement within the administration that any policy toward Bosnia would have to be supportive of, or at least not undermine, relations with Moscow.
41. Drew, *On the Edge*, p. 157.
42. See Drew, *On the Edge*, p. 158; Walker, *The President We Deserve*, p. 266.

option and that we expect them to support us."[43] No one, not even the most vociferous supporters of air strikes, spoke up in favor of the "raw power approach." Pressuring the Europeans to support lift and strike risked a major confrontation with the allies and would make the United States solely responsible for Bosnia. Said one official, "If we'd bet the ranch, said to the French and English, 'This threatens a fundamental breach in our relationships,' we could perhaps have got the Europeans—kicking and screaming—involved. But this would have made it an American problem. We would have taken over."[44] No one in the administration, least of all the president, was prepared to take full responsibility for the conflict given that the costs of doing so would involve spending political capital and other resources that Clinton needed to further the domestic policy agenda on which he was elected. Hence while Clinton would remark as late as May 14 that lift and strike was "still on the table,"[45] it was clear that this policy was effectively dead.

Once internal support for lift and strike had dissipated, containment of the Bosnian conflict rather than intervention to resolve it became the name of the game. As Christopher, who had worked especially hard to get Bosnia off the front pages of the newspapers, later recalled, "although lift and strike remained formally on the table, attention turned to how we could keep the conflict from spreading and deal with the humanitarian problems it had created."[46]

In what would become a pattern in the administration's approach to Bosnia in these early years, the failure of a U.S. policy initiative was soon followed by Washington adopting the approach favored by the Europeans. In this case, the new policy consisted of defending six Muslim enclaves that the UN on May 6 had declared "safe areas." There was much wrangling among the allies over how to defend the enclaves. The Europeans called on the United States and Russia to provide troops to protect the areas, a call Washington firmly rebuffed—with Clinton emphasizing that he would not send U.S. troops into "a shooting gallery."[47]

---

43. Christopher, *In the Stream of History*, pp. 346–47.

44. Cited in Drew, *On the Edge*, p. 156.

45. "Press Conference by the President" (White House, Office of the Press Secretary, May 14, 1993).

46. Christopher, *In the Stream of History*, p. 347.

47. "Remarks by the President in a Photo Opportunity with the Cabinet" (White House, Office of the Press Secretary, May 21, 1993).

Agreement on a new policy direction was finally reached on May 22. Under an arrangement known as the Joint Action Plan, the United States, Russia, Spain, Britain, and France agreed to:[48]

—Protect the six "safe areas" with force, if necessary (with the United States committed only to provide air support);

—Establish an international war crimes tribunal;

—Place monitors on the Serbian border to ensure Belgrade was honoring the international embargo of the Bosnian Serbs; and

—Increase the international presence in Kosovo and Macedonia to help contain the conflict.

There was no mention of lifting the arms embargo or of air strikes. The focus had shifted from intervention to containment.

Enter NATO: Air Strikes and "Safe Areas"

While the Joint Action Plan managed to paper over the differences between the United States and its allies, it did little to calm the situation in Bosnia. By early July 1993, reports of Serb shelling and the deteriorating humanitarian situation were again making headlines. The situation in and around Sarajevo was particularly bad, as Serb artillery shells rained down from the surrounding mountains preventing international relief supplies from getting through. Gruesome tales of people resorting to eating raw sewage and the rapid spreading of highly contagious diseases were appearing in newspapers. Graphic pictures of the horrible conditions in the city that had hosted the winter Olympics less than a decade before were beamed by CNN around the world.

Among those watching in growing shock and disbelief was President Clinton, who was attending the annual meeting of the Group of Seven (G-7) countries in Tokyo. Appalled by the reports and images, the president pressed his secretary of state and national security adviser to develop viable military options to avert an even worse disaster in the coming winter. Clinton explicitly told Lake that he wanted him to look at all options—including the use of American ground forces. Lake believed that the president was committed this time, and he asked Aspin to order up a full panoply of military options to address the situation in Sarajevo and

---

48. "Text of Joint Action Program Released by the Office of the Spokesman," May 22, 1993, in U.S. Department of State, "Opening Statement at News Conference on Bosnia Office of the Spokesman" (May 22, 1993).

other enclaves under siege by Bosnian Serb forces. Sensing a new opening for a more assertive policy, officials in the State Department began to push a more muscular approach as well. Christopher, who had run hot and cold over Bosnia policy since becoming secretary of state, now ran hot, prodded in part by his staff and in part by Clinton's renewed engagement on the issue.[49]

Upon their return from Asia, the principals met to hear a briefing from Joint Chiefs of Staff Vice Chairman Admiral David Jeremiah on the available military options. Jeremiah contended that it would take roughly 70,000 troops to relieve the pressure on Sarajevo. The large force requirement was due to the fact that the airport's closure meant that the troops would have to traverse hostile territory to get to the city before they could lift the siege. Although in subsequent discussions Powell indicated that only 25,000 troops might be needed for the more limited mission of helping to bring relief supplies into the city, few principals believed it likely that sufficient congressional and public support could be garnered to make even this a realistic option.[50]

The alternative to deploying ground troops was, once again, the use of air power. Two distinct purposes for using air power had emerged in the initial deliberations. Officials in the State Department were arguing in favor of threatening air strikes to end the "strangulation" of Sarajevo and possibly of the other Muslim enclaves under attack by Bosnian Serb forces. In contrast, Lake and his NSC staff suggested that, in addition to assuaging the humanitarian situation, air power could be used to force the Serbs into serious peace negotiations. As Lake said later, "The idea was, if we're going to use power for the sake of diplomacy, let's relate it directly to the diplomacy."[51] After several more rounds of feverish discussions, the principals agreed that a new push for air strikes made sense. Their aim would be to end the Bosnian Serb "strangulation" of Sarajevo and the other UN "safe areas" as well as to place "air power in the service of diplomacy" by

49. Interview with a senior administration official, October 21, 1997; Drew, *On the Edge*, pp. 273–74; and Daniel Williams, "Grim Balkans Outlook Affected U.S. Position," *Washington Post*, August 19, 1993, pp. A1, A24.

50. Madeleine Albright was the only principal to argue strongly in favor of the ground troops proposal, believing that such action could be explained to the American people. At times, Christopher supported Albright, especially if it involved a decision to go it alone if necessary. See Drew, *On the Edge*, pp. 274–75; and Mark Matthews, "U.S. Nears Sarajevo Rescue," *Baltimore Sun*, July 14, 1993, p. A14.

51. Quoted in Drew, *On the Edge*, p. 275.

forcing them to commence serious negotiations on the basis of an agreed cease fire.[52]

One key issue remaining was who would make the threat and, if necessary, implement it. Christopher, in particular, hesitated about having to get the allies on board. With his European trip of the previous May still fresh on his mind, the secretary of state was reluctant to get too far out in front of a policy, only again to be undermined by European opposition. Christopher's concerns were eased when it was agreed that, while allied agreement would be sought, the United States would proceed unilaterally if necessary, making clear the consequences for the alliance if the Europeans did not go along. In a play on the administration's policy toward gays in the military, one official described the new approach as, "Don't ask, tell."[53]

On the weekend of July 24–25, 1993, Lake and Bartholomew secretly flew to Europe to talk with British and French officials. In making the administration's latest argument for air strikes, Lake did not adopt the consultative mode that Christopher had used three months earlier. Instead, Clinton's national security adviser made clear that "the President had decided" that a new policy was needed. That policy consisted of air strikes to end the siege of Sarajevo and other "safe areas" and to force the Bosnian Serbs to engage in serious negotiations. To underscore U.S. determination, Lake made clear that the future of the alliance was on the line. If nothing was done and Sarajevo collapsed, the NATO summit scheduled for January 1994 would be a farce and transatlantic relations would be severely damaged. Moreover, Lake stressed, acquiescing in the ethnic cleansing of the Bosnian Muslims would have broad implications for Western interests throughout the Muslim world.[54] The British liked the plan, but the French expressed reservations. It was agreed that further discussions were needed.

Discussions between top U.S., British, and French officials continued in Washington immediately upon Lake's return from Europe. By the end of the week, there appeared sufficient agreement among these key allies to try to get a formal NATO decision in Brussels. The North Atlantic Council (NAC) met on August 2 to discuss the threat and possible use of air strikes. After a marathon, sixteen-hour session that, according to one U.S.

52. Drew, *On the Edge*, pp. 275–76; and Williams, "Grim Balkans Outlook Affected U.S. Position," p. A24.

53. Michael Gordon, "Rebuffed Once, U.S. Takes a Forceful Tack toward Allies on Approach to Balkan War," *New York Times*, August 3, 1993, p. A1.

54. Interview with a senior administration official, October 21, 1997. See also Drew, *On the Edge*, p. 277.

official, was "as bitter and rancorous a discussion as has ever taken place in the alliance," the allies finally reached agreement.[55] The NAC communiqué stated:

> —The Alliance has now decided to make immediate preparations for undertaking, in the event that the strangulation of Sarajevo and other areas continues, including wide-scale interference with humanitarian assistance, stronger measures including air strikes against those responsible, Bosnian Serbs and others, in Bosnia-Herzegovina.
>
> —These measures will be under the authority of the United Nations Security Council and within the framework of relevant UN Security Council resolutions, and in support of UNPROFOR in the performance of its overall mandate. For that purpose, full coordination will be carried out with the United Nations, including appropriate arrangements between the NATO Military Authorities and UNPROFOR and consultation with UNHCR (the United Nations High Commissioner for Refugees).
>
> —The Council has accordingly asked the NATO Military Authorities urgently to draw up, in close coordination with UNPROFOR, operational options for air strikes, including the appropriate command and control and decision-making arrangements for their implementation.[56]

The administration trumpeted the agreement as a major success, but that proved to be an overstatement. In the end, Washington gained NATO's support for threatening air strikes only at a heavy price: while the allies would support the use of NATO air power in case of the continued strangulation of Sarajevo, the decision on whether to conduct such strikes was to be shared by NATO and the UN, giving both organizations an effective veto.[57] Thus was born the infamous "dual-key" arrangement under which

---

55. Quoted in Barton Gellman and Trevor Rowe, "NATO Prepares Bosnia Target Lists," *Washington Post*, August 4, 1993, p. A1.

56. "Press Statement by the Secretary General," following the Special Meeting of the North Atlantic Council (Brussels: NATO Headquarters, August 2, 1993).

57. See Barton Gellman and Trevor Rowe, "U.S. Agrees to UN Veto on Bombing," *Washington Post*, August 7, 1993, p. A1; and Douglas Jehl, "U.S. Cedes to UN an Air Strike Veto," *New York Times*, August 7, 1993, p. A4. At the last minute during the August 2 meeting of the North Atlantic Council, the British (who until that time had been fully supportive of the U.S. position) argued that in view of the large UN pres-

the UN secretary general (or his designated representative) would have to approve the initiation and scope of any NATO air action. Given dominant British and French roles in the UNPROFOR command, the dual-key provided London and Paris with a way to manipulate the air strikes threat to their own purposes. While often agreeing with the United States and others in NATO that air strikes were desirable and necessary, London and Paris were able to use their dominant roles in the UN to veto or restrict the scope of NATO action. In the end, the acceptance of a UN role, which was necessitated by the need to reach a NATO consensus, would prove to be a major stumbling block in future attempts to use air power in punitive strikes.

The Sarajevo Ultimatum

In what would become a well-known pattern, the Bosnian Serbs responded to NATO's latest threat by easing up their military assault on Sarajevo and other "safe areas." Prospects for a negotiated compromise throughout the fall brightened, further undermining allied support for air strikes. However, once the wind had been taken out of NATO's sails, prospects for peace waned. By the end of 1993, the Bosnian Serbs had again dramatically increased their pressure on the Muslim "safe areas," attacking UN humanitarian relief efforts and resuming the heavy artillery shelling of Sarajevo.

As before, the NATO allies were deeply divided as to how to respond to the latest Bosnian Serb assault. A compromise statement was issued at the NATO summit on January 11, 1994, but its strong rhetoric could not hide the continuing and fundamental disagreement among the allies on what needed to be done.[58] These disagreements boiled over two weeks later when, at a Paris meeting with Secretary Christopher, French Foreign Minister Alain Juppé strongly urged the United States to take a more aggressive role in Bosnia. Juppé argued that if Washington refused to put troops on the ground, then it should at least be prepared to push the Bosnian

---

ence on the ground, the United Nations should have a role in the decision on launching air strikes. Interview with a senior administration official, October 21, 1997.

58. "Declaration of the Heads of State and Government," Press Communiqué M-1(94)3, Ministerial Meeting of the North Atlantic Council, North Atlantic Cooperation Council (Brussels: NATO headquarters, January 11, 1994).

Muslims into accepting a deal that was less than Sarajevo was hoping to attain.[59] In so doing, Paris exposed the fundamental contradiction of the U.S. position on Bosnia. While the Clinton administration supported the Bosnian Muslim contention that nothing less than the status quo ante—including the reversal of the Serb war gains—was an acceptable outcome of negotiations, it was unwilling to run the military risks necessary to bring this about. Washington would neither put its troops on the ground to support the Muslim cause nor push Sarajevo into accepting an outcome considerably less favorable than the one it sought. As Clinton stated publicly after the Paris meeting had concluded, "I don't think that the international community has the capacity to stop people within the nation from their civil war until they decide to do it."[60]

As pressure on the United States to do more increased, those within the Clinton administration who had long supported a U.S. leadership role began to mobilize. Upon returning from a post–NATO summit trip to central and eastern Europe, Madeleine Albright was convinced that the Bosnia imbroglio had begun to hurt the development of democracy in the region. In a passionate report, she warned the president of the dire consequences to the administration's Europe policy and the credibility and effectiveness of NATO and the United Nations. Tony Lake had separately come to the same conclusions and began an internal NSC review to determine what could be done. At a meeting with the president and his principal foreign policy advisers in late January 1994, a consensus emerged that a more aggressive U.S. approach to the negotiations was necessary, including putting air power in the service of diplomacy.[61] Christopher was asked to put the set of ideas into a coherent strategy. A paper reflecting input from Lake, Albright, and the new secretary of defense, William Perry, was sent to the president on February 4. It called for a U.S. leadership role in trying to find a diplomatic solution by both threatening the Serbs with air strikes if Pale refused to negotiate seriously and strengthening the Bosnian negotiating position by forging an alliance between the Muslims and Croats. In a private cover letter to the president, Christopher pleaded for a new approach: "I am acutely uncomfortable with the passive position we are now in, and believe that now is the time to undertake a new

59. Elaine Sciolino, "U.S. Rejects Plea to Act in Bosnia," *New York Times*, January 25, 1994, pp. A1, A8.

60. "Remarks by the President in Press Availability" (White House, Office of the Press Secretary, January 24, 1994).

61. Interview with a senior administration official, October 21, 1997.

initiative. . . . It is increasingly clear there will likely be no solution to the conflict if the United States does not take the lead in a new diplomatic effort."[62]

Then, just as the policy process was getting into gear, the situation on the ground provided an unexpected boost for a proactive U.S. policy, albeit in a most unwelcome fashion. On February 5, an artillery shell landed in a crowded Sarajevo marketplace, killing 68 and wounding about 200 others. In a meeting that afternoon with his foreign policy advisers, President Clinton expressed outrage and sought ideas on how to respond. While all agreed that air strikes were in order if there were evidence that the shell came from Serb artillery, the lack of definitive proof made some officials reluctant to recommend immediate retaliation. Unsure how to proceed and concerned that the United States not move too far ahead of the allies, Clinton tasked Albright to work through the UN to determine responsibility for the attack and ordered the U.S. military to help evacuate the wounded from Sarajevo. Meanwhile, Secretary Christopher would consult with the allies to determine an appropriate course of action.[63]

One of the ideas to come out of Christopher's discussions with the allies was a French proposal to use air power to establish and enforce a demilitarized zone around Sarajevo. While the U.S. officials liked the concept and were encouraged by France's newfound willingness to threaten air strikes, the Pentagon in particular believed that the quarantine requirements were too ambitious. The French plan would impose a heavy weapons exclusion zone extending thirty kilometers from the center of Sarajevo and require many thousands of additional ground troops to enforce compliance. As a result, during two painstaking meetings, the principals reworked the French ideas in a way that would permit enforcement of the protected zone without the deployment of additional ground forces. The modified plan reduced the weapons exclusion zone to a twenty-kilometer radius and required the parties (including the Bosnian Muslims) to withdraw or place under UN control all heavy weapons within ten days, or face air strikes. In the interim, any further attacks on civilians within the demilitarized zone would be met with immediate air strikes.

After extensive intra-alliance discussions, the North Atlantic Council endorsed the U.S. concept and issued the Sarajevo ultimatum on February 9,

62. Elaine Sciolino and Douglas Jehl, "As U.S. Sought a Bosnia Policy, the French Offered a Good Idea," *New York Times*, February 14, 1994, pp. A1, A6; here p. A6.
63. Sciolino and Jehl, "As U.S. Sought a Bosnia Policy."

which was to go into effect at midnight the following day.[64] Over the next ten days, a flurry of diplomatic activity sought to assure that the parties would abide by the directive's requirements and prevent NATO from having to engage in combat operations for the first time in its forty-five year history. On February 10, a UN negotiated cease-fire went into effect. A week later, Russian negotiators secured the Bosnian Serbs' agreement to abide by the NATO deadline and the Serbs began turning over their weapons within the zone to the UN.[65] When the ultimatum deadline expired on February 21, NATO determined that the requirements set on February 9 had been met. The siege of Sarajevo had been lifted.

The Washington Agreement

In addition to NATO's newfound willingness to implement air strikes, another significant outcome of the discussions leading up to the issuance of the Sarajevo ultimatum was the U.S. decision to become actively involved in the diplomatic negotiations. Concurrent with the Sarajevo ultimatum, the president had dispatched Undersecretary of State Peter Tarnoff and Charles Redman, who had replaced Reginald Bartholomew as special envoy to the Balkans, to London, Paris, and Bonn to consult with the allies and underscore the new U.S. determination to find a political solution. Previously, the United States had distanced itself from European negotiation efforts on the basis that the territorial divisions envisaged in the European proposals short-changed the Muslims and legitimized "ethnic cleansing." However, under the new U.S. diplomatic initiative, the administration proved more willing to engage the Bosnian government in discussions on what sorts of arrangements the Muslims could reasonably expect to get out of any negotiation. As one State Department official described the effort, "We will be talking to the Muslims about their bottom line. . . . If they want an intact Bosnia, well, we'll just have to see."[66]

64. "Decisions Taken at the Meeting of the North Atlantic Council," Press Release (94)15 (Brussels: NATO headquarters, February 9, 1994).

65. For details on these deliberations, see Dick Leurdijk, *The United Nations and NATO in the Former Yugoslavia, 1991–1996: Limits to Diplomacy and Force* (The Hague: Netherlands Atlantic Commission, Netherlands Institute of International Relations, Clingendael, 1996), pp. 41–47.

66. Ann Devroy and Daniel Williams, "Clinton Seeks NATO Deadline for Removal of Serb Artillery," *Washington Post*, February 9, 1994, p. A16.

Redman believed that a key to the success of any new diplomatic effort was to end the Muslim-Croat conflict. This conflict, which developed in the spring of 1993 when the parties began battling over Croat-controlled lands in central Bosnia, complicated the peace negotiations in two important ways. First, having three rather than two parties involved in the negotiations made it inherently more difficult to reach a settlement. Second, the Muslim-Croat conflict had left the Serbs with a decisive military advantage and little incentive to concede territory during negotiations. U.S. officials saw a possible Muslim-Croat alliance as a means to improve the military balance of power on the ground and thereby achieve a better (and more acceptable) settlement for the Bosnian Muslims.

Intensive negotiations took place between the Muslims and Croats in February and March 1994, with Redman playing a key mediating role. The basic framework that emerged called for the creation of a joint Muslim-Croat federation that would consist of about half of Bosnia's territory and be linked in an economic confederation with Croatia. The Bosnian Serbs would constitute their own entity alongside the Muslim-Croat federation within a united Bosnia. A final deal was struck on March 18 after four days of intense discussions in Washington. Although many details remained unresolved (including the drafting of a constitution and the specifics of military integration), the basic elements of a new power-sharing arrangement were agreed by the Bosnian Muslim and Croat sides. On that same day, President Clinton congratulated the sides on having established their federation in what came to be known as the Washington Agreement—the administration's first successful Bosnian initiative.[67]

The Contact Group

With the Washington Agreement, the Clinton administration succeeded in isolating the Serbs at the negotiating table. But this was just a first step, for peace between the Bosnian Croats and Muslims would mean little if the Bosnian Serbs could not also be brought on board. After all, although the Muslim-Croat federation was to consist of roughly 50 percent of

---

67. "Remarks by President Clinton, President Izetbegovic of Bosnia-Herzegovina, President Tudjman of Croatia in Signing of Peace Agreement" (White House, Office of the Press Secretary, March 18, 1994). See also Burg and Shoup, *The War in Bosnia-Herzegovina*, pp. 292–98; and Laura Silber and Allan Little, *Yugoslavia: Death of a Nation* (New York: TV Books, distributed by Penguin USA, 1996), pp. 319–23.

Bosnian territory, at present the two combined controlled only 30 percent. How to get the Bosnian Serbs to the table and then agree to give up large parts of their ill-gotten gains was a major preoccupation of negotiations throughout the remainder of 1994.

Assistance in this effort came from an unexpected corner. Starting in early 1994, Russia became a major player in Balkan diplomacy. In mid-February, Russian envoy Vitaly Churkin had helped convince the Bosnian Serbs to withdraw their guns from Sarajevo and two weeks later he persuaded them to reopen the airfield in Tuzla for humanitarian relief flights.[68] Moreover, when the Bosnian Serbs turned up the pressure on the "safe area" of Gorazde in early April, Russia joined with NATO in compelling the Serbs to back off the assault.

The emergence of Washington and Moscow as major players on the Bosnian peace-negotiating scene suggested that the EU-UN arrangements that had been in place since late 1991 were no longer up to the task. To ensure their inclusion, a new negotiating forum known as the Contact Group was formed in April 1994. It consisted of representatives of the United States, Russia, Britain, France, and Germany. The Contact Group offered each of the five members particular advantages. For the Europeans, the arrangement proved to be a way to ensure that the United States would not move too far ahead of the prevailing consensus. For Washington, the Contact Group provided the ability to avoid complex processes that would involve all twelve EU members and the unwieldy—and, in Washington's eyes, no longer trustworthy—UN system. For Moscow, finally, the group offered a way to confirm Russia's continuing international standing as a major power.

Throughout the spring and early summer of 1994, Contact Group discussions focused on a map of the territorial division among the parties in a peace settlement. Drawing largely on the efforts of David Owen and Thorvald Stoltenberg (who had replaced Cyrus Vance as the UN representative), the map eventually used by the Contact Group envisioned a territorial division that provided the Muslim-Croat federation 51 percent of the territory, and the Bosnian Serbs the remaining 49 percent. By providing the Muslim-Croat federation a majority of the territory, yet allowing the Serbs to maintain their occupation of significant swaths of previously Muslim lands, U.S. officials viewed the proposal as a compromise between justice and reality. The details of the peace agreement, such as the

---

68. Elaine Sciolino, "U.S. and Russians Broker New Pacts for a Bosnia Peace," *New York Times*, March 2, 1994, p. A1.

Figure 1. *The Contact Group Plan*

constitutional arrangements, would be worked out later in direct talks between the parties. As Redman described the plan, "It's a reasonable solution, but it's one that will not please everyone."[69] In particular, the

69. William Drozdiak, "Big Powers Give Final Endorsement to Partition Plan for Bosnia," *Washington Post*, July 6, 1994, p. A21.

map accepted the de facto division of Bosnia, long the aim of the Serbs and a premise of European effort, but antithetical to the idea of a multiethnic and territorially intact Bosnia. Its acceptance thus represented a major U.S. change of heart.

On July 6, 1994, the Contact Group formally presented its plan to the parties on a take-it-or-leave-it basis, giving them two weeks to accept the proposal. If either party refused to accept the plan, the Contact Group warned of punitive actions. The Muslims and Croats agreed to the plan almost immediately. Characteristically, the Bosnian Serbs delayed their response to the very last minute and then couched the terms of their acceptance in so many conditions as to be tantamount to a rejection.[70] After the deadline expired on July 20, the Contact Group urged the Serbs to reconsider for a second and third time, but to no avail.

As a result of the Bosnian Serb rejection, the Contact Group was forced to consider punitive measures that it hoped would compel the Serbs to accept the agreement. Throughout the Contact Group discussions, Washington—partly due to congressional pressure and partly in order to gain leverage over the Serbs—had pushed for lifting the arms embargo if Pale refused to accept the plan. However, the allies were quick to remind Washington that such action meant the UN forces would have to be withdrawn, a consequence no one was prepared to accept.[71] Another measure that had more support was the tightening of sanctions on Serbia. Given his longstanding political and material support to the war effort, Serbian President Slobodan Milosevic had long been seen as central to getting the Bosnian Serbs to sign a peace agreement. In a memorandum to the EU foreign ministers, David Owen wrote:

> The key as always is Milosevic. He understands power and he will only pressurize the Bosnian Serbs further if the Contact Group convince him that they are serious. He must receive a sharp reminder . . . that we expect him to act against the Bosnian Serbs, and that if he does not deliver, we will take further action against him.[72]

70. See David Ottaway, "Bosnian Serb Reply to Peace Plan Seeks More Talks on Map, Six Issues," *Washington Post*, July 22, 1994, p. A20.

71. See Owen, *Balkan Odyssey*, p. 290.

72. Ibid., p. 287.

When Milosevic's entreaties in Pale failed to convince the Bosnian Serbs, the Serb president agreed to sever ties with Pale in return for relief from international sanctions.[73] Although economic assistance to the Bosnian Serbs was largely cut off, military assistance continued to flow across the Drina River.

Bihac

Throughout the summer and into the fall of 1994, the Contact Group continued its efforts to get the Bosnian Serbs to sign on to its proposal. By October, however, the situation on the ground had changed dramatically, further undermining the prospects for a negotiated solution. The Bosnian Muslims had launched an ill-advised offensive from the Bihac "safe area," and the Serbs responded with a major counterattack. By November, some 2,000 to 4,000 Croatian Serb troops had joined 10,000 Bosnian Serbs in the assault. The new fighting risked a major escalation of the war, not least by possibly dragging Croatia directly into the Bosnian conflict. Whereas the United States worried about an escalation of the conflict to a region-wide war, the allies were less concerned. British and French officials blamed the Bosnian government for starting the fighting and they viewed the Serb counterattack as little more than an attempt to reacquire lost territory.

Aside from disagreeing about the risks posed by the escalating fighting around Bihac, the United States and its major European allies also differed more generally over how to proceed in the search for an end to the Bosnian conflict. One major source of conflict was the question of the arms embargo, which the Clinton administration announced it would no longer enforce. The president had agreed to this action in negotiations with Congress in order to prevent passage of a law that would have unilaterally lifted the embargo against the Bosnian Muslims. Days before the president's announcement on November 10, 1994, that the United States would no longer enforce the embargo, Clinton had suffered a stunning electoral defeat when the Republicans captured both houses of Congress for the first time in forty years. The new Republican leadership—with the Senate's

---

73. John Pomfret, "Yugoslavia Orders End of Ties to Bosnian Serbs," *Washington Post*, August 5, 1994, p. A23; and Barbara Crossette, "UN Eases Curbs on Yugoslavia after Serbian Peace Concessions," *New York Times*, September 24, 1994, p. 1.

new majority leader Robert Dole (R-Kans.) at the forefront—had long favored lifting the embargo, unilaterally if necessary. Clinton was therefore in no position to ignore congressional sentiment on the embargo question.[74]

The allies, of course, did not see it this way. To them, the possible inflow of new arms to any party represented additional risk to their forces. It was therefore particularly infuriating for the United States, which did not share this risk, to end enforcement of the arms embargo. The French reaction to the U.S. announcement was particularly angry. A foreign ministry spokesman said, "This action by the Americans could ruin chances of maintaining a common approach and lead to a lot of nasty finger-pointing across the Atlantic. . . . If fighting spreads and the European troops are forced to pull out, the Americans will have to shoulder the responsibility for what comes next."[75]

A second, related source of disagreement concerned the question of air strikes in response to the Bosnian Serb assault on the UN safe area of Bihac. At NATO's urging and with the UN's reluctant assent, NATO launched limited air strikes against an airfield in Croatia from which Croatian Serb aircraft were flying missions against Bihac, as well as against a number of Serb surface-to-air missile sites in Bosnia. Subsequent NATO and UN threats of further escalation did not deter the Bosnian Serb forces. To the contrary, the Serbs responded with a series of countermeasures, including blockading 200 UN peacekeepers stationed at nine weapons collection sites around Sarajevo, detaining 50 Canadian troops, and stopping the movement of all other UN military observers throughout Bosnia. The Bosnian Serb leader, Radovan Karadzic, underscored these actions with a blunt warning to the UN: "If a NATO attack happens, it will mean that further relations between yourselves and our side will be rendered impossible because we would have to treat you as our enemies. All United Nations Protection Force personnel as well as NATO personnel would be treated as our enemies."[76]

While the United States insisted that NATO proceed with further air

---

74. See Michael R. Gordon, "President Orders End to Enforcing Bosnian Embargo," *New York Times*, November 11, 1994, p. A1; and Craig R. Whitney, "Move on Bosnia by U.S. Alarms Allies in NATO," *New York Times*, November 12, 1994, p. A1.

75. Bradley Graham and William Drozdiak, "Bosnia Hails Arms Ban Shift by U.S.: Europeans' Warn Step May Strain Alliance," *Washington Post*, November 12, 1994, p. A21.

76. Roger Cohen, "Fighting Rages as NATO Debates How to Protect Bosnian Enclave," *New York Times*, November 25, 1994, p. A16.

strikes to try to save Bihac, those allies with troops on the ground and vulnerable to Serb retaliation were in no mood to accept additional risks. Discussions in Brussels and allied capitals made clear that the Europeans had reached the end of the road: either the United States would deploy the additional troops to Bosnia necessary for the UN to do its job effectively, or the UN forces would limit their activities to protecting humanitarian agencies and supplies. As British Defense Minister Malcolm Rifkind commented, "Those who call for action by the world must match words [by] deeds, and that doesn't require just a few aircraft."[77]

By Thanksgiving 1994, the differences within NATO over Bosnia policy that had simmered for months below the surface had come to a full boil, creating the worst crisis within the Atlantic alliance since 1956. It was clear that the Clinton administration had to make a real choice: either Washington would go ahead with air strikes (unilaterally, if necessary) in support of the Bosnian Muslims and defense of the UN "safe area" in Bihac or it would have to abandon the prospect of further air strikes to avoid precipitating the withdrawal of European and other UN forces from Bosnia. Initially air strikes might save Bihac from a Serb onslaught, but it threatened to undermine not only the most successful military alliance in history, but also one that provided the essential glue for the U.S. military presence in Europe and its leadership of NATO. Forgoing air strikes might save the alliance, but at the possible cost of a Bosnian Serb victory in Bihac that would not only leave many thousands of innocents at the mercy of marauding Serb forces, but also call into question the very safe-area concept around which support for the use of NATO air power had originally coalesced.

Faced with the possibility that NATO might be torn asunder by the rift over Bosnia policy, the administration decided to put NATO unity first and abandon any effort to convince the allies or the United Nations that air strikes remained necessary to turn the military tide in Bosnia.[78] Lake argued in a memorandum to the president, "to use NATO air strikes to prevent the fall of Bihac has only intensified the trans-Atlantic friction. . . . Bihac's fall has exposed the inherent contradictions in trying to use NATO

77. Robin Knight, "On the Road to Exhaustion," *U.S. News and World Report,* December 5, 1994, p. 64.

78. For a more in-depth review of U.S. policymaking on Bosnia during this period, see Ivo H. Daalder, *Anthony Lake and the War in Bosnia,* Pew Case Studies in International Affairs, no. 467-95-N (Washington, D.C.: Institute for the Study of Diplomacy, 1995).

air power coercively against the Bosnian Serbs when our allies have troops on the ground attempting to maintain impartiality in performing a humanitarian mission." Lake concluded that since "the stick of military pressure is no longer viable," it should be abandoned.[79]

Instead of air strikes, the administration decided that henceforth the objective of U.S. policy toward Bosnia would be, first, to mend the rift in the alliance; second, to contain the war in Bosnia and prevent its spread throughout the Balkans; and, only third, to help preserve the territorial integrity of Bosnia through negotiation.[80] As one senior official explained, the "principals agreed that NATO is more important than Bosnia. . . . Our objective, we pretty much accept at this point, is containment. Bosnia is a tragedy. A greater Balkan war would be a disaster."[81] Said another, "We are not downplaying Bosnia. . . . The problem is that we have no maneuver room. This time we have no leverage with the Europeans unless we agree to put peacekeeping troops on the ground."[82]

The administration realized that abandoning the threat of military pressure on the Serbs would complicate the search for a diplomatic solution. To enhance prospects for success, the principals agreed that a cease-fire of three to six months would be necessary. That meant pressuring Sarajevo to halt its mostly unsuccessful attempts to regain lost territory and making concessions to get the Serbs to the bargaining table. After all, Pale had refused to accept the Contact Group plan even as the basis for negotiation, and it was bound to continue to reject it now that the prospect for effective military pressure had disappeared. The concessions agreed to by the principals were threefold:

—First, territorial modifications to the Contact Group map dividing Bosnia 51-49 percent between the Muslim-Croat Federation and the Bosnian Serb entity would be acceptable so long as the parties agreed;

79. Cited in Michael Gordon, Douglas Jehl, and Elaine Sciolino, "Conflict in the Balkans: The Policy; Colliding Missions—A Special Report: U.S. and Bosnia: How a Policy Changed," *New York Times*, December 4, 1994, pp. A1, A20.

80. Michael Gordon, "U.S., in Shift, Gives Up Its Talk of Tough Action against Serbs," *New York Times*, November 29, 1994, p. A16; and Norman Kempster and Jim Mann, "U.S. Says Talks Remain Best Option in Bosnia," *Los Angeles Times*, November 30, 1994, p. A1.

81. Michael Kelly, "Surrender and Blame," *The New Yorker*, December 19, 1994, p. 51.

82. Gordon, "U.S., in Shift, Gives Up Its Talk of Tough Action against Serbs," p. A16.

—Second, constitutional links between the Bosnian Serbs and Serbia proper would be possible—so long as these were balanced by similar links between the Federation and Croatia;

—Third, contacts with the Bosnian Serb leadership in Pale would resume, thus providing it with a degree of legitimacy that the leadership had long desired.

Charles Redman was sent to Pale in early December to present this list of concessions directly to the Bosnian Serb leadership.[83]

Notwithstanding these significant concessions, the Bosnian Serbs showed little interest in negotiations. Rather than agreeing to engage directly with the United States or other Contact Group countries, Pale sought to bypass the normal diplomatic channels and engage former President Jimmy Carter, who in previous months had played the peacemaker in North Korea and Haiti.[84] Although skeptical that Carter could succeed, the Clinton administration did not oppose the former president's trip to Pale to determine whether negotiations were possible. Carter succeeded in gaining both sides' agreement to halt military activities until April 30, 1995, but his trip did little to move negotiations closer to a breakthrough.[85]

Containing "the Problem from Hell"

By the end of 1994, the Clinton administration's policy toward Bosnia had reached a virtual dead end. The many months of debate within the Atlantic alliance had shown that further U.S. pressure on the allies to allow the use of air power would likely call the continued utility of NATO into question. Bihac proved to be the last straw. As one senior official said at the time:

> We have been putting straws on the back of NATO solidarity over Bosnia for the last two years. We have been pushing them over and over to use military force, to the point where we have come to threaten

83. Roger Cohen, "Maps, Guns, and Bosnia: Redrawn Map Is Unlikely to Please," *New York Times*, December 6, 1994, p. A1. See also Gordon, "U.S., in Shift, Gives Up Its Talk of Tough Action against Serbs," pp. A1, A16.

84. See James Wooten, "The Conciliator," *New York Times Magazine*, January 29, 1995, p. 28.

85. For a review of the Carter mission, see Douglas Brinkley, *The Unfinished Presidency: Jimmy Carter's Journey beyond the White House* (Viking Books, 1998), pp. 443–53.

the destruction of the transatlantic treaty. We decided that we are not going to do that anymore. We are not going to make this a manhood test. We are not going to break NATO over this.[86]

Once the administration decided that NATO was more important than Bosnia and that effective military pressure would no longer be available to influence the course of events there, it was logical to adopt a more flexible negotiating stance—including one that would be seen by many as rewarding the aggressor. That led to the decision to engage in direct contact with Pale and to relax the previous, non-negotiable strictures of the Contact Group plan. When that proved insufficient to bring the Bosnian Serbs back to the table, few minded handing off the task to others, including to former President Carter. By that time, most of the administration's foreign policy players had come to believe that Bosnia, in Secretary Christopher's memorable words, was "the problem from hell"[87] and therefore better avoided. The new goal became containment of the problem in the hope that this would provide time to turn foreign policy attention elsewhere. The only real question was whether the actors in Bosnia would allow U.S. attention to be diverted for long.

86. Quoted by Kelly, "Surrender and Blame," p. 51.

87. "Statement of Warren Christopher, Secretary of State," *Foreign Assistance Legislation for Fiscal Year 1994 (Parts 1 and 8)*, Hearings and markup before the House Foreign Affairs Committee, 103 Cong. 1 sess. (Government Printing Office, 1993), p. 94.

CHAPTER TWO

From Containment
to Engagement

THE WINTER OF 1995 proved to be a relatively quiet one for U.S. policy toward Bosnia. Winter was usually marked by lulls in the fighting in Bosnia. The four-month cease-fire negotiated by former President Jimmy Carter in late December went into effect January 1, 1995, and, with only minor exceptions, held into early spring. The United Nations Protection Force (UNPROFOR) continued to assist civilian agencies in delivering humanitarian supplies to the many hundreds of thousands of people in need. Diplomatic efforts to entice the Bosnian Serbs to the negotiating table continued both by relaxing some constitutional and territorial strictures of the Contact Group plan and by engaging the Pale leadership directly. When these proved insufficient to persuade Pale to abandon its insistence on independence for Republika Srpska— the Bosnian Serb "republic," which occupied nearly 70 percent of Bosnian territory—the Contact Group countries turned to Serb President Slobodan Milosevic as an alternative to securing Bosnian Serb participation in the negotiations.

The relative military and diplomatic quiescence of the first months of 1995, however, turned out to be the calm before the storm—a storm that, in this case, proved to be definitive for Bosnia's future. The Bosnian Muslims used the cease-fire to import illicit arms and train their forces in time for the spring offensive.[1] The Bosnian Serbs, meanwhile, were readying

1. See Thomas Lippman and Daniel Williams, "U.S. Is Allowing Iran to Arm Bosnian Muslims," *Washington Post*, April 14, 1995, p. A1; and Daniel Williams, "Washington Foresees More Bosnia Combat; Acquiescence on Iran Arms Taken as an Indicator," *Washington Post*, April 15, 1995, p. A12.

their own offensive, designed to end the war by summer. Disquieting rumblings were heard across the border in Croatia as well. In mid-January, President Franjo Tudjman announced that the status quo in his country was no longer acceptable. He warned that Croatia would end its consent for the UN presence in Croatia when UNPROFOR's mandate expired on March 31, 1995, and forcefully establish Croatian control over the four UN-protected sectors inhabited by Serbs.[2] Although a slightly modified mandate for a renamed UN presence was accepted by the Croats after intervention by Vice President Al Gore in March,[3] Tudjman's warning suggested that Croatia's patience was wearing thin and that it might resort to military action. In May Croatia swept into western Slavonia (the UN's sector West) and in August forcefully established control in the Krajina (sectors North and South).

The military developments that were to take place in the spring and summer of 1995 would be decisive for Bosnia. The war was going to end that year; the question was whether the end would come through an outright military victory for one side, a negotiated agreement, or a combination of the two. Policymakers in Washington were not always sure. As developments threatened to spin out of control, the Clinton administration tried for the first time in the three-year-old conflict to seize the moment by exploiting events on the ground to its own advantage.

Turning toward Milosevic

The United States and its allies in the Contact Group believed that the four-month cease-fire would provide the last opportunity to get the parties to the bargaining table and negotiate an end to the war. That was why Washington had agreed in December 1994 to relax its strictures against negotiating with the Pale leadership and offered to consider changes in the constitutional and territorial provisions of the Contact Group plan that were acceptable to all parties. Notwithstanding this flexibility, the Bosnian

2. Roger Cohen, "Croatia Is Set to End Mandate of UN Force on Its Territory," *New York Times*, January 12, 1995, p. A4.

3. Barbara Crossette, "Croatian Leader Agrees to Continuation of UN Force," *New York Times*, March 13, 1995, p. A9. On March 31, 1995, the UN peacekeeping operation in the former Yugoslavia was renamed the UN Peace Force (UNPF). This was subdivided into three separate operations: UNCRO (which was deployed in Croatia); UNPROFOR (deployed in Bosnia); and UNPREDEP (deployed in Macedonia).

Serbs refused to budge. They rejected any effort to negotiate on the basis of the Contact Group plan.

The prospects for commencing negotiations now rested on the ability of the Contact Group to persuade Milosevic to force the Bosnian Serbs to the table.[4] The principal Western leverage over Milosevic was the prospect of the suspension or even the lifting of economic sanctions first imposed on Belgrade in May 1992. Accordingly, in February 1995 the Contact Group offered to suspend sanctions immediately if Serbia agreed to: recognize Croatia and Bosnia unequivocally; endorse the Contact Group plan for a Bosnian settlement; and accept the U.S. plan as the basis for negotiating a solution to the situation in Croatia. In addition, sanctions enforcement mechanisms would be kept in place and the suspension of sanctions would not apply to loans or assistance from international financial institutions or the European Union.[5]

In making this offer, the United States decided to try the approach long advocated by its European and Russian Contact Group partners, namely, to get results at the negotiating table by offering inducements rather than making threats.[6] Yet positive inducements proved no more successful than limited pressure. Many months of fruitless negotiations followed between the Serb president and the U.S. Contact Group representative, Deputy Assistant Secretary of State for European Affairs Robert Frasure. At first, Milosevic indicated that he could not recognize Bosnia and Croatia until the conflicts there had been resolved.[7] After a modified proposal for sanctions relief was put on the table in May,[8] negotiations foundered over the

4. For details on the negotiations, consult Jan Willem Honig and Norbert Both, *Srebrenica: Record of a War Crime* (Penguin Books, 1996), pp. 160–73.

5. Roger Cohen, "Allies Agree on a Proposal to Belgrade," *New York Times*, February 15, 1995, p. A9; and Daniel Williams, "U.S. Revises Approach to Sanctions on Serbia," *Washington Post*, February 15, 1995, p. A15.

6. Not everyone in the administration agreed with this approach. U.S. Ambassador to the United Nations Madeleine Albright opposed the move, continuing to argue in favor of military pressure. Vice President Gore's influential national security adviser, Leon Fuerth, who ran the interagency sanctions task force, also opposed any suspension of sanctions in the belief that, once suspended, sanctions would be difficult to reimpose. See Williams, "U.S. Revises Approach to Sanctions on Serbia," p. A15.

7. Roger Cohen, "Serb Leader Rejects U.S.-Backed Proposal," *New York Times*, February 21, 1995, p. A8; and Roger Cohen, "Yugoslavia Rules Out Recognition of Croatia or Bosnia Soon," *New York Times*, February 23, 1995, p. A6.

8. Under this Contact Group proposal, sanctions on all but oil, arms, and access to international financial assistance would be suspended in return for Milosevic's recognition of Bosnia's borders (rather than its government's) and allowing the United Na-

mechanism for reimposing sanctions in case of Serb noncompliance. The United States insisted that any UN Security Council member could demand that sanctions be reimposed, while Milosevic argued that the UN secretary general be given the sole right to determine when and how sanctions would be reimposed.[9] In late May after Milosevic seemed emboldened by the Bosnian Serb military advances, Frasure recommended to Washington that the diplomatic dance be ended and the negotiations be left to the Europeans, now led by former Swedish prime minister Carl Bildt, who had replaced David Owen as the European Union's chief negotiator for the former Yugoslavia.[10]

War Returns

While diplomats maneuvered in Belgrade and various Contact Group capitals, developments on the ground in Bosnia were soon to overtake their efforts.[11] With the melting snow, fighting resumed. In February and March, 1995, there were isolated outbreaks of fights in a number of key strategic areas around Bosnia, indicating that both sides were preparing for a full-scale resumption of the war when the cease-fire expired on April 30.[12] Indeed, in May fighting erupted in full force not only in Bosnia, but also in Croatia, where Serb forces launched cluster-bomb attacks against Zagreb and the Croatian army prepared to retake control of western Slavonia. Sporadic shelling resumed in Sarajevo, one of the six UN-declared "safe areas," and on May 7 an artillery shell exploded in the center of the city, killing eleven. U.S. pressure on the UN and its allies to respond forcefully to the latest Serb attack was resisted in UN headquarters in New

tions to place monitors on the Serb-Bosnian border. See Steven Greenhouse, "U.S. Gives New Offer to Serbian," *New York Times*, May 18, 1995, p. A6.

9. Stephen Engelberg, "U.S. Says It Plans to Propose New Concessions to Serbia," *New York Times*, June 1, 1995, p. A12; and Stephen Kinzer, "U.S.-Serb Talks Suspended," *New York Times*, June 8, 1995, p. A10.

10. Richard Holbrooke, *To End a War* (Random House, 1998), p. 63.

11. For a good overview of these developments, see Tihomir Loza, "From Hostages to Hostiles: How the West Dropped Its Policy of Neutrality and Took on the Bosnian Serbs," *War Report*, no. 43 (July 1996).

12. See Roger Cohen, "Fighting Erodes Cease-fire in Bosnia," *New York Times*, February 13, 1995, p. A8; "Bosnia Army, on the Attack, Breaking Truce," *New York Times*, March 21, 1995, p. A1; and "Bosnian Serbs Shell a Town and Steal Arms," *New York Times*, March 22, 1995, p. A8.

York and by the UN command in the region, which overruled a request for NATO air strikes by Lieutenant General Rupert Smith, the UNPROFOR Commander.[13]

The UN's failure to react only emboldened the Serbs and increased the incentives for the Bosnians to launch their own offensives. On May 22, Serb forces seized artillery stored in a containment depot near Sarajevo within the twenty-kilometer heavy weapons exclusion zone established in February 1994. This time, the civilian UN leadership backed up General Rupert Smith's demand that unless the weapons were returned to the depots within forty-eight hours, NATO would respond with air strikes. When the forty-eight hours expired without a positive response from the Bosnian Serbs, NATO bombers went into action, destroying two ammunition bunkers. Pale responded with defiance—threatening UN peacekeepers and shelling the northern Bosnian city of Tuzla, also a UN-declared "safe area," killing seventy-one young people at an outdoor café. NATO responded by attacking six more ammunition sites, leading the Bosnian Serbs to take hundreds of UN peacekeepers hostage. General Smith's request for additional air strikes was rejected by the UN military and civilian command for fear of the safety of the hostages and UN personnel in the region. In an emergency session of the UN Security Council no one pushed to continue with NATO air strikes.[14]

The spectacle of seeing French, Canadian, and other UN peacekeepers being held hostage on television sets around the world proved to be sobering in two important respects. First, it demonstrated once and for all the contradiction between using air power to punish the Bosnian Serbs and deploying lightly armed and widely dispersed troops on what essentially was a peacekeeping mission (even though there was precious little peace

13. David Rohde, "New Battles Risk Wider Balkan War," *Christian Science Monitor,* May 3, 1995, p. 1; Barbara Crossette, "UN Overrules New Calls for Air Strikes against Serbs," *New York Times,* May 9, 1995, p. A8; and Alison Mitchell, "U.S. Lobbied Allies for Weeks before NATO Attack on Serbs," *New York Times,* May 26, 1995, p. A8.

14. See, especially, Stephen Engelberg and Eric Schmitt, "NATO Bombing and Serb Hostage-Taking Now Mark Turning Point in War," *New York Times,* July 16, 1995, p. 8. See also Roger Cohen, "NATO May Be Called on to Silence Guns in Sarajevo," *New York Times,* May 25, 1995, p. A14; "NATO Jets Bomb Arms Depot at Bosnian Serb Headquarters," *New York Times,* May 26, 1995, p. A1; Joel Brand, "NATO Jets Hit Serb Site in Bosnia; Rebels Strike Back after Bombing Raid," *Washington Post,* May 26, 1995, p. A1; and Stephen Engelberg and Alison Mitchell, "A Seesaw Week for U.S. Policy in the Balkans," *New York Times,* June 5, 1995, pp. A1, A8.

to keep).[15] Indeed, it was to preserve the latter that the UN and the troop-contributing nations repeatedly rejected calls by the United States for more forceful action. Second, the sight of helpless soldiers held hostage by swashbuckling Bosnian Serb forces was deeply embarrassing to the countries contributing troops, notably France and Great Britain, two major powers with proud military histories. This embarrassment forced London and Paris to re-examine their participation in UNPROFOR. The choice was clear: either their troops would be withdrawn or UNPROFOR should be beefed up and deployed in a more defensible manner.

The Rapid Reaction Force

With the evident failure of NATO air strikes to convince the Bosnian Serbs to end their military actions and with nearly 400 UN peacekeepers still held hostage, the UN believed it had little choice but to put the safety of its troops first and reject demands for additional air strikes—whether they came from local commanders or from the United States. Washington had come to the same conclusion. At a meeting in late May, the principals agreed to "quietly" suspend the use of air strikes, a position that Secretary of State Warren Christopher conveyed to his Contact Group counterparts two days later when they met in The Hague.[16]

But while the United States favored suspending NATO air strikes, the UN had gone further. To gain the hostages' release, the UN force com-

---

15. Remarkably, U.S. officials had been caught by surprise by the hostage-taking, even though a similar sequence of events had occurred following the NATO air strikes in Bihac the previous November. See Engelberg and Mitchell, "A Seesaw Week for U.S. Policy in the Balkans," p. A8.

16. Interview with an administration official, August 13, 1998; and "Key Bosnia Meeting/Event Chronology" (White House paper prepared for media backgrounders on evolution of U.S. policy toward Bosnia, August 1995), p. 2. See also Joel Brand, "Bosnian Serbs Seize More UN Troops," *Washington Post*, May 29, 1995, p. A1. In so doing, the administration rejected the advice of Richard Holbrooke, which he had phoned in before the meeting from Budapest, where he was about to get married. According to Holbrooke's account, he recommended "that we give the Serbs forty-eight hours to release all the hostages unharmed, and tell them if they don't, we will bomb Pale. And then do so if necessary." In response to the deafening silence from Ambassador Albright, John Kornblum (Holbrooke's deputy), and Tom Donilon (Christopher's chief of staff), who were listening on the other end of the line, Holbrooke said, "I'm serious, but now I have to get married." Holbrooke, *To End a War*, p. 64.

mander apparently had promised the Bosnian Serbs that the UN would not authorize any further NATO air strikes. On June 4, French General Bernard Janvier, the United Nations Peace Force commander, met secretly with General Ratko Mladic, the commander of the Bosnian Serb forces. During their meeting Mladic prepared a letter that stated:

1. The Army of Republika Srpska will no longer use force to threaten the life of and safety of members of UNPROFOR;
2. UNPROFOR commits to no longer make use of any force which leads to the use of air strikes against targets and territory of Republika Srpska; and
3. The signing of this agreement will lead immediately to the freeing of all prisoners of war.[17]

Mladic then asked Janvier to deliver the letter to UN headquarters in Zagreb for approval. Although no documentary evidence has surfaced to prove that an agreement was concluded, a suspicious series of events followed the June 4 meeting. On June 9, UN Special Representative Yasushi Akashi met with Generals Janvier and Smith to discuss the use of air power against the Bosnian Serbs. Smith argued strongly in favor of the use of air strikes to discourage further Serbian aggression but was overruled by Janvier, who believed that the Serbs wanted to "modify their behavior, be good interlocutors." After the meeting, Akashi publicly affirmed that the UN would return to "traditional peacekeeping principles."[18] In the weeks following the June 4 meeting, Janvier and Akashi denied repeated requests for close air support by Dutch peacekeepers in Srebrenica, who were being overrun by Bosnian Serb forces. Separately, two days after Janvier met with Mladic, French General Bertrand de Lapresle was dispatched from Paris to meet secretly with the Bosnian Serbs in Pale. The next day, 111 hostages were released. Reports also began to surface that Serbian president Milosevic had received assurances from French president Jacques Chirac that there would be no further air strikes against the Bosnian Serbs. On June 17, Milosevic met with Akashi in Belgrade. Akashi reported that "Milosevic stated that he had been advised by President Chirac of Presi-

17. Quoted in David Rohde, *Endgame: The Betrayal and Fall of Srebrenica, Europe's Worst Massacre since World War II* (Farrar, Straus, and Giroux, 1997), p. 361.
18. Ibid., pp. 420, 422.

dent Clinton's agreement that air strikes should not occur if unacceptable to Chirac."[19]

Whatever the particular reasons for ruling out further air strikes once the hostages were freed, the United Nations faced a clear choice in responding to the continued fighting: it could either withdraw UNPROFOR or strengthen the force by adding firepower and redeploying vulnerable troops to more defensible positions in central Bosnia. The decision would be up to those countries contributing troops as well as those, like the United States, that would need to support the UN force during the withdrawal or redeployment.

It was France, under the reinvigorated leadership of its newly elected president, Jacques Chirac, that took the lead. In a conversation with President Clinton on May 27, the French president argued that there needed to be a forceful response to the humiliation of UNPROFOR troops being taken hostage by the Bosnian Serbs.[20] He proposed adding a well-armed, rapid reaction component, with the purpose of protecting less well-armed UNPROFOR troops and ending the Serb siege of Sarajevo by opening up a six-mile corridor between the Sarajevo airport and Bosnian-controlled territory in the capital. Chirac further proposed that UNPROFOR forces be "reconfigur[ed] and redeploy[ed]. . . in ways that make them less vulnerable."[21] A written version of the French proposal arrived at the White House the following day, just as the principals were meeting to discuss the next steps in U.S. policy. Since Chirac's proposal made no mention of a possible U.S. troop contribution to the Rapid Reaction Force (RRF), as the force came to be known, the principals decided that Washington should

19. See Roger Cohen, "France Held Secret Talks with Serbs," *New York Times*, June 23, 1995, p. A7; Roy Gutman, "UN's Deadly Deal," *New York Newsday*, May 29, 1996, pp. A7, A24–A25, A31; and Rohde, *Endgame*, pp. 359–64. The French government, Akashi, and Janvier have repeatedly denied that any deal was reached with the Bosnian Serbs regarding the release of hostages and air strikes. A detailed UN review of this period also concluded that there was no evidence of an agreement on the release of hostages in exchange for suspending airstrikes. See *Report of the Secretary-General Pursuant to General Assembly Resolution 53/35 (1993)*, para. 197.

20. The conversation occurred the same day that French UN troops in Bosnia had engaged in a serious firefight to retake an observation post that had been seized by Serbs in a brazen assault by troops dressed as blue-helmeted peacekeepers. See Roger Cohen, "2 French Killed as Sarajevo Battle Takes New Course," *New York Times*, May 28, 1995, p. 1; Joel Brand, "French Units Attack Serbs in Sarajevo," *Washington Post*, May 28, 1995, p. A11; and Rohde, *Endgame*, p. 27.

21. Todd S. Purdum, "U.S. Backs French on Moving Peacekeepers," *New York Times*, May 29, 1995, p. A5.

support the proposal and be prepared to offer logistical, intelligence, and other support.[22] In a rare demonstration of allied policy cohesion and a clear indication that those concerned with the Balkans were desperate for a different policy direction, Chirac's proposal was endorsed by the Contact Group on May 30, by NATO on June 3, and by the UN Security Council on June 16. The 10,000-strong RRF consisting of French, British, and Dutch troops was deployed by early July.[23]

There was much skepticism in Washington about the RRF, however. Some officials worried that the force would not execute its mandate in the robust fashion that Washington desired. As Defense Secretary William Perry warned, "A fair conclusion is that the addition of these 10,000 troops would still not put UNPROFOR in a position to confidently carry out all of the missions of this mandate."[24] Others were concerned that its deployment was designed principally to enable the extraction of the UN force rather than its strengthening.[25] Nevertheless, the RRF's deployment served the important purpose of bolstering UNPROFOR at a time when many in the United States and Europe feared that the UN would decide to withdraw the peacekeepers. Indeed, the UN secretary general had implied as much when he ordered a "fundamental review" of UNPROFOR in mid-May.[26]

22. Interview with an administration official, July 7, 1998. See also Craig R. Whitney, "Diplomatic Moves Pressed by Paris," *New York Times*, May 28, 1995, p. 1; Engelberg and Mitchell, "A Seesaw Week for U.S. Policy in Balkans," p. A8; Michael Dobbs, "U.S. Push for Airstrikes Shown as Miscalculation," *Washington Post*, May 29, 1995, p. A1; Joint Statement by William J. Perry, secretary of defense, and John M. Shalikashvili, chairman, Joint Chiefs of Staff, *Situation in Bosnia*, Hearings before the Senate Committee on Armed Services, 104 Cong. 1 sess., June 7, 1995 (GPO, 1996), pp. 17–20; and Elizabeth Drew, *Showdown: The Struggle between the Gingrich Congress and the Clinton White House* (Simon and Schuster, 1996), pp. 244–45.

23. Steven Greenhouse, "Allies Resolve to Bolster UN Peacekeeping in Bosnia; U.S. Weighs a Ground Role," *New York Times*, May 30, 1995, p. A1; Michael Dobbs, "U.S., Europeans to Beef Up, Regroup UN Force in Bosnia," *Washington Post*, May 30, 1995, p. A1; William Drozdiak and Bradley Graham, "European Force Set for Bosnia; U.S. to Provide Support for Rapid-Reaction Unit, but No Ground Troops," *Washington Post*, June 4, 1995, p. A1.

24. Statement by Perry and Shalikashvili, *Situation in Bosnia*, p. 31.

25. Interview with a State Department official, July 15, 1998. See also Elaine Sciolino and Craig R. Whitney, "Costly Pullout in Bosnia Looms unless UN Can Prove Effective," *New York Times*, July 9, 1995, p. A1.

26. William Drozdiak, "Total Review of Peacekeeping Ordered by UN," *Washington Post*, May 13, 1995, p. A17; Barbara Crossette, "New Role Sought for U.N. Bosnia Force," *New York Times*, May 17, 1995, p. A6. See also UN Security Council, *Report*

UNPROFOR's withdrawal was not something Washington could ignore. Not only would its departure eliminate whatever limited deterrent value it retained in preventing a full-scale conflict, but Washington also had been committed for some time to assist in the withdrawal, if necessary by using U.S. ground troops. It was the prospect of having to fulfill this NATO commitment—which, according to the alliance's contingency plans, could entail up to 25,000 U.S. troops—that proved deeply worrisome to key policymakers in the State and Defense Departments, and strengthened their resolve to do what was necessary to ensure that UNPROFOR would remain deployed in Bosnia. Indeed, the more senior officials learned about the alliance's contingency plan—known in the NATO parlance as operations plan (or OPLAN) 40104—the stronger their resolve became to keep UNPROFOR in place.

U.S. Troops in Bosnia?

Since early 1993, when the prospects of a negotiated peace agreement first appeared to brighten, NATO military commanders and staff had examined the force requirements and drew up a variety of contingency plans to assist in the enforcement of a peace agreement.[27] However, when it became clear in late summer 1994 that the Bosnian Serbs were unlikely to agree to negotiate a peace agreement, NATO planners shifted their efforts. They drew up plans to help the UN extract exposed peacekeepers and help UNPROFOR withdraw completely if conditions in Bosnia (or Croatia) continued to deteriorate.[28] The debacle in Bihac in November 1994—which both demonstrated the UN's impotence in the face of a determined adversary and exposed a serious rift within the alliance—underscored that UNPROFOR's withdrawal was not just a theoretical possibility. Thus when the principals decided in late November 1994 to put NATO

---

of the Secretary General Pursuant to Security Council Resolutions 982 (1995) and 987 (1995), S/1995/444 (May 30, 1995). Document is available at gopher:// gopher.undp.org:70/00/uncurr/sgrep/95_06/444 (accessed October 1999).

27. Gregory L. Schulte, "Former Yugoslavia and the New NATO," Survival, vol. 39 (Spring 1997), p. 24.

28. The plans to extract UN personnel in an emergency focused primarily on forces deployed in the eastern enclaves. See Statement of Lieutenant General Wesley J. Clark, director, strategic plans and policy, Joint Chiefs of Staff, Situation in Bosnia, Hearings before the House Committee on International Relations, 104 Cong. 1 sess., June 8, 1995 (GPO, 1995), p. 13.

ahead of Bosnia, they also acknowledged that it was necessary to evaluate the nature and extent of any U.S. military commitment to a NATO operation designed to assist UNPROFOR in withdrawing from Bosnia. The U.S. commitment to NATO could mean nothing less than that the United States would have to participate, with troops on the ground, in any such operation.

President Clinton accepted the recommendation of his senior advisers on December 7, 1994, and informed the NATO allies and Congress the next day that the United States would in principle be prepared to supply about half the force necessary for a worst-case extraction operation: some 20,000–25,000 troops.[29] In making this decision, the administration hoped to reassure NATO allies contributing the vast majority of forces to the UN operation that the United States, as the alliance leader, would stand ready to assist allies in need, and thus to provide them an incentive to keep their forces in Bosnia. A senior administration official commented, "This is a demonstration that the United States will assist our NATO allies if their forces are in danger. We hope that it is an operation that does not have to be implemented. . . . We do not believe a withdrawal is imminent. Nor do we believe it is justified or wise. But if it occurs, we are prepared to participate."[30]

The Clinton administration conditioned the participation of U.S. forces in a withdrawal operation on the understanding that such an operation would be under the clear and sole command of NATO; there could be no dual-key arrangement, as existed for the use of NATO air power. The NATO extraction force would also have to have robust rules of engagement. In January 1995, high-level UN and NATO officials agreed that while the UN Security Council would have to request NATO's assistance in helping UNPROFOR withdraw and while the North Atlantic Council (NAC) would have to approve the UN's request, once underway, the command and control of this operation would be in NATO's hands. On the

29. Douglas Jehl, "25,000 U.S. Troops to Aid UN Force If It Quits Bosnia," *New York Times*, December 9, 1994, p. A1; and Ann Devroy and Bradley Graham, "U.S. to Send Forces If UN Quits Bosnia," *Washington Post*, December 9, 1994, p. A1. For a good overview, see also Dick Leurdijk, *The United Nations and NATO in Former Yugoslavia, 1991–1996: Limits to Diplomacy and Force* (The Hague: Netherlands Atlantic Commission, Netherlands Institute of International Relations, Clingendael, 1996), pp. 64–67.

30. Cited in Devroy and Graham, "U.S. to Send Forces If UN Quits Bosnia," p. A41.

basis of this agreement, UN Secretary General Boutros Boutros-Ghali formally requested NATO in February 1995 to begin planning for a possible UNPROFOR withdrawal.[31]

NATO contingency planning proceeded apace during the first half of 1995. Computer simulations of an evacuation were conducted in February and some pre-positioning of communications equipment and expertise was undertaken in May. By then, the basic structure of the operations plan governing withdrawal (OPLAN 40104)—including its 1,300 pages and 24 annexes—was more or less in place, with only technical issues remaining to be resolved.[32] In its most extensive configuration, the NATO force required to assist in the withdrawal could have involved as many as 82,000 NATO troops, with the United States providing 25,000 of the total. The operation would have lasted up to twenty-two weeks, at a cost to the United States of $700 million.[33] In short, the U.S. and NATO commitment was extensive—and dangerous.

An Uneasy U.S. Commitment

Until the resumption of fighting in early spring 1995, this major commitment was largely a theoretical one. However, once fighting escalated throughout Bosnia and NATO air power was effectively checkmated by Serb hostage-taking, the prospect of actually having to fulfill the commitment was becoming quite real. The Clinton administration confronted two critical questions. First, would OPLAN 40104 in fact accomplish its objective of getting the 24,000 UN troops out safely? Second, with the UN command and the major allies rejecting the use of NATO air strikes

31. UN Security Council, *Report of the Secretary-General Pursuant to Security Council Resolutions 982 (1995) and 987 (1995)*, para. 74.

32. See Gilbert Lewthwaite, "U.S. Experts Go to Croatia to Aid in UN Pullout," *Baltimore Sun*, May 3, 1995, p. A6; and Leurdijk, *The United Nations and NATO*, pp. 66–67.

33. The main U.S. force, the 1st Armored Division, was assigned the most difficult task: to extract lightly armed forces from the three isolated enclaves in eastern Bosnia. Interview with a Pentagon official, July 20, 1998. See also testimony of Lieutenant General Howell Estes II, USAF, director for operations, Office of Joint Chiefs of Staff, in *Briefing on the F-16 Shootdown in Bosnia and Current Operations*, Hearing before the Senate Committee on Armed Services, 104 Cong. 1 sess. (July 13, 1995), p. 20; testimony of General John Shalikashvili, U.S. Army, chairman, Joint Chiefs of Staff, *Situation in Bosnia*, Senate hearings, pp. 23–26; Gilbert A. Lewthwaite, "NATO Could Send U.S. Troops to Balkans under Evacuation Plan for U.N. Forces," *Baltimore Sun*, July 5, 1995, p. A4; and Eric Schmitt, "Plans for UN Pullout Paint Bleak Picture Full of Pitfalls," *New York Times*, July 13, 1995, p. A1.

except in the most grave of circumstances, what sort of assistance short of a full-scale withdrawal should the United States be prepared to provide those UNPROFOR troops that found themselves in dire straits? As the situation on the ground in Bosnia began to deteriorate in mid-May, both questions were beginning to be addressed at the highest levels of the U.S. government.

The president's senior advisers met at least three times in mid– to late May, amidst the latest assaults on Sarajevo and the escalation of fighting throughout Bosnia, to discuss the issues raised by the NATO planning process. None who attended was sanguine about the implementation of 40104; all understood that this was a risky and dangerous undertaking. The operation would be a logistical nightmare, having to operate in rugged, mountainous terrain with only a few, badly maintained roads, most of which were mined. U.S. forces would have to travel from Germany by train to port and by ship to the Croatian Adriatic ports of Split and Ploce. From there, they would have to cross the length of the country to Tuzla in the north and then hook back down toward the eastern enclaves.[34] In addition, there was a series of more tangible issues that needed to be considered:

—How to deal with large refugee movements, particularly from the eastern enclaves, of people who would be abandoned by the removal of what were admittedly token UN forces;

—How to respond to continued Serb aggression against the Muslims, even if the UN and NATO forces were not targeted directly;[35]

—How to react in case civilians—women and children—obstructed the exit paths, pleading for protection;

—How to get the troops out of Bosnia after the UN force had been withdrawn, given that NATO's departure was almost certain to return Bosnia to the carnage witnessed at the war's outset in the summer of 1992;

—How to get the American people and the Congress to support such a mission, one in which little public relations groundwork had been laid.

In view of these uncertainties, the principals decided that the NATO force should have a narrow and well-defined mission—to assist in the withdrawal and emergency extraction of the UN force. It would not engage in helping refugees, provide humanitarian support, or prepare for

34. Interview with a Pentagon official, July 20, 1998, and a senior NATO official, August 7, 1998.

35. Under the robust rules of engagement of the NATO force (including the UN forces that would be operating under NATO command), direct attacks on the forces would meet with a devastating response from ground and, if necessary, air forces.

and participate in operations subsequent to the withdrawal of UNPROFOR. That said, the magnitude of the problems associated with 40104 convinced these same officials that however inadequate UNPROFOR had become in fulfilling its mandate or improving the situation on the ground, keeping the UN force in Bosnia was preferable to any of the alternatives. As National Security Adviser Anthony Lake recalled, "We all agreed that collapse would mean that American troops would have to go into Bosnia in order to rescue UNPROFOR, which meant that we were going in the context of a defeat. And nobody wanted that. It would have had huge consequences."[36] The principals thus agreed to make a concerted effort to convince the allies to keep their forces in place—an effort aided considerably when, a few days later, Chirac proposed the deployment of the RRF.[37]

Of course, the decision on whether UNPROFOR would stay or not, though one the administration could try to influence, was not one Washington could make. And while many in the administration were skeptical that the Chirac plan for the RRF was serious—and some saw it as a cynical move to cover the imminent withdrawal of the UN force—it was believed that Washington's support for the force and UNPROFOR more generally would at the very least delay a decision in London, Paris, and elsewhere to pull the troops out. As a result, the administration fully supported the RRF's deployment—and committed to back it with close air support, strategic lift, an intelligence cell, and certain types of weapons and other equipment not readily available to the allies (including AC-130 gunships and Cobra attack helicopters, artillery-locating radar, satellite-linked navigation devices, and night-vision equipment).[38]

36. Loza, "From Hostages to Hostiles," p. 17.

37. Interviews with a senior administration official, October 21, 1997, and an administration official, August 13, 1998. See also statement by Shalikashvili, *Situation in Bosnia*, Senate hearings, p. 24; Dana Priest, "U.S. Planners Fear Heavy Pullout Costs," *Washington Post*, July 14, 1995, p. A26; and Schmitt, "Plans for UN Pullout Paint Bleak Picture Full of Pitfalls," p. A1.

38. Statement by Perry, *Situation in Bosnia*, Senate hearings, p. 17; and Drozdiak and Williams, "European Force Set for Bosnia," p. A25. Because of congressional opposition, it proved difficult for the administration to provide the requisite financial assistance. At a June 3 defense ministers' meeting in Paris attended by Secretary of Defense Perry, France initially proposed placing the RRF under the command of its contributing nations to avoid the UN bureaucracy, a notion that was eventually rejected on the basis that it would create too many chains of command. Instead, it was decided that the force should be formally integrated into UNPROFOR. However, Perry left the session before this agreement had been reached and, upon returning to Washington, briefed key members of Congress that the force would be deployed under national command, with each participant funding its own contingent. As a result,

The principals met on Sunday, May 28, 1995, to determine what the United States would bring to the table when Christopher met with his Contact Group and NATO counterparts in the Netherlands the following two days. During the meeting, which in Anthony Lake's absence was chaired by Deputy National Security Adviser Samuel R. (Sandy) Berger, the principals reaffirmed the commitment the United States had made to NATO and UNPROFOR in case the UN determined that the force needed to be withdrawn. However, Defense Secretary Perry and Joint Chiefs of Staff Chairman General John Shalikashvili wanted to expand the U.S. commitment to include assisting in a possible redeployment of UN troops within Bosnia to more defensible positions. While none of the allies had formally asked NATO or the United States to assist in the redeployment of their troops, some of which were stationed in highly vulnerable positions in the eastern enclaves, allied and NATO military officials had informally raised the question of a possible U.S. role in case such a redeployment became necessary. Moreover, a UN redeployment would also reduce their vulnerability to possible Serb reprisals in the event of a NATO and UN decision to launch air strikes.[39] In response to Perry's and Shalikashvili's urging, Secretary Christopher asked whether such an operation could involve the use of American ground troops. Perry answered affirmatively, "Yes." Although Christopher warned that there "would be no support in the Congress or among the public for deeper involvement," the principals agreed that the U.S. commitment to assist UNPROFOR should apply to the possible "relocation" of UN forces from untenable positions, particularly if such assistance would strengthen allied resolve to remain in Bosnia.[40]

---

vehement opposition arose when Congress learned that the RRF would be part of the UN peacekeeping operation and that, as a result, Washington would be responsible for 31.7 percent of its $300 million cost. This prompted Senator Joseph Biden (D-Del.) to deem the RRF the "rapid ripoff force." When it became clear that Congress would not approve funding for the plan, Clinton decided to pay for it with $50 million out of the existing defense department budget. See Michael Sheridan, "Policy Wrecked on the Rocks of U.S. In-fighting," *The Independent*, June 22, 1995, p. 13; Michael Dobbs, "Congress Skeptical of 'Voluntary' Plan for Bosnia Funding," *Washington Post*, June 23, 1995, p. A31; and Michael Dobbs, "U.S. Plans to Fund Bosnia Force without Seeking Hill Approval," *Washington Post*, June 29, 1995, p. A34.

39. Interview with a senior administration official, May 18, 1999.

40. Interview with an administration official, July 7, 1998, and with a senior administration official, March 1, 1999. See also Engelberg and Mitchell, "A Seesaw Week for U.S. Policy in the Balkans," pp. A1, A8; Michael Dobbs, "U.S. Push for Airstrikes Shown as Miscalculation," *Washington Post*, May 29, 1995, p. A21; and Drew, *Showdown*, p. 245.

In subsequent days, there was considerable uncertainty about what exactly had been decided. According to a detailed account in the *New York Times*, Lake recommended in a memo to Clinton that the president consult with Congress on "a new contingency plan to send American ground troops as part of a NATO force to help redeploy United Nations units that had to be removed from untenable positions."[41] The purpose of such a redeployment would be to enhance the viability of UNPROFOR and thereby avoid the need for its precipitous withdrawal. At the same time, officials in the Pentagon—including Perry—were indicating a more limited mission for the possible use of U.S. ground forces, namely an "emergency evacuation" of an endangered UN peacekeeping unit.[42] The confusion was compounded when, on May 31, the president for the first time publicly explained the nature of the U.S. commitment in a commencement address at the United States Air Force Academy:

> A strengthened United Nations operation is the best insurance against an even worse humanitarian disaster should they leave. We have a longstanding commitment to help our NATO allies, some of whom have troops in the UN operation in Bosnia, to take part in a NATO operation to assist them in a withdrawal if that should ever become necessary. And so, if necessary, and after consultation with Congress, I believe we should be prepared to assist NATO if it decides to meet a request from the United Nations troops for help in *a withdrawal or a reconfiguration and a strengthening of its forces.*
>
> We have received no such request for any such assistance, and we have made no such decision. . . . We have obligations to our NATO allies, and I do not believe we can leave them in the lurch. So I must carefully review any requests for an operation involving a temporary use of our ground forces.[43]

Both the specific wording of the speech and the inclusion of a reference to the temporary use of ground forces were controversial. According to several detailed accounts, in an Oval Office meeting on May 30 called to discuss a draft of the speech, Tony Lake argued that the president's ad-

---

41. Engelberg and Mitchell, "A Seesaw Week for U.S. Policy in the Balkans," p. A8.

42. See, for example, Perry's statement cited in Alison Mitchell, "U.S. Set to Offer Aid to Reinforce UN Bosnia Troops," *New York Times*, May 31, 1995, p. A1.

43. "Remarks by the President at the U.S. Air Force Academy Graduation Ceremony" (Colorado Springs: White House, Office of the Press Secretary, May 31, 1995), p. 4, emphasis added.

dress to the Air Force Academy include a reference to Bosnia, given that events on the ground were resulting in daily headlines. Everyone at the meeting agreed. Later that day, the president also approved the recommendation by Lake, Perry, and Shalikashvili, set forth in the Lake memorandum of May 29, "that if requested by NATO, we should provide assistance to our allies to redeploy from the eastern enclaves, provided we can get Congress to go along." Clinton indicated that he agreed with Lake's recommendation "as you have set forth."[44] The president's decision was reported—in some instances, in an overblown fashion—by major newspapers on May 31, the day of the president's speech in Colorado Springs. While traveling to Colorado, Lake and Clinton concluded that the president needed to address the issue by including "a complete, nuanced explanation of how far the administration was prepared to go." Christopher, who had dissented from Lake's original recommendation, strongly disagreed. He believed that too much had already been said. Christopher called Air Force One from The Hague to express his views to Lake and warned that any announcement by the president would be misconstrued by Congress and in Europe. Clinton nevertheless decided to speak out.[45]

However complete and nuanced, Clinton's statement was especially vague regarding the purpose of any temporary deployment of U.S. forces—including not only a withdrawal, but also a "reconfiguration and a strengthening" of UNPROFOR. The reason for the vagueness was partly the result of a lack of clarity on the part of the president and his major advisers on the circumstances that might call for a temporary deployment. It was also a consequence of the multiple audiences the president was trying to reach. On the one hand, the administration was attempting to reassure the European allies that in a crunch the United States would be there.[46] On the other hand, it sought to reassure a reluctant Congress and uncertain pub-

44. Quotations are from notes by a senior administration official consulted during an interview on March 1, 1999.

45. The quotation is from Engelberg and Mitchell, "A Seesaw Week for U.S. Policy in the Balkans," p. A8. See also Mitchell, "U.S. Set to Offer Aid to Reinforce UN Bosnia Troops," p. A1; Ann Devroy and Rick Atkinson, "U.S. to Allow Ground Forces in Bosnia," *Washington Post*, May 31, 1995, p. A1; Ann Devroy and Bradley Graham, "Seeking to Reassure Europe, Clinton Alarmed Congress," *Washington Post*, June 5, 1995, p. A1; Doyle McManus, "Clinton Zigzag on Balkans May Underscore His Unease," *Los Angeles Times*, June 6, 1995, p. A1; Ann Devroy, "Nailing Down a Bosnia Policy," *Washington Post*, June 7, 1995, p. A28; and Drew, *Showdown*, p. 246.

46. For that reason, Clinton's statement was well received in Europe. See John Darnton, "Clinton's Offer of Troops Pleases Europe," *New York Times*, June 2, 1995, p. 11.

lic about the limits of any U.S. military involvement. Thus instead of achieving greater clarity, the administration succeeded principally in leaving everybody confused about what exactly it was prepared to do with U.S. troops in Bosnia.

A raucous Washington frenzy followed with administration critics, defenders, and the press all vying to interpret the latest twists in U.S. policy. Many speculated about the bureaucratic infighting that may have underpinned the confusion.[47] Critics on Capitol Hill and elsewhere immediately seized on Clinton's speech, which they assumed entailed a significant new commitment, as indicating a major shift in U.S. policy.[48] To quiet the storm, the president addressed the issue again in his radio address to the nation on June 3. This time, he left no room for misinterpretation:

> I want to make it clear again what I have said about the use of our ground forces. We will use them only if, first, if there is a genuine peace with no shooting and no fighting. . . . Second, if our allies decide they can no longer continue the UN mission and decide to withdraw, but they cannot withdraw in safety, we should help them to get out. . . . [Third,] I have decided that if a UN unit needs an

47. Anonymous sources—presumably from the State Department—pointedly noted that Christopher had warned against a presidential statement on the issue, and blamed Lake for having misunderstood what the principals had decided in the May 28 meeting, which was to assist in an emergency extraction of UN peacekeepers only, not to help reconfigure or strengthen UNPROFOR. The situation inside the administration was not helped when on June 2 the president met with Secretary Perry, General Shalikashvili, and White House aides in the Oval Office to receive a briefing on both NATO's OPLAN 40104 and the Pentagon's proposal to assist the RRF by supplying equipment and providing other support. Neither the State Department nor representatives from the U.S. mission at the United Nations were invited to the meeting. Complaints from Deputy Secretary of State Strobe Talbott that neither he nor Christopher was invited were dismissed by the White House, which maintained that the meeting constituted merely a military briefing. See Devroy and Graham, "Seeking to Reassure Europe, Clinton Alarmed Congress," p. A1; McManus, "Clinton Zigzag on Balkans May Underscore His Unease," p. A1; Devroy, "Nailing Down a Bosnia Policy," p. A28; and Drew, *Showdown*, p. 247.

48. For example Bob Dole (R-Kans.), Senate majority leader and Clinton's likely Republican opponent during the 1996 elections, noted that this was a "significant policy shift" which was "nothing more than a policy of reinforcing failure." Dole suggested an alternative: "lift the immoral arms embargo on Bosnia . . . because it is the best alternative to continuing an irretrievably flawed peacekeeping operation." Cited in John Harris, "Clinton Vows Help for UN Troops in Bosnia," *Washington Post*, June 1, 1995, p. A1. See also Katharine Seelye, "Many in Congress Reluctant to Widen U.S. Role in Bosnia," *New York Times*, June 2, 1995, p. A1.

emergency extraction, we would assist, after consulting with Congress. This would be a limited, temporary operation, and we have not been asked to do this.[49]

Clinton's statement and subsequent testimony before both houses of Congress by Secretary Perry and General Shalikashvili resolved any confusion surrounding administration policy on the circumstances under which the United States would deploy American troops to Bosnia. These were restricted to three situations: to implement a negotiated peace agreement, assist in the withdrawal of the UN force, and help in an emergency extraction of a UN unit under attack or in substantial danger.[50]

In clarifying its policy on when U.S. troops would be sent to Bosnia, the administration reaffirmed its commitment to NATO to assist in the withdrawal of the UN force if and when such a request came from the United Nations. Indeed, Clinton approved the basic outlines of the NATO contingency plan, as set forth in OPLAN 40104, following a June 2 briefing by General Shalikashvili.[51] Of course, the final decision on both the implementation of the operations plan and any U.S. participation therein was deferred until such time as it was necessary to make the decision. Only when a request from the United Nations to NATO had in fact been made, would the North Atlantic Council—and through it, the sixteen member states—decide whether to accede to the request and implement the plan. In this sense, NATO never formally approved OPLAN 40104, although everyone knew that if the UN requested assistance, the operation would most likely be approved.[52]

49. "Radio Address by the President to the Nation" (White House, Office of the Press Secretary, June 3, 1995). At the suggestion of his political adviser, Dick Morris, who worried about a public backlash with opinion polls running 80 percent against sending ground troops to Bosnia, the president departed from this prepared text and added, "I think it is highly unlikely that we would be asked to do it." See George Stephanopoulos, *All Too Human: A Political Education* (Little, Brown, 1999), p. 355. Quotation from *Public Papers of the Presidents of the United States: William J. Clinton, 1995: Book I, January 1 to June 30, 1995* (GPO, 1996), p. 805.

50. Statement by Perry, *Situation in Bosnia*, Senate hearings, p. 15.

51. "Key Bosnia Meeting/Event Chronology," p. 2. See also Devroy and Graham, "Seeking to Reassure Europe, Clinton Alarmed Congress," p. A1.

52. NATO issued two, identical statements on OPLAN 40104, following NAC meetings on June 14 and 28, 1995, respectively. Both statements read as follows:

—NATO strongly supports the continued presence of UN forces in the former Yugoslavia. It believes that the UN Peace Forces perform an essential mission and that withdrawal can be considered only as a last resort;

Clinton, Holbrooke, and the U.S. Commitment

This detailed account of the origins and extent of the U.S. commitment to assist in the withdrawal of the UN is important in view of the somewhat different rendition that appears in Richard Holbrooke's writings on the subject, including his book on the origins of Dayton.[53] Holbrooke notes that he did not fully appreciate the scope and dangerous nature of the U.S. commitment implied in OPLAN 40104 until he received a briefing from the Pentagon in the second week of June, after he returned from his honeymoon in Europe. According to Holbrooke, the plan, as briefed, was "bold and dangerous" and suggested an "operation likely to produce casualties." Immediately after the briefing, Holbrooke went to Christopher and insisted he get the same briefing. "When he heard it, Christopher was equally amazed."[54] What particularly disturbed both officials was

---

—NATO's planning for a possible UN withdrawal is therefore on a contingency basis only. In this context, following intensive work in the Military Committee on contingency planning for withdrawal, the Council is fully engaged in the process of considering and approving the planning as a matter of priority;

—NATO's planning will be continuously updated and will only be finally approved by Council if and when a withdrawal operation needs to be implemented following a UN request.

"Statement by the NATO Spokesman Following NAC," Press Release (95)63 (Brussels: North Atlantic Treaty Organization, June 14, 1995); and "Statement by the NATO Spokesman Following NAC," PL267 (Brussels: North Atlantic Treaty Organization, June 28, 1995).

53. See Richard Holbrooke, "Why Are We in Bosnia?" *The New Yorker*, vol. 74 (May 18, 1998), pp. 40–41, and the slightly different account in Holbrooke, *To End a War*, pp. 66–68. Part of the story Holbrooke recounts first appeared in Bob Woodward, *The Choice* (Simon and Schuster, 1996), p. 255.

54. Holbrooke, *To End a War*, p. 66. It is not clear why Christopher, in particular, should have been amazed. All the principals had had ample opportunity to discuss the details of the plan. Indeed, according to a senior aide to one principal, OPLAN 40104 was discussed in numerous interagency meetings. His principal was well briefed, in part because of the numerous memoranda on the subject this senior aide wrote during the first half of 1995. "If Christopher didn't know about the details of 40104, then his staff let him down. There was no reason why he should not have known." Interview with a senior administration official, June 8, 1998. Moreover, as recounted earlier, the contingency plan had been discussed in detail during at least three high-level meetings in mid- to late May at which Christopher was present, and many of the plan's complexities and dangers had been addressed during these meetings. Indeed, that was why the principals concluded that Washington should leave no stone unturned to convince the allies to keep their troops in Bosnia, thus avoiding the need to fulfill the commitment to NATO and the UN.

their apparent belief that there was a high degree of automaticity in the decision to send U.S. troops. As Holbrooke describes it:

> [The OPLAN] had already been [formally] endorsed by the NATO Council. According to complicated Cold War procedures that had never been tested, if the NATO Council gave the order to assist the UN's withdrawal, the planning document [OPLAN 40104] would become an operational order, adjusted for specific circumstances. Thus if the UN withdrew, OpPLAN 40-104 [sic] would trigger the immediate deployment of 20,000 American troops in the heart of the Balkans as part of the NATO force. . . . The president would still have to make the final decision to deploy U.S. troops, but his options had been drastically narrowed. If, in the event of a UN withdrawal, he did not deploy American troops, the United States would be flouting, in its first test, the very NATO process it had created. The resulting recriminations could mean the end of NATO as an effective military alliance.[55]

This interpretation is flawed in important respects. On a minor point, the North Atlantic Council had not, in fact, formally endorsed the OPLAN, but instead declared on June 14, and again on June 28, that it was "fully engaged in the process of considering and approving the planning as a matter of priority."[56] No formal endorsement of the plan was needed until the UN requested NATO's assistance. In this sense, the "complicated Cold War procedures" would be set in motion *only* if the UN requested NATO's assistance, at which time the NAC—and the member states individually— would have to approve the execution of the plan. Moreover, the notion that 20,000 U.S. troops would be automatically deployed was a possibility—but hardly a certainty. This was the worst-case scenario, properly included in a military contingency plan. The nature and extent of the NATO—and U.S.—military commitment would depend on the circumstances prevailing at the time the UN decided to withdraw (for example, whether the RRF was already in place or not). Finally, however, there is the somewhat bizarre notion that U.S. credibility in the eyes of its NATO allies depended upon the execution of a complex NATO process. Surely,

55. Holbrooke, *To End a War*, pp. 66–67.

56. "Statement by NATO Spokesman Following North Atlantic Council," Press Release (95)63; "Statement by NATO Spokesman Following North Atlantic Council," PL267.

U.S. credibility was at stake not because of admittedly "complicated Cold War procedures," but because the United States, as the leader of NATO, had long ago, repeatedly, and publicly committed itself to assist its NATO allies contributing troops to UNPROFOR in case of need. It was that commitment that lay at the heart of the NATO planning process, which would not have proceeded in December 1994 if the president had not decided to make it in the first place.

This distinction between a complicated NATO process and an explicit, overt commitment in explaining the degree of automaticity in the U.S. pledge to send troops to Bosnia helps to place a critical and oft-cited anecdote recounted by Holbrooke in its proper context. According to Holbrooke, a "pre-brief" in the Oval Office prior to French President Chirac's first visit to Washington on June 14 "quickly degenerated into an angry and contentious discussion of Bosnia. The presentation given by members of the National Security Council staff was, in my view, misleading as to the situation, and especially the degree of American 'automaticity' in assisting a UN withdrawal." However, Clinton cut off the discussion before Holbrooke could make his case. The opportunity to do so arose later that evening, after a dinner for Chirac, when the Clintons approached Holbrooke, Christopher, Berger, and Madeleine Albright, who were standing in front of the North Portico. Holbrooke records what happened next:

> The president joined us and broke the ice. "What about Bosnia?" he asked suddenly.
>
> "I hate to ruin a wonderful evening, Mr. President," I began, "but we should clarify something that came up during the day. Under existing NATO plans, the United States is already committed to sending troops to Bosnia if the UN decides to withdraw. I'm afraid that we may not have that much flexibility left."
>
> The President looked at me with surprise. "What do you mean?" he asked. "I'll decide the troop issue if and when the time comes."
>
> There was silence for a moment. "Mr. President," I said. "NATO has already approved the withdrawal plan. While you have the power to stop it, it has a high degree of automaticity built into it, especially since we have committed ourselves publicly to assisting NATO troops if the UN decides to withdraw."
>
> The President looked at Christopher. "Is this true?" he said. "I suggest that we talk about it tomorrow," Christopher said. "We have a problem." Without another word, the President walked off.[57]

57. Holbrooke, *To End a War*, pp. 67–68.

Whether wittingly or not, this anecdote portrays a president who is in the dark as to the nature and extent of the U.S. troop commitment to NATO and Bosnia.[58] Crucial to this inference is Holbrooke's contention, apparently shared by Christopher, that the president seemed surprised by the extent to which the United States was already committed to assisting in UNPROFOR's withdrawal as a result of the near-automaticity of NATO's decisionmaking process. Not having been present that evening, nor having been able to confirm or contradict Holbrooke's account in interviews, it is impossible for me to determine the degree to which Clinton was truly surprised. Yet Holbrooke's inference appears to be mistaken.

There are at least two reasons to think that either Holbrooke misread Clinton's surprise or the expression of surprise reflected the president's annoyance in being confronted with an unpleasant reality that he had wished to put aside, at least at that moment.[59] First, it is not credible to infer, assume, or otherwise believe that the president was not fully aware of either the commitment to the NATO allies or its implications for the deployment of American ground forces. Clinton had publicly reiterated the commitment only days before, in his speech to the Air Force Academy and his radio address to the nation. He had been briefed by his chief military adviser, General Shalikashvili, about the contents and the nature of the U.S. military commitment on June 2. And for weeks the newspapers had been full of stories about the commitment—the number of troops that

58. Nearly all reviews of Holbrooke's book uncritically—if amazingly—accept Holbrooke's contention that the president was unaware of the extent of the U.S. commitment. See, for example, Mark Danner, "Slouching toward Dayton," *New York Review of Books*, vol. 45 (April 23, 1998), pp. 59–61; Jim Hoagland, "Holbrooke's Prophetic Memoir," *Washington Post*, April 9, 1998, p. A25; Tom Gjelten, "Bickering toward Peace," *Washington Post: Book World*, June 7, 1998, p. 1; Chris Hedges, "The Peacemaker," *New York Times Book Review*, June 14, 1998, p. 6; "Junkyard Dogs," *Economist*, June 13, 1998, p. 6; Roger Cohen, "After the Vultures: Holbrooke's Bosnia Peace Came Too Late," *Foreign Affairs*, vol. 77 (May/June 1998), pp. 106–11; David Rieff, "Almost Justice," *The New Republic*, vol. 219 (July 6, 1998), p. 36; and Paul Wolfowitz, "The Man Who Saved the Day—Sort Of," *National Interest*, no. 53 (Fall 1998), p. 104.

59. According to someone who knew Clinton well, the president sometimes acted surprised when confronted with situations he did not like. He also hated interpersonal conflict. These behavioral traits appear to be a form of defensiveness on Clinton's part. Finally, the president was aware that Christopher was still unhappy about the earlier agreement by the president on the conditions under which the United States would send forces to the region. All of these could help explain Clinton's surprised expression. Interviews with an administration official, August 13, 1998, and a senior administration official, February 5, 1999.

might have to be involved, the danger of the operation, and the problems the administration faced on the Hill. To imply that Clinton, a policy wonk and a person who can absorb seemingly endless amounts of data, did not fully appreciate the consequence of his own public commitment to NATO is simply not credible.

Second, whereas Holbrooke, Christopher, and much of the State Department seemed to have believed that UNPROFOR's withdrawal represented an unmitigated disaster that was to be avoided at almost any cost, the White House (and the president himself) had by this time concluded that the UN forces were likely to be withdrawn sooner rather than later. In the short term, the White House was prepared to expand the necessary effort and resources to keep UNPROFOR in place—whence the decision to provide equipment and air assets to bolster the RRF and the willingness to send U.S. troops to assist in an emergency extraction. In the long run, however, the president, Lake, and others on the NSC staff were coming to the conclusion that UNPROFOR's withdrawal might represent an opportunity to implement a more forceful policy. What Clinton and others feared was not UNPROFOR's withdrawal *per se*, but being blamed for the departure, because this would make the United States rather than Europe primarily responsible for the Bosnia issue. These considerations were clearly captured in Clinton's press conference at the Group of Seven summit in Halifax less than forty-eight hours after the encounter on the North Portico. Much of the conference was devoted to reassuring the allies that Washington would support the RRF, a force that would provide UNPROFOR with a new lease on life. But the president also pointedly noted that, while he would do nothing to precipitate the UN's departure, "if the UN mission does fail, if our allies decide to leave, I would strongly support lifting the arms embargo. It's the best alternative at that moment."[60] With this, Clinton underscored his belief that if UNPROFOR went, its departure would provide an opportunity to set a new direction for U.S. policy.

Holbrooke's account does, however, underscore an important point. The United States was clearly boxed in by its commitment to NATO. The president would have had little choice but to go ahead with the operation outlined in the NATO OPLAN if and when the UN decided to withdraw. It may not have mattered that a refusal to participate would have flouted "the very NATO process" the United States had created, but the failure to

60. "Remarks by the President at Press Availability" (Halifax, Nova Scotia: White House, Office of the Press Secretary, June 16, 1995).

assist allies in need would certainly have raised a large question mark over the Atlantic alliance. To be sure, the president and his senior foreign policy advisers were well aware of this, which is why they decided in December 1994, following the debacle in Bihac, to make the commitment in the first place. Moreover, whereas Holbrooke and Christopher feared the consequences of a withdrawal, Clinton and Lake were coming to see in it an opportunity for a more forceful U.S. policy.

Congress and the Arms Embargo

While conditions on the ground were influencing allied decisions on whether to retain their troops in Bosnia, one other consideration determining whether the United States would have to send forces to the region was being played out in the corridors of power in Washington. Congress had long been critical of the Clinton administration's policy on Bosnia—and never more so than after the 1994 elections, when the Republicans seized control of both houses. A central issue in contention was the arms embargo, which had remained in place on Bosnia and the other former Yugoslav republics that had become independent since it was first imposed by the UN Security Council in September 1991.[61] The Clinton administration had come to office pledging to seek an end to the embargo, but had failed to convince the European allies to go along. Ever since, the administration remained rhetorically committed to the *multilateral* lifting of the embargo, but rejected efforts to end it unilaterally. Not so the Congress, which had consistently pushed to lift the embargo. In late 1994, Congress had succeeded in forcing an end to U.S. enforcement of the embargo. And in early 1995, it was evident that a Republican-led Congress would challenge the president on the embargo issue. Among its very first

61. UN Security Council, Resolution *S/RES/713 (1991)*, September 15, 1991. The Bosnian government argued that the arms embargo violated Bosnia's right to self-defense as stipulated under Article 51 of the UN Charter, and was therefore illegal. However, according to Chapter VII of the UN Charter, Article 51 applied only until the Security Council had taken "measures necessary to the maintenance of international peace and security." The arms embargo was applied to the territories of the Federal Republic of Yugoslavia under a Chapter VII measure, and therefore remained in effect after the republics became independent. Under Article 25 of the UN Charter, all states agree to be bound by Chapter VII resolutions, thereby providing the Security Council sole authority for lifting the embargo. See James Gow, *Triumph of the Lack of Will: International Diplomacy and the Yugoslav War* (Columbia University Press, 1997), p. 38.

acts was the introduction on January 4, 1995, of a bill by Senate majority leader Bob Dole to lift the arms embargo under one of two conditions: if the Bosnian government asked it to be lifted; or once the four-month cease-fire expired on April 30, 1995. In either case, the embargo would be lifted unilaterally.[62]

The administration vehemently opposed the Dole bill, arguing that it would precipitate an allied decision to withdraw their forces and place responsibility for Bosnia's future squarely on Washington.[63] Such an allied decision would mean that U.S. troops would go to Bosnia as part of a NATO effort to assist in UNPROFOR's withdrawal. Moreover, once the UN was gone, Bosnia would be America's responsibility. The international and non-governmental agencies providing for the humanitarian needs of the Bosnian population would either leave or require protection by other, presumably U.S., forces. In addition, if the Serbs responded to the UN's departure and the imminent arrival of new weapons by launching an all-out assault for fear that the balance of arms might soon shift against them, then the United States would face the choice of seeing the Bosnian government defeated or having to intervene itself.[64]

Administration opposition, the relative quiet in Bosnia, and a laser beam–like focus on domestic issues in the Republican-led Congress combined to shelve the Dole bill through the winter and early spring of 1995. However, once the situation on the ground in Bosnia deteriorated in May, the issue returned with a vengeance. As senior Clinton officials debated the intricacies of when, how, and under what circumstances U.S. forces might need to be deployed to rescue a hapless UN presence in Bosnia, congressional sentiment for lifting the arms embargo as the preferred alternative once again rose in full force. Senate Republicans drafted a resolution authorizing the use of U.S. troops to help UNPROFOR withdraw and then to lift the arms embargo.[65] Much of the support for the resolution came from

62. "Bosnia and Herzegovina Self-Defense Act of 1995," S. 21, 104 Cong. 1 sess., January 4, 1995.

63. Allied reaction to the introduction of the Dole bill had been both swift and predictable. The French and British foreign ministers traveled to Washington and warned that, if enacted, France and Britain would pull their troops out of Bosnia, signaling the collapse of UNPROFOR. See Elaine Sciolino, "Bosnian Asks G.O.P. Lawmakers to Help End Arms Embargo," *New York Times*, January 31, 1995, p. A3.

64. See, for example, the statement of White House Press Secretary Michael McCurry cited in Elaine Sciolino, "Dole Offers Foreign Policy Initiatives," *New York Times*, January 5, 1995, p. A3.

65. Donna Cassata, "Congress Bucks White House, Devises Its Own Bosnia Plan," *Congressional Quarterly*, June 10, 1995, p. 1653.

Senate Democratic circles, with many senior Senators indicating that they wished to see a course correction.[66] In the House of Representatives, meanwhile, an amendment to the foreign aid bill was approved on June 8 by a three-to-one margin (318 to 99) to lift the embargo if the Bosnian government so requested. Although that version was unlikely ever to become law since it was attached to a bill the president had already promised to veto for other reasons, the vote nevertheless indicated the degree of opposition to the administration's Bosnia policy.

Of course, the congressional actions provided no clear road map for how to resolve the conflict in Bosnia. It was more an expression of frustration with administration policy and a strong belief that the Bosnians possessed a moral right of self-defense than a ready policy course to follow. As one perceptive analyst noted, "Not one of the bills or resolutions generated by lawmakers this year would send the Muslims so much as a squirt gun. . . . The oratory and maneuvering say more about American politics than foreign affairs."[67] At the same time, while playing politics with a difficult issue and avoiding responsibility for charting a clear and achievable course of action, Congress was putting the administration on notice that time was running out and that if the situation continued to deteriorate it might take matters into its own hands.

As it happened, developments in Bosnia forced Congress into action sooner rather than later. Once the UN's failure to halt the Serb attack against the eastern enclaves had become fully evident following the conquest of the towns of Srebrenica and Zepa in mid-July, Congress acted swiftly to force the administration's hand. On July 26, the Senate voted 69-29 to end U.S. participation in the arms embargo.[68] The House followed suit on August 1, voting 298-128 to send the Senate bill to the president for his signature or veto.[69] Nine days later, Senator Dole and Senator Jesse Helms (R-N.C.) introduced a bill to provide Bosnia with

66. See Elaine Sciolino, "Clinton's Policy on Bosnia Draws Criticism in Congress," *New York Times*, June 8, 1995, p. A10; and Cassata, "Congress Bucks White House, Devises Its Own Bosnia Plan," pp. 1653–44. See also, more generally, Drew, *Showdown*, pp. 248–49.

67. Elaine Sciolino, "Congress Arms Bosnia with Gas," *New York Times*, June 18, 1995, p. 1.

68. Elaine Sciolino, "Defiant Senators Vote to Override Bosnian Arms Ban," *New York Times*, July 27, 1995, p. A8.

69. Elaine Sciolino, "House Like Senate, Votes to Halt Bosnia Embargo," *New York Times*, August 2, 1995, p. A6.

$100 million in military assistance (half in cash; half in-kind) and to create an international coalition to help arm the country.[70]

The specific provisions of the bill sent to the president on August 1 provided the administration with some room to maneuver. The bill stated that the United States would end participation in the embargo only after UNPROFOR had been withdrawn or twelve weeks after the Bosnian government had asked UNPROFOR to withdraw. The provision could also be waived by the president for an unlimited number of thirty-day periods if he certified that this was necessary to ensure a safe withdrawal. Finally, the president was required to seek a multilateral lift of the embargo in the UN Security Council prior to abandoning it unilaterally.[71]

Still, the message sent by Congress was clear: the bill passed both houses of Congress by margins sufficient to override a presidential veto. Continued reliance on UNPROFOR as the main instrument of U.S. policy toward Bosnia should be abandoned in favor of assisting the Bosnians with arms—although not with American troops. It was one more indication that administration policy had reached a dead end and that a fundamental reevaluation of both the aim and the means of that policy was necessary. The final indication had come in the days just prior to the congressional vote, with the brutal assault on Srebrenica and the unexpected decision by the NATO allies to take the steps necessary to make sure this was the last time that the Bosnian Serbs would succeed militarily.[72]

A Final Serb Offensive

It was not long after he arrived in Sarajevo in January 1995 that British Lieutenant General Rupert Smith realized that 1995 was to be the decisive year of the war and, thus, for the UN troops that he was to command as the new head of UNPROFOR's forces in Bosnia. Smith arrived at this conclusion on the basis of his assessment that the Bosnian Serbs were

70. *Multilateral Bosnia and Herzegovina Self-Defense Fund*, S. 1157, 104 Cong. 1 sess., August 10, 1995 (GPO); Adam Clymer, "Dole-Helms Bill Asks $100 Million in Arms Aid for Bosnia," *New York Times*, August 11, 1995, p. A3.

71. See Sciolino, "Defiant Senators Vote to Override Bosnian Arms Ban," p. A8.

72. Clinton vetoed the arms embargo bill on August 11, 1995, after he had agreed to a new policy and after he had sent his national security adviser to Europe to advise the major allies of his decision. See "Statement by President Clinton on Veto of Lifting of Bosnia Arms Embargo" (White House, Office of the Press Secretary, August 11, 1995).

Figure 2. *Bosnia and the UN-Declared "Safe Areas"*

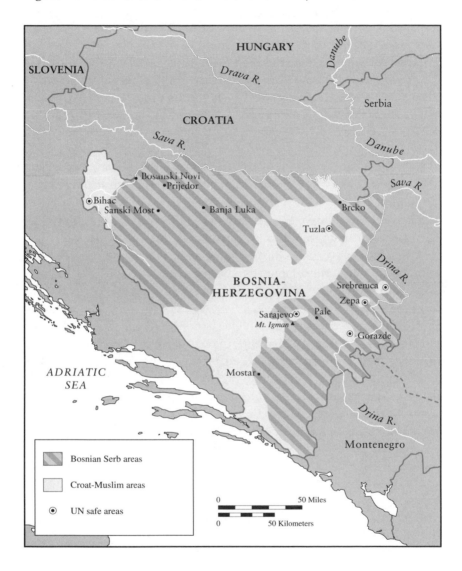

feeling increasingly squeezed on all sides. Although Milosevic's August 1994 decision to cut off supplies to the Bosnian Serbs had not been fully implemented, the supply lines were appreciably less reliable than they had been before Belgrade's announcement. Pale also believed, quite rightly, that the Bosnian Croats and Muslims viewed the cease-fire of the first four months of 1995 as a convenient pause to prepare for taking the fight to the Serbs. Given this strategic predicament, Smith believed that the Bosnian Serbs would sooner rather than later attempt to settle the war on their own terms. The key to that strategy would be to take over the three eastern enclaves, whose existence posed a strain on Bosnian Serb soldiers—the one area in which the Bosnian Muslims and Croats enjoyed a major advantage. As Smith told his military and civilian superiors in early June, "Our analysis of the Serbs' intentions is to finish the war this year and to take every risk to achieve it. . . . They will destroy the eastern enclaves this year."[73]

Smith's assessment was correct. In early March 1995, the Bosnian Serb political and military leadership had met to assess their strategic predicament and agreed to "launch a final campaign in an attempt to force their Bosnian and Croat opponents to settle the war before the year was out." The eastern enclaves were top on the list.[74] Accordingly, the end of the cease-fire on May 1 signaled the beginning of the final phase in the Bosnian war. The Bosnian Serbs responded to Bosnian Muslim and Croat attempts to cut Serb supply lines by increasing pressure on the "safe areas." The Serbs shelled Sarajevo on May 7, killing eleven. When the UN command in Zagreb turned down Smith's request for NATO air strikes, Pale felt sufficiently emboldened to challenge the weapons exclusion zone around Sarajevo. Pinprick air strikes followed and the Serbs took nearly 400 UN peacekeepers hostage. While Smith pressed to continue the use of NATO air power, he was rebuffed by the UN command, which instead issued a new set of guidelines severely circumscribing the circumstances under which NATO air strikes would be requested or approved.[75]

From this point on, it was clear to the Bosnian Serbs that the United Nations, which on June 9 had indicated that UNPROFOR would return

73. Gutman, "The UN's Deadly Deal," p. A3.
74. Jan Willem Honig and Norbert Both, *Srebrenica* (Penguin Books, 1996), pp. 141–42; quotation from p. 141. See also Rohde, *Endgame*, p. 372.
75. Under the new guidelines, issued by the UNPF Commander, General Janvier, the authority to approve large-scale NATO air strikes of the kind launched days earlier would now rest with UN Secretary General Boutros Boutros-Ghali rather than his special representative for the former Yugoslavia, Yasushi Akashi. As for close air support (CAS) to defend UN peacekeepers, authority for which had rested with Smith, Janvier would have to approve each individual request. The reason for the change was clearly stated in the new guidelines: "The execution of the mandate is secondary to the security of UN personnel." See Rohde, *Endgame*, pp. 27–28, with quotation on p. 28.

to "traditional peacekeeping principles,"[76] would not interfere with their efforts to end the war by finishing off the eastern enclaves. Within a month, they were well on their way to success. In the early morning hours of July 6, 1995, the attack on the UN "safe area" of Srebrenica began in earnest. After the UN turned down air strike requests from Dutch peacekeepers, the small UN force could do little to prevent a disaster. In ten days, the Bosnian Serbs, led by their commander, General Ratko Mladic, engaged in the worst war crimes in Europe since the end of World War II. Some 23,000 women and children were herded like cattle out of the enclave and sent to Bosnian Muslim territory near Tuzla. In harrowing scenes since described in detail, almost 8,000 men and boys were summarily executed en masse.[77] Although most intelligence agencies had misjudged Serb intentions, believing that this attack was but the latest in a series of probes to make life in the UN "safe area" uncomfortable, it was soon evident that this was something different. The dimensions of both the attack and the brutality (described by one Dutch UN peacekeeper as a "combination of *Schindler's List* and *Sophie's Choice*")[78] were generally known in the days during and immediately following the attack—and confirmed in deeply disturbing newspaper accounts that soon appeared.[79] However, the extent of the massacre—indeed, the very fact of its occurrence—was not fully

76. The statement was issued by Yasushi Akashi following a meeting with General Janvier and General Smith in Split, Croatia, at which Smith had vehemently argued for the resumption of air strikes even though many hostages still remained in Serb hands, only to be overruled by Janvier and Akashi. Detailed excerpts of a transcript from the meeting are in Rohde, *Endgame*, pp. 419–422n8; Akashi's statement is on p. 422.

77. The single best account of what happened in these ten days is by David Rohde in *Endgame*. In addition, consult Honig and Both, *Srebrenica*; Chuck Sudetic, *Blood and Vengeance* (W. W. Norton, 1998), pp. 251–325; Frank Westerman and Bart Rijs, *Srebrenica: Het Zwartste Scenario* (Amsterdam: Uitgeverij Atlas, 1997); Mark Danner, "The U.S. and the Yugoslav Catastrophe," *New York Review of Books*, vol. 44, November 20, 1997, pp. 56–64; and Danner, "Bosnia: The Great Betrayal," *New York Review of Books*, vol. 45, March 26, 1998, pp. 40–52.

78. Quoted in Honig and Both, *Srebrenica*, p. xvii.

79. See, for example, Stephen Kinzer, "Terrorized Human Tide Overwhelms Relief Camp," *New York Times*, July 15, 1995, p. 4; Kinzer, "Bosnian Refugees' Accounts Appear to Verify Atrocities," *New York Times*, July 17, 1995, p. A1; and Kinzer, "Bosnia Lets Refugees Leave Camp but 20,000 Others Are Missing," *New York Times*, July 16, 1995, p. 1; Stephen Engelberg, Tim Weiner, Raymond Bonner, and Jane Perlez, "Srebrenica: The Days of Slaughter," *New York Times*, October 29, 1995, p. A1; and Michael Dobbs and R. Jeffrey Smith, "New Proof Offered of Serb Atrocities," *Washington Post*, October 29, 1995, p. A1.

appreciated until some weeks later, when satellite photographs showed the freshly bulldozed earth around the Srebrenica pocket presumably containing the thousands of bodies that had been slaughtered.[80]

Chirac's Challenge

With the fall of Srebrenica on July 16, the Bosnian Serbs turned their aim south-east, to another UN "safe area" around the town of Zepa. With Zepa about to fall, General Mladic felt confident enough to make his strategy public: "By the autumn, we'll take Gorazde, Bihac and in the end Sarajevo and we'll finish the war."[81] This challenge confronted the United Nations, NATO, and especially the leading member states with a fundamental choice. They could act to oppose what was unfolding before them by force of arms or they could declare defeat, withdraw the UN force, and hope for the best. French President Jacques Chirac posed the issue starkly on July 13: "It is . . . indispensable to bring a halt to the abandonment of the enclaves by a firm, yet limited military action. [If] such a military action proved impossible, France would be bound, in conjunction with its partners and the UN secretary general, to draw all the relevant consequences."[82]

80. Despite numerous first-hand refugee accounts taken within days of the fall of Srebrenica, it was not until August 4 that the U.S. intelligence community was able to provide policymakers evidence that the massacres had been committed. On July 13, Washington first learned of the possibility of atrocities in a phone call from Bosnian Foreign Minister Mohamed Sacirbey to Ambassador Madeleine Albright. At Sandy Berger's suggestion, Albright subsequently tasked the intelligence community to look for proof. On July 17, the CIA's Bosnia Task Force reported that numerous refugee accounts "provide details that appear credible" about atrocities being committed, but "we lack authoritative, detailed information to substantiate this information." Over the coming days, additional first-hand accounts were received by John Shattuck, assistant secretary of state for democracy, labor and human rights, after Secretary Christopher had received a cable from U.S. Ambassador to Croatia Peter Galbraith that detailed testimony of Serb atrocities by a survivor that had escaped to Tuzla. On August 2 an intelligence analyst was able to piece together the first evidence of the massacres from satellite imagery taken days and weeks earlier. The classified report was published two days later in the *National Intelligence Daily*. It was made public on August 10, after Albright briefed a closed session of the UN Security Council. See Dobbs and Smith, "New Proof Offered of Serb Atrocities," p. A1; and Engelberg and others, "Srebrenica: The Days of Slaughter," p. 1.

81. Quoted in David Evans, "Muted Threat Falls Short of Summit Hopes," *The Times*, July 22, 1995, p. 1.

82. Cited in William Echikson, "France Wants Action to Halt Attacks," *Boston Globe*, July 14, 1995, p. A8.

The French president's admonition was more than rhetoric; it came with a proposal—to make a firm and final stance in Gorazde, a UN "safe area" east of Sarajevo that was home to some 50,000 to 60,000 Bosnians, half of them refugees from nearby towns.[83] The specific suggestion was to deploy around 1,000 troops to Gorazde, drawn from the soon-to-be-deployed Rapid Reaction Force, in order to deter a possible attack. Although Paris did not expect Washington to send U.S. ground troops, France did propose that the United States provide air cover for the operation, as well as air and helicopter transportation to ferry the troops into Gorazde.[84]

The French proposal posed a difficult challenge to the United States, a challenge that was debated by President Clinton's senior national security advisers for two-and-a-half hours on July 14. The principals confronted a basic predicament. On the one hand, the French proposal was risky and U.S. military participation crossed a critical line that could draw the United States in more deeply than was desirable. On the other hand, President Chirac had effectively put the ball in Washington's (and London's) court by deciding that military action was necessary and making sure that others would be blamed if no action was forthcoming. The principals therefore decided that the United States should not reject the French proposal to reinforce Gorazde. But rather than accepting it, they raised a series of questions designed to turn the option away from a ground reinforcement of the enclave toward an allied consensus to use air power in a strategically significant manner in the event that the Bosnian town was attacked. Indeed, according to one participant, Secretary Perry was particularly forceful and eloquent in pressing for significant air strikes, arguing that the debacle in Srebrenica provided the United States the policy opening it had

83. Earlier, Chirac had offered the use of French troops to recapture Srebrenica if the UN Security Council so decided. While Britain rejected the proposal as impractical, as late as July 13 President Clinton called on the UN forces "to go back in there and re-establish the safe area"—a statement his aides later described as a mistake. For Chirac's statement and the British reaction, see Eric Schmitt, "U.S. and NATO Face Unhappy Choices for UN Force in the Balkans," *New York Times*, July 12, 1995, p. A6; and Fred Barbash, "London Rebuts Paris Bosnia Stand," *Washington Post*, July 16, 1995, p. A25. For Clinton's statement, see "Remarks by the President Following Welfare Reform Meeting" (White House, Office of the Press Secretary, July 13, 1995). See also Laura Silber and Allan Little, *Yugoslavia: Death of a Nation* (New York: TV Books, distributed by Penguin USA, 1996), pp. 351–52.

84. See Craig R. Whitney, "France Asks Allied Forces to Help Hold 'Safe Areas,'" *New York Times*, July 14, 1995, p. A1; and Alison Mitchell, "U.S. Weighs a Response to French Call on Bosnia," *New York Times*, July 15, 1995, p. A4.

long sought to convince the allies to support the kind of air campaign that was now needed.[85] To this end, President Clinton decided to send General Shalikashvili to London to meet with his British and French counterparts to discuss the French proposal and work out a response that was militarily feasible and realistic, including a possible NATO air campaign.[86]

In London, General Shalikashvili posed a series of probing questions designed to convince his French counterpart, Admiral Jacques Lanxade, that the idea of reinforcing Gorazde from the ground was militarily untenable. According to a U.S. official who was present, the central point of Shalikashvili's argument was that ensuring the safety of the helicopters and aircraft transporting the troops required destroying the Bosnian Serb air defense systems capable of attacking them—before sending forces to Gorazde.[87] If that were the case, the U.S. general asked, why not threaten that kind of devastating strike to deter an attack on the enclave in the first place? Why not draw a line by making clear that any threat or attack against Gorazde would lead to a devastating response by NATO air power? Shalikashvili made clear that, to be effective, such air strikes would have to be extensive and could not be subject to the "dual-key" arrangement that had characterized air operations in Bosnia up to this point. To reduce the possibility of Serb reprisals against UN forces, UN military observers in Serb-controlled territory should also be withdrawn.[88]

85. Interview with a senior administration official, August 7, 1998. See also "Key Meeting/Event Chronology," p. 3.

86. See "Press Briefing by Mike McCurry" (White House, Office of the Press Secretary, July 14, 1995). See also Mitchell, "U.S. Weighs a Response to French Call on Bosnia," p. 4; Ann Devroy and William Drozdiak, "Clinton Agrees to Plan Defense of 'Safe Areas,'" *Washington Post*, July 15, 1995, p. A17; Art Pine, "Military Chiefs to Meet, Review Bosnia Options," *Los Angeles Times*, July 15, 1995; and Drew, *Showdown*, p. 250.

87. Interview with a Pentagon official, March 26, 1998. NATO planners had developed an air campaign that included attacks to suppress enemy air defenses (SEAD) within a specific theater inside Bosnia. Two zones of action (ZOA) were drawn up for the SEAD mission—a southeastern zone around Sarajevo and a northwestern zone around Banja Luka—dividing Bosnia into two distinct theaters of action in case air strikes were approved. See Robert C. Owen, "Summary," in Owen, study director, *DELIBERATE FORCE: A Case Study in Effective Air Campaigning*, Final Report of the Air University Balkans Air Campaign Study, School of Advanced Airpower Studies (Maxwell Air Force Base, Ala.: SAAS, 1998), Chapter 12, p. 12. It was on the basis of these studies that Shalikashvili argued that the use of NATO and U.S. aircraft required an extensive SEAD campaign to assure their safety.

88. Interview with a Pentagon official, March 27, 1998. The "dual key" arrangement stemmed from a series of NATO consultations that took place in early August 1993. See pp. 22–23 above.

According to the same U.S. official, an extensive discussion of Shalikashvili's ideas followed, but it was clear that the United States still needed to do much convincing.[89] The British Chief of the Defense Staff, Field Marshal Sir Peter Inge, explained that while London sought to keep its forces in Bosnia and was willing to strengthen UNPROFOR, air strikes would inevitably lead to a pull-out of all British troops. Inge seemed to favor consolidating the UN forces in more defensible and central positions, even if this meant that Gorazde (and perhaps even Bihac) would be left unprotected.[90] The French, while conceding the logic of Shalikashvili's argument, nevertheless insisted that the only possible solution was a ground reinforcement of Gorazde and that doing so required not just a NATO air cover, but also the use of U.S. helicopters to ferry personnel into the area. As for air strikes, Lanxade agreed that an attack on air defense systems would be required, but only in case any of the helicopter or other air assets actually came under fire.

Drawing the Line in Gorazde

The day after the meeting of the British, French, and U.S. chief military officers, the principals met for their regular weekly breakfast in Tony Lake's office.[91] At issue was both long-term U.S. policy toward Bosnia and the more immediate question of what the U.S. position should be at the upcoming London conference, which had been called by British Prime Minister John Major in the immediate aftermath of the fall of Srebrenica.

89. Interview with a Pentagon official, March 26, 1998, and "Key Meeting/Event Chronology," p. 3. See also William Drozdiak, "Allies Set to Prod U.S. into Role in Bosnia," *Washington Post*, July 19, 1995, p. A17.

90. Given that Zepa was already under attack, there was a general assumption in Washington, London, Paris, and New York that this UN "safe area" had already been lost.

91. In addition to Principals Committee meetings in which there were formal agendas, papers, and summaries of conclusions circulated to the participants prior to and after each meeting, during the Clinton administration, some principals met regularly in an informal setting in Lake's West Wing office. There was a weekly luncheon with the secretaries of state and defense—known as the "CPL" lunch (after Christopher, Perry, and Lake) in both State and the NSC, and as the "PCL" (pronounced "pickle") in Defense—prior to which an agenda of issues had been agreed. There also was a weekly breakfast that included, in addition, Ambassador Albright and General Shalikashvili. The principals' breakfasts did not have an agenda, and no substitutes were allowed; the principals came when possible, but could not send anyone in their place. It was in these meetings that much of the principals' discussion of U.S. Bosnia policy took place. Interview with a senior administration official, April 27, 1998.

Shalikashvili's meeting had made clear that there were three distinct options for the London conference:

—The French proposal, to reinforce Gorazde with 1,000 troops to be ferried in by U.S. air and helicopter transport;

—The British inclination to continue with the status quo by beefing up UNPROFOR with the deployment of the RRF, redeploying UN forces in more defensible positions by withdrawing exposed UN personnel from isolated enclaves, and enforcing the UN mandate more robustly (although *not* with air strikes);

—The U.S. proposal for a vigorous air campaign with clear rules of engagement and without a "dual key" to defend both Gorazde and Sarajevo.

Of the three proposals, the British idea of muddling through was clearly unacceptable to the principals. It offered neither an adequate response to the French proposal to reinforce Gorazde nor represented the kind of decisive action that the situation required. As for the French proposal, principals agreed that it was risky—a "Dien Bien Gorazde," as Richard Holbrooke called it when he first heard of the proposal, referring to the French entanglement in Vietnam in the mid-1950s.[92] At the same time, it was clear from Shalikashvili's meeting on July 16 that British and French acceptance of the U.S. plan would require much arm-twisting. Accordingly, the principals decided to present two options for the president's consideration at an Oval Office meeting on July 18. The U.S. plan called for defending Gorazde and Sarajevo by threatening a large-scale air campaign with robust rules of engagement and no "dual key." A modified French plan proposed combining the air strikes option with helicopter support to transport 1,000 French troops to Gorazde.[93]

The meeting in the Oval Office turned out to be an emotional one, according to an account by Bob Woodward. Vice President Al Gore spoke at length on the need to respond forcefully to the brutality the world had just witnessed in Srebrenica: "The worst solution would be to acquiesce to genocide and allow the rape of another city and more refugees." Gore

92. Interview with an administration official, July 15, 1998.
93. Interviews with an administration official, August 13, 1998; Pentagon official, March 26, 1998; and senior administration official, October 21, 1997. See also Carla Anne Robbins, Thomas E. Ricks, and Mark M. Nelson, "U.S. Seeks Vigorous Bosnian Airstrikes," *Wall Street Journal*, July 18, 1995, p. A2; Ann Devroy and Michael Dobbs, "U.S.: Unity Must Precede Balkan Action," *Washington Post*, July 18, 1995, p. A17; and Eric Schmitt, "U.S. Sees French Plan as Taking It to Brink of War," *New York Times*, July 18, 1995, p. A7.

recalled the story that had appeared over the weekend of a young woman, who had committed suicide by hanging herself in a camp for refugees from Srebrenica. "My 21-year-old daughter asked about that picture," Gore said. "What am I supposed to tell her? . . . My daughter is surprised the world is allowing this to happen." Gore added carefully, "I am too." Clinton agreed with Gore's assessment that "we have to come up with something practical to make military sense. Acquiescence is not an option." It was clear that the French proposal did not meet the test of practicality and military sense. To the president, Shalikashvili's argument in London remained convincing—that if air strikes were needed to enable helicopters to transport troops safely, then why not try air strikes alone first. "The situation underscores the need for robust airpower being authorized," Clinton concluded. "The United States can't be a punching bag in the world anymore."[94]

A Success in London

To turn an agreement on the authorization of robust air power into operational reality, Christopher, Perry, and Shalikashvili needed to nail down four points at the London conference:

—NATO air power would be used in an air campaign against air defense systems and other targets of strategic significance in order to draw a clear and unambiguous line in defense of Gorazde and the other UN "safe areas";

—Clear rules of engagement would be necessary to determine when NATO air power would be used;

—The "dual-key" arrangement would have to be modified, so that the decision to use NATO air power would rest with the UN and NATO military commanders directly involved; and

—Air strikes would continue even if UN peacekeepers or civilians (including Americans) were taken hostage (although some UN forces might have to be redeployed to reduce their vulnerability to hostage-taking).[95]

94. Woodward, *The Choice*, pp. 262–63.

95. Interview with a Pentagon official, March 26, 1998. See also Robbins, Ricks, and Nelson, "U.S. Seeks Vigorous Bosnian Airstrikes," p. A2; Michael Dobbs and John F. Harris, "U.S. Favors 'Aggressive' NATO Airstrikes in Bosnia," *Washington Post*, July 19, 1995, p. A1; R. W. Apple Jr., "U.S. Rejecting French Plan, Urges Air Attacks in Bosnia," *New York Times*, July 20, 1995, p. A1; John Darnton, "U.S. Wins Support from Britain for Plan to Bomb Bosnian Serb Units," *New York Times*, July 21, 1995, p. A1; and David Evans, "American Deal Sours over Dinner," *The Times*, July 22, 1995.

Although there was agreement to push the allies hard on accepting the U.S. proposal for a vigorous air campaign, not everyone thought it likely that the delegation traveling to London would succeed. Some officials at the State Department, in particular, thought the meeting would be a disaster. They felt the British did not have a clear objective in mind when they had called the conference on July 14. There would also be too many participants for a fruitful discussion (including not just NATO members but all countries contributing troops to UNPROFOR).[96] Pentagon officials—notably Secretary Perry and General Shalikashvili—were more optimistic. They strongly believed that Srebrenica posed a fork in the road leaving only two options: either the UN would withdraw in failure, in which case the United States would have to send up to 25,000 troops to assist in the evacuation, or the United States and its allies would agree to use overwhelming force in response to future provocations. They were confident that once presented with this choice, the allies would not accept defeat and instead agree to make a final stand in Gorazde.[97] The White House, too, was committed to doing everything possible to get an agreement, and the president spent many hours on the phone with President Chirac and Prime Minister Major to convince them to adopt the U.S. plan.[98] Although

96. Interview with an administration official, August 13, 1998. Those in the State Department's European Affairs Bureau who had dealt with Bosnia for a long time were particularly worried about the meeting, having seen many previous efforts fail in the past. According to one official, this view was shared by Richard Holbrooke, who could not attend the London conference because of a serious ear infection. (Interview with an administration official, July 15, 1998.) This may explain why Holbrooke's account of how the decisions at London were actually made is wrong. In *To End a War* (p. 71), Holbrooke claims that the U.S. delegation traveled to London without a clear sense of its aims and that the outlines of the policy were only drafted by Christopher's key staff en route to London. As the account above makes clear, however, the idea of a decisive air campaign had first been raised by Secretary Perry with his colleagues on July 14. Subsequently, principals met numerous times (often with the president) to decide both the details of such a campaign and how allied support could be garnered. To ensure the latter, Clinton and his advisers had also had innumerable conversations with their European counterparts to get the allies on board. The turning point came on July 18—that is, three days *before* the meeting in London—when French President Chirac finally relented, telling Clinton that while he continued to favor a ground operation, France would not stand in the way of a consensus in favor of the U.S. proposal for a decisive air campaign. Interview with a senior administration official, August 7, 1998, and "Key Bosnia Meeting/Event Chronology," p. 4.
97. Interviews with a senior administration official, July 20, 1998; an administration official, August 13, 1998; and a senior administration official, May 18, 1999.
98. Interview with a senior administration official, October 21, 1997. See also Dobbs and Harris, "U.S. Favors 'Aggressive' NATO Airstrikes in Bosnia," p. A1;

some in the State Department remained skeptical, Christopher also worked the phones. His primary focus was London, and Christopher met with the then British Foreign Secretary Malcolm Rifkind four times in four days in both Washington and London.[99]

In the end, the London conference was a success. Three key agreements were reached that, once fully operationalized by NATO in subsequent discussions, would fundamentally alter the scope and extent of NATO air power in Bosnia. First, NATO would respond to an attack against Gorazde with a significant air campaign, which could include targets throughout Bosnia, not just limited strikes in the immediate vicinity of the "safe area." Second, NATO could respond in this manner not only when the Bosnian Serbs attacked the Gorazde enclave as they had Srebrenica and Zepa, but as soon as it was clear that they were preparing to do so. Third, the command-and-control arrangements were streamlined. Authority for calling in NATO close air support to protect individual peacekeepers or units would rest with the local commander of the unit, while authority for more extensive NATO air strikes to deter attack against Gorazde would rest with General Smith, the UNPROFOR commander.[100] The agreement provided the basis for the first sustained NATO air campaign in Bosnia, Operation Deliberate Force, which was to commence on August 30, 1995.

Apple, "U.S. Rejecting French Plan, Urges Air Attacks in Bosnia," p. A1; and Darnton, "U.S. Wins Support from Britain for Plan to Bomb Bosnia Serb Units," p. A1.

99. Interview with a senior administration official, January 11, 1999.

100. The specific command-and-control arrangements agreed to depended upon the types and location of targets to be struck. Close air support (or "Option 1") targets included only those within a twenty-kilometer exclusion zone that directly threatened the UN forces. Strikes against these targets could be authorized by the local UN commander and NATO commander in Aviano, Italy, where the aircraft that would conduct the air strikes were based. In case of an attack on Gorazde, a more extensive target set (so-called "Option 2" targets) could be struck within one of the two zones of action that divided the Bosnian theater of operations. Authority for these strikes rested with the UNPROFOR Commander (General Smith) and the NATO AFSOUTH commander (Admiral Leighton "Snuffy" Smith). Finally, a theater-wide air campaign, that included targets throughout Bosnia ("Option 3" targets) would require approval from the NAC and, probably, from the UN secretary general. Interviews with a senior NATO official, August 7, 1998; and a Pentagon official, March 26, 1998. See also Evans, "American Deal Sours over Dinner"; John Darnton, "Allies Warn Bosnian Serbs of 'Substantial' Airstrikes if UN Enclave Is Attacked," *New York Times*, July 22, 1995, p. 1; Stephen Engelberg, "Advancing Bosnian Serb Troops Would Be First Bombing Targets," *New York Times*, July 22, 1995, p. 1; and Michael Dobbs and Fred Barbash, "Allies Warn Serbs to Avoid Gorazde," *Washington Post*, July 22, 1995, p. A1.

Initially, the significance of these agreements remained obscured by somewhat differing statements from key participants on what exactly had been decided. Clarity was also undermined by a subsequent debate among the allies concerning the operational details of implementing the agreement.[101] On the former, the conference chairman's statement summarizing the meeting's conclusions was less robust than U.S. statements, in part because the Russians refused to endorse any call for NATO air strikes.[102] The operative paragraph of that statement noted that the "meeting therefore warned that in order to deter any attack on Gorazde, any such action will be met with a substantial and decisive response. There was strong support for this to include the use of air power, but there was also great concern expressed."[103] In contrast, Secretary Christopher characterized "what the United States believes to be the central elements of today's agreement" as follows:

> Bosnian Serb leaders are now on notice that an attack on Gorazde will be met by substantial and decisive air power. . . . Any air campaign in Gorazde will include significant attack on significant targets. There'll be no more pin-prick strikes. Moreover, existing command-and-control arrangements for use of NATO air power will be significantly adjusted to ensure that responsiveness and unity— our purposes—achieved.[104]

101. As a result, congressional reaction to the conference was highly negative, with Senate Majority Leader Bob Dole taking to the Senate floor and denouncing the London meeting as a "dazzling display of ducking the problem." Dole moved immediately to bring his resolution on lifting the arms embargo to the floor for a vote. Dole's statement is cited in Dobbs and Barbash, "Allies Warn Serbs to Avoid Gorazde," p. A1.

102. Russia's public posture in opposition to any military action was not as vehement in private. This became evident during Perry's meeting with Russian Defense Minister Pavel Grachev during the London conference. According to one participant, Grachev, reading his talking points, was scathing in his denunciation of the U.S. plan for an air campaign. Once he had finished the points, however, Grachev's mood noticeably changed and, turning to Perry, he said, "You know, we've looked at Yugoslavia a lot. It's very difficult. There are no good targets there!" Interview with a senior administration official, July 20, 1998.

103. "Excerpts from Statement on Bosnia," New York Times, July 22, 1995, p. A4.

104. Warren Christopher, "The International Conference on Bosnia: Now We Must Act," Opening Remarks at a Press Briefing, reprinted in Dispatch, vol. 6 (July 24, 1995), p. 583.

Immediately following the London meeting, moreover, it was clear that differences among key allies remained concerning important operational aspects of the mission. Of particular note was the question of command and control. Though he had attended the conference, UN Secretary General Boutros-Ghali refused to hand over his "key" to the military commanders. France, meanwhile, insisted that the UN key be delegated to French General Janvier, the UNPF Commander, rather than to his subordinate, British General Smith, the UNPROFOR commander. Britain also continued to have doubts and indicated that it had agreed to the decision in London primarily in the hope that it would suffice to deter the Serbs from attacking Gorazde and therefore would not have to be carried out. For that reason, London also opposed extending the threat of air strikes to cover the defense of other "safe areas."[105]

These issues were addressed in a marathon session of the North Atlantic Council on July 25. After thirteen hours of debate, the essential elements of what the Clinton administration had believed were agreed in London remained intact. Specifically, the NAC agreed:[106]

—The trigger for NATO air strikes in defense of the Gorazde "safe area" would include not just an actual attack on the area, but also the threat of an attack, as indicated by the massing of Bosnian Serb forces.[107]

—Authority for requesting NATO air strikes in case UN peacekeepers or units were attacked or Gorazde was threatened or attacked would rest with the UN Force Commander, General Janvier, but not with UN civilian personnel. A decision on the role of the UN secretary general to authorize

105. See Craig R. Whitney, "NATO Diplomats Question Details for Air Raids," *New York Times,* July 23, 1995, p. 1; John Darnton, "Ambiguous Ultimatum: Allies Show Differences," *New York Times,* July 24, 1995, p. A6; and Craig R. Whitney, "Allies Search for the 'Key' in Bomb Plan," *New York Times,* July 25, 1995, p. A6.

106. The statement is quoted in full in "Bosnia: NATO Is Determined to Carry Out Air Strikes to Protect Gorazde and Possibly Other Safe Areas," *Atlantic News,* no. 2739 (July 28, 1995), p. 1. See also Leurdijk, *The United Nations and NATO in the Former Yugoslavia,* p. 76; and Owen, "Summary," Chapter 12, p. 13.

107. According to NATO Secretary General Willy Claes, "NATO's planning is designed to ensure that military preparations by the Bosnian Serbs which are judged to present a direct threat to Gorazde, or direct Bosnian Serb attacks on Gorazde, will be met with the firm and rapid response of NATO's air power." *Atlantic News,* no. 2739, p. 1. See also Donald L. Dittmer and Stephen P. Dawkins, *Deliberate Force: NATO's First Extended Air Operation* (Alexandria, Va.: Center for Naval Analysis, July 1998), p. 10.

a theater-wide air campaign against military-related civilian infrastructure throughout Bosnia was deferred until such time as the NAC would have to consider a request for such use of NATO air power.[108]

—There would be three sets of targets: Option 1 targets, relating to integrated air defense systems and Bosnian Serb forces in the field; Option 2 targets, including command-and-control facilities, supply depots, munition sites, radar and missile sites, and force concentrations; Option 3 targets, including military-related civilian infrastructure.[109]

—Air strikes in defense of the Gorazde "safe area" would involve strikes against the Bosnian Serb air defense network throughout Bosnia; this would help ensure that NATO aircraft could strike their targets without interference from air defense capabilities on the ground. These latter targets would be confined to the southeast zone of action, an area that encompassed much of eastern Bosnia, including Mostar, Gorazde, Sarajevo, Tuzla, and Brcko.[110]

—Air strikes would continue even if UN personnel were taken hostage (although the UN would be encouraged to take steps to avoid hostage-taking).[111]

108. Even after the NATO meeting, Boutros-Ghali refused to relinquish his key, and it took the personal intervention of Secretary Christopher in three phone calls, including "two firm phone conversations" on July 26, before he relented. See Christopher, *In the Stream of History*, p. 349; confirmed in interview with a senior administration official, January 11, 1999. The following day, Boutros-Ghali wrote to the Security Council that "to streamline decisionmaking within the United Nations chain of command when air strikes are deemed to be necessary, I have decided to delegate the necessary authority . . . to the Force Commander of the United Nations Peace Forces with immediate effect. . . . As regards close air support to defend United Nations peacekeepers, my special representative has today delegated the necessary authority to the Force Commander (General Janvier), who is authorised to delegate it further to the commander of the United Nations Protection Force (UNPROFOR) when operational circumstances so require." See S/1995/623, July 27, 1995, as quoted in Leurdijk, *The United Nations and NATO in the Former Yugoslavia*, p. 77.

109. Dittmer and Dawkins, *Deliberate Force*, pp. 10–11.

110. A map of Bosnia depicting the Zones of Action can be found in Christopher Campbell, "The DELIBERATE FORCE Air Campaign," in Owen, *DELIBERATE FORCE*, Chapter 4, p. 10.

111. Boutros-Ghali reported to the Security Council that he had "already issued instructions to my special representative to take all measures necessary to protect United Nations personnel in the theatre and to reduce their vulnerability to retaliation and hostage-taking." Quoted in Leurdijk, *The United Nations and NATO in the Former Yugoslavia*, pp. 77. Moreover, as Claes reported, "There is a strong feeling among the Allies that such operations, once they are launched, will not lightly be discontinued. In the face of the inherent risks, the Alliance is determined." *Atlantic News*, no. 2739, p. 1.

—NATO's Military Committee was charged with determining how (not whether) these provisions (known as the "Gorazde rules") could be extended to apply to the defense of the remaining three "safe areas": Bihac, Sarajevo, and Tuzla.

On August 1, the NAC approved the planning to deter attacks on the remaining "safe areas." The NATO Secretary General announced, "NATO is ready to take the same robust action to defend the other safe areas in Bosnia. . . . As is the case already for Gorazde, our planning will ensure that military preparations which are judged to represent a direct threat for the UN Safe Areas or direct attacks upon them will be met with the firm and rapid response of NATO's airpower."[112] Nine days later, the commanders of AFSOUTH (Admiral Leighton "Snuffy" Smith) and the UN Peace Forces (General Janvier) signed a memorandum of understanding on the circumstances for NATO air strikes in case of a threat or attack against any UN "safe area" and the targets to be struck in case such strikes were deemed necessary.[113] From this point on, the United Nations and NATO were prepared to conduct the type of air campaign the United States had long sought and that was finally executed following the shelling of the Sarajevo market place on August 28, 1995.

The Need to Seize Control

It was clear by the end of July 1995 that the new understandings reached through the London conference and NATO agreements were still insufficient to extricate the administration's policy from the bind it was in. The Bosnian Serbs remained triumphant following their brutal but strategically successful assaults on Srebrenica and Zepa. The European allies, while seemingly committed to strengthening the UN's presence and enforcing its mandate as a result of the new French President's lobbying, still remained on the verge of deciding to withdraw their forces before the onset of an-

112. "Press Statement by the Secretary General following NAC Meeting on 1st August 1995" (Brussels: NATO Press Service, August 1, 1995).

113. Owen, "The Balkan Air Campaign Study: Part I," p. 22. According to a briefing by USAF Brigadier General Chuck Wald, the MOU's objective was to set forth the process by which to "deter attacks or threats of attack against 'safe areas' and to be ready, should deterrence fail, to conduct operations to eliminate any threat or defeat any force engaged in an attack on a 'safe area.'" Wald, "Air Power in Bosnia-Herzegovina–'Operation Deliberate Force,'" presentation at Defense Forecasting International, Washington, July 17, 1998.

other winter. The United States, having committed its forces to a NATO evacuation operation in case the UN decided to withdraw, confronted the increasing likelihood of having to send American troops to Bosnia either to fulfill this commitment or to assist materially in efforts to provide backbone to the European and UN resolution to stay. The U.S. Congress, meanwhile, challenged the administration to take the morally correct route of helping Bosnia defend itself—although it was unwilling either to provide the means for doing so or to guarantee that American troops would be ready in case Bosnia's ability to defend itself proved inadequate.

In short, the Clinton administration was boxed in by an unworkable diplomatic strategy that sought to substitute Milosevic for the Bosnian Serbs (who would have to be a party to any negotiated settlement), by its own refusal to put U.S. troops on the ground, by allied resistance to using force so long as their troops could be taken hostage, by a UN command that insisted on "traditional peacekeeping principles" even though a war was raging, and by a Congress bent on taking the moral high ground without, however, taking responsibility for the consequences of doing so. The president, facing re-election the next year, felt caught between bad and worse options. He was increasingly frustrated that he was not in control of events—or even of his own policy. Tempers boiled over one July day. While chipping golf balls onto the green behind the White House, Clinton engaged in one of his celebrated rages for forty-five minutes. "This can't continue," he exclaimed as his two deputy national security aides, Sandy Berger and Nancy Soderberg, watched helplessly, kicking golf balls back for Clinton to putt. After a series of profanities, Clinton finally concluded: "We have to seize control of this."[114]

What was needed was a new policy—a bold new direction that would abandon the staid assumptions that had guaranteed inaction in the past. A meeting with the president and his foreign policy team was scheduled for August 7 in the Cabinet room to discuss various policy options that the principals and their agencies had developed in the weeks before. This would be one of three meetings the president would have on Bosnia policy that week. By the time the final meeting took place on the morning of August 9, a new course had been charted, one that would end with an agreement in Dayton, Ohio. That agreement committed the United States to deploy 20,000 troops in Bosnia one year before the president was to face the electorate.

114. Woodward, *The Choice*, p. 260.

CHAPTER THREE

The Endgame
Strategy

THE SEARCH FOR A NEW U.S. strategy for Bosnia was driven primarily by the White House and, in particular, the National Security Council (NSC) staff. There was undoubtedly a significant political motivation behind this search. After all, with an election year approaching, the president and his advisers were well aware of the political implications of deploying perhaps tens of thousands of American troops into what many believed would be a quagmire. One senior adviser noted in 1995, "I don't think the President relishes going into the 1996 election hostage to fortune in the Balkans, with the Bosnian Serbs able to bring us deeper into a war."[1] But while politics inevitably lurks below the surface of any major policy discussion in the White House, the president's reelection was not the sole or even the most important motivation for the policy review. For one, those pushing

1. Cited in Stephen Engelberg, "How Events Drew U.S. into the Balkans," *New York Times*, August 19, 1995, p. A1. One political adviser who took credit for pushing the president to take charge of his Bosnia policy was Dick Morris. Morris claimed to be primarily responsible for getting Clinton focused on seizing the reins of his own policy by convincing French President Jacques Chirac and British Prime Minister John Major to endorse massive NATO air strikes in the summer of 1995. Morris's claims were scoffed at by other White House officials, one of whom pointedly noted, "If we knew how to fix this don't you think we'd have done it before now?" See Dick Morris, *Behind the Oval Office: Winning the Presidency in the 1990s* (Random House, 1997), pp. 254–55; and Thomas Lippman and Ann Devroy, "Clinton's Policy Evolution: June Decision Led to Diplomatic Gamble," *Washington Post*, September 11, 1995, p. A1, where the quotation is found. On Morris's role, see also George Stephanopoulos, *All Too Human: A Political Education* (Little, Brown, 1999), pp. 380–83.

the review had long advocated a more active U.S. engagement in Bosnia and were able to exploit the prevailing circumstances to press their views more effectively. For another, the policy that emerged from the review was hardly without risk, especially because it meant seizing primary responsibility for Bosnia from the Europeans and the United Nations. Moreover, one way or another, the new policy would lead to the very deployment of U.S. forces in Bosnia that two successive administrations had sought to avoid.

The driving force behind the policy review was Clinton's national security adviser, W. Anthony (Tony) Lake, who was in turn strongly supported by his staff, especially his senior director for European affairs, Alexander (Sandy) Vershbow. Lake was a foreign service veteran who rose to prominence during the Nixon administration when he resigned from Henry Kissinger's NSC staff in protest over the invasion of Cambodia. He subsequently served as the policy-planning director in Cyrus Vance's State Department in the late 1970s, providing much of the intellectual scaffolding for Vance's foreign policy approach. During the 1980s, Lake had moved to academia and worked with various nongovernmental organizations on a host of issues. He had also coauthored an important critique of American foreign policymaking, arguing in part that the role of the national security adviser was primarily to broker policy differences among the president's senior advisers while eschewing the more activist and confrontational role that Henry Kissinger and his Democratic successor, Zbigniew Brzezinski, had played in the 1970s.[2]

Lake would ignore that advice on Bosnia. A self-described "pragmatic neo-Wilsonian,"[3] Lake had played a crucial role in the 1992 presidential campaign, serving together with Samuel R. (Sandy) Berger as the chief foreign policy advisers to the Democratic candidate. In that capacity, Lake and Berger convinced Clinton to take a forceful stance on Bosnia, charging the Bush administration with failure to take a leadership role and advocating the use of NATO air power as a way to halt the brutal Serb advances.

Once in office, however, Lake found he had few allies for implementing the course candidate Clinton had outlined during the campaign. (Madeleine K. Albright, then the U.S. representative to the United Nations, was an

---

2. I. M. Destler, Leslie Gelb, and Anthony Lake, *Our Own Worst Enemy: The Unmaking of American Foreign Policy* (Simon and Schuster, 1984), especially pp. 278–79.

3. Quoted in Thomas Friedman, "Clinton's Foreign Policy: Top Advisor Speaks Up," *New York Times*, October 31, 1993, p. A8.

important exception.) Chief among the obstacles was a political one. Clinton had been elected on a platform of domestic renewal and had pledged upon his election to "focus like a laser beam" on the economy.[4] Such a preoccupation made it difficult to countenance a major escalation of U.S. involvement in Bosnia. This decision became evident on February 10, 1993, when Secretary of State Warren Christopher announced that U.S. policy toward Bosnia was premised on *not* deploying U.S. troops to Bosnia under any circumstances other than to help enforce a peace agreement negotiated and agreed to by the parties.[5] Lake and his allies also faced bureaucratic obstacles. The Pentagon was dominated by the doctrinal preferences of the chairman of the Joint Chiefs of Staff, General Colin Powell, who insisted on using force decisively and for clear and attainable objectives—which in the case of Bosnia required numbers of ground forces that were politically excluded.[6] The State Department, after the first failed foray into Balkan diplomacy in May 1993, adopted a cautious, almost hands-off approach designed primarily to contain what Christopher would describe as "the problem from Hell."[7] The intelligence community consistently argued both that a unified and multi-ethnic Bosnian state could not survive on its own and that limited military intervention was more likely to embolden than subdue the Bosnian Serbs.

Despite some notable U.S. successes in forging a consensus in favor of a more assertive policy toward Bosnia—including the August 1993 NATO decision to support UNPROFOR with air strikes and the February 1994 ultimatum that temporarily ended the shelling of Sarajevo—most efforts ended in failure. At one point, Lake wrote a memo to Clinton arguing

4. Interview on "Nightline: ABC News," November 4, 1992, cited in R. W. Apple Jr., "Clinton, Savoring Victory, Starts Sizing Up Job Ahead," *New York Times*, November 5, 1992, p. A1.

5. Warren Christopher, "New Steps toward Conflict Resolution in the Former Yugoslavia," Opening statement at a news conference, Washington, D.C., February 10, 1993. Reprinted in *Dispatch*, vol. 4 (February 15, 1993), p. 81.

6. For a good statement of Powell's views, see Colin L. Powell, "U.S. Forces: Challenges Ahead," *Foreign Affairs*, vol. 71 (Winter 1992/93), pp. 32–45. For an assessment of the implications of what I have termed this "new orthodoxy," see Ivo H. Daalder, "The United States and Military Intervention," in Michael E. Brown, ed., *The International Dimensions of Internal Conflict* (MIT Press, 1996), pp. 469–76.

7. Warren Christopher, *In the Stream of History: Shaping Foreign Policy for a New Era* (Stanford University Press, 1998), p. 344. Christopher records that these "early attempts to grapple with Bosnia affected the course and content of our diplomacy over the next two years. . . . In developing U.S. positions over those years, we kept coming back to core questions of acceptable risks and political will," p. 347.

"that the administration's weak, muddle-through strategy in Bosnia was becoming a cancer on Clinton's entire foreign policy—spreading and eating away at its credibility."[8] To Lake, the November 1994 crisis in Bihac and the administration's constantly shifting response represented the metastasizing of the cancer from Bosnia to Clinton's foreign policy as a whole. As he admitted some months later, "I'm really worried that Bosnia will again come to be the definition of American foreign policy and obscure all the other things we've done."[9]

Following the Bihac crisis, Lake concluded it was no longer possible to forge a U.S.—let alone an allied—consensus to do anything other than submit to the reality on the ground. The European allies refused to take even the most minimal coercive steps for fear of retaliation against their peacekeepers. The warring parties themselves could neither be forced to come to the negotiating table nor be persuaded to seek a diplomatic rather than military solution. As for the U.S. government itself, with both the State and Defense Departments favoring containment over engagement, there was little prospect that a new initiative for concerted action could gain the required degree of bureaucratic support. Confronted with these obstacles, Lake was ready to give up on trying to forge a more activist Bosnia policy, if not on his NSC position itself. It was just too hard to do.[10]

Within weeks, however, it was clear that as far as Bosnia was concerned, it was impossible to ignore the issue and focus on other aspects of foreign policy. Lake's analysis had been correct. Bosnia was—or, at least, was widely perceived to be—U.S. foreign policy writ large. The cancer image had been exactly right: you just could not ignore it; you had to fight it tooth and nail. Lake instinctively understood this, but the Bihac debacle had left him without the energy necessary to take on the fight. Clinton also knew this, and he would not let his national security adviser ignore Bosnia, however difficult the issue had become. The president was deeply interested and very much engaged in Bosnia policy. It was the first issue he raised during the daily national security briefings, and Lake often felt as if

8. Bob Woodward, *The Choice* (Simon and Schuster, 1996), p. 253.

9. Quoted in Jason DeParle, "The Man inside Bill Clinton's Foreign Policy," *New York Times Magazine*, August 20, 1995, p. 57.

10. Interview with a senior administration official, April 27, 1998. See also Ivo H. Daalder, *Anthony Lake and the War in Bosnia*, Pew Case Studies in International Affairs, no. 467 (Washington, D.C.: Institute for the Study of Diplomacy, Georgetown University, 1995).

a big "B" was imprinted on his forehead when he walked into the Oval Office each weekday morning.[11]

It was Lake's chief European policy aide, Sandy Vershbow, who convinced him that giving up on Bosnia was simply not an option. Vershbow had worked on Bosnia issues almost from the beginning: first as the number two in the U.S. mission at NATO; then as the principal deputy to Stephen Oxman, Richard Holbrooke's predecessor as assistant secretary of state for European and Canadian affairs; and finally as the senior director for European affairs at the NSC. In each position, Vershbow had pushed a hard line, arguing that force was a necessary ingredient of an effective strategy for Bosnia and that reliance on force required concerted U.S. leadership. He did the same at the NSC, at every opportunity cajoling Lake to accept the need to push ahead on Bosnia and not to give up.

Following some weeks of doubt, Lake accepted the need to come up with a workable strategy for Bosnia in early 1995. As was his wont as national security adviser, Lake turned to the regular inter-agency process—a process that had produced the framework for Clinton's Bosnia policy in the first weeks of the administration and that subsequently led to the promulgation of the "lift and strike" policy. As it became clear that this regular process would not produce the results he sought, Lake embarked on a different, less inclusive process that used his physical proximity to the president to get his way. Instead of trying to force a consensus within the bureaucracy, he worked with a small coterie on his staff to develop a new strategy designed to break the impasse in America's Bosnia policy. Once he had Clinton's support for a new policy direction, Lake opened up the process in order to ensure that the president would have available to him the full spectrum of advice and options. The resulting policy review would create a consensus decision in support of his preferred strategy. Once embraced by the president and his foreign policy team, Lake's strategy laid the basis for the diplomatic effort that Richard Holbrooke would pursue to a successful conclusion in Dayton.

The Interagency Process and Bosnia

The formal process for making U.S. foreign and national security policy in the Clinton administration is set forth in Presidential Decision Directive

11. Interview with a senior administration official, April 27, 1998. See Stephanopoulos, *All Too Human*, p. 383.

No. 2 (PDD-2).[12] Although by statute the National Security Council is the formal advisory body to the president,[13] in recent administrations the main policymaking body became the Principals Committee (PC) or its equivalent. In the Clinton administration, PC meetings were chaired by the national security adviser; members included the secretary of state, secretary of defense, U.S. ambassador to the United Nations, director of Central Intelligence, and chairman of the Joint Chiefs of Staff. In 1995, these were respectively Anthony Lake, Warren Christopher, William Perry, Madeleine Albright, John Deutch, and General John Shalikashvili. The PC's role was to review, coordinate, and monitor the development and implementation of foreign and national security policy. Supporting the PC was the Deputies Committee (DC), which reviewed and monitored work of the NSC interagency process, acted as a day-to-day crisis management body, and oversaw policy implementation, including periodic reviews of the major policy initiatives. The DC was chaired by the deputy national security adviser and included the deputies to the principals who were members of the PC, as well as the vice president's national security adviser. In 1995, these were respectively Sandy Berger, Strobe Talbott, John White, David Scheffer, George Tenet, Admiral William Owens, and Leon Fuerth. Finally, the interagency process was supported by a series of permanent and ad hoc Interagency Working Groups (IWGs), covering both regional and functional issues. IWGs met at the assistant secretary level and were chaired either by a departmental representative of State or Defense or by a senior director of the NSC staff. In the case of Bosnia, the IWG was chaired from 1994–97 by Sandy Vershbow and met daily to review developments and coordinate the formulation and implementation of Bosnia policy.

12. "Presidential Decision Directive No. 2: Organization of the National Security Council" (White House, Office of the Press Secretary, January 21, 1993).

13. Under the National Security Act of 1947, membership in the NSC is restricted to the president, vice president, and the secretaries of state and defense. The director of Central Intelligence and chairman of the Joint Chiefs of Staff serve as statutory advisers to the NSC. Under PDD-2, NSC membership in the Clinton administration also includes the secretary of the treasury, the U.S. ambassador to the United Nations, the assistants to the president for national security affairs and economic affairs, the chief of staff, and (in matters under her jurisdiction, including covert action) the attorney general. There have been few formal NSC meetings in the Clinton administration. Instead, Clinton prefers to meet informally with his advisers in what are called foreign policy team meetings.

At the start of the Clinton administration, a series of Presidential Review Directives (PRDs) was issued requesting interagency reviews of important policy issues confronting the incoming administration. Reflecting the administration's priorities and concerns, PRD-1 dealt with Bosnia. The PRD tasked an interagency group to develop options for meeting the administration's key objectives in Bosnia: delivering relief supplies; stopping further Serb advances; rolling back Serb territorial gains; and strengthening the hands of negotiators trying to arrange cease-fires and a peace settlement. The intensive review produced a draft Presidential Decision Directive by early February 1993, which was reviewed by the Deputies Committee and Principals Committee before being forwarded to the president. Its conclusions were announced by Secretary Christopher on February 10.

When it was clear that the initial policy directive had not achieved its objective by mid-April, a similar review process was used to produce additional policy options for the president's consideration. The outcome was the lift and strike policy Secretary Christopher tried to sell in Europe that May. When that effort failed, the interagency process moved from developing policy options to managing the crisis on a day-to-day basis. Deputies Committee and, less frequently, Principals Committee meetings were used to discuss the minutiae of daily developments in and around Bosnia. The deputies and principals themselves began to micromanage the policy process, in effect becoming the action officers for Bosnia. As a result, U.S. policy became largely tactical and reactive, leaving much of the initiative to the warring parties, the Europeans, and the United Nations.

In early 1995, Lake sought to get away from micromanagement of the policy process and to revive an interagency process able to generate real policy options. In February 1995, he ordered a review of all policy options for responding to the likely resumption of fighting in Bosnia once the cease-fire expired on April 30. Following meetings of the Bosnia IWG, Vershbow drafted a paper presenting four possible options:[14]

—*Status Quo*. The United States should focus on containing the conflict and mitigate its humanitarian consequences, continue to support the Bosnian Muslims, and proceed with diplomatic efforts.

14. Interview with a senior administration official, October 21, 1997; and "Key Bosnia Meeting/Event Chronology" (White House paper prepared for media backgrounders on evolution of U.S. policy toward Bosnia, August 1995), p. 1.

—Active Containment. Recognizing the realities on the ground, the United States should adopt a neutral stance on the terms of any settlement, and end or suspend further Contact Group activities.

—A Quarantine of the Bosnian Serbs. The border between Bosnia and Serbia should be sealed to cut off all supplies—military, economic, and humanitarian—to the Bosnian Serbs.

—Lift, Arm, Train, and Strike. Following withdrawal of UNPROFOR, the arms embargo should be lifted, Muslim forces armed and trained, and air strikes conducted during the transition period to ensure the Bosnian Serbs would not exploit any interim military advantage.

The State Department supported the status quo option, while the Pentagon favored a policy of active containment. The quarantine option was favored by Leon Fuerth, reflecting his role as chairman of the interagency sanctions task force. The fourth option was nominally supported by Lake and Albright. The NSC options paper was reviewed by the Deputies Committee and sent to the principals in March 1995. According to one official who was present at the meeting, the principals reviewed the paper and agreed that with the cease-fire still holding, this was not the time to rock the boat. Instead, they agreed to more modest attempts to manage the situation, to focus on convincing the parties to maintain the cease-fire past the April 30 deadline, and to reengage Slobodan Milosevic to see whether he would put pressure on the Bosnian Serbs to negotiate in good faith.[15]

This decision confirmed that following the Bihac debacle much of the steam for addressing the Bosnia issue had gone out of the administration. Nevertheless, Lake contended that the majority's preference for muddling through was unacceptable in the long run. Sooner or later the administration would have to make a decision. Lake believed that doing so after a careful review of the options and their consequences was better than reacting to the ebb and flow of daily events, as most of his colleagues seemed to prefer. So in early spring 1995, he turned again to Sandy Vershbow. He asked him to take a look at what the United States could do if UNPROFOR withdrew and the arms embargo were lifted—either unilaterally, as mandated in a bill introduced by Senator Robert Dole (R-Kans.) in January, or multilaterally, following the UN's departure.

Vershbow worked closely with his key staff person, Nelson Drew, an Air Force colonel who had worked at NATO and had just spent a year

15. Interview with a senior administration official, October 21, 1997.

examining the Bosnia issue while on leave at the National Defense University. Their paper was premised on the belief that the time had come for a review of the fundamental principles guiding U.S. Bosnia policy and argued that it was necessary to shape events before U.S. strategic choices were completely dictated by the situation on the ground.[16] They argued that because of the dangers associated with deploying American troops to assist in the withdrawal of UNPROFOR, it was necessary in the short run to support the UN presence and restore its credibility through a policy of "retrench and reinvigorate": that is, by withdrawing UN peacekeepers deployed in untenable positions in the eastern enclaves and robustly enforcing the UN mandate. In the long run, however, UNPROFOR's presence posed more problems than it solved and its withdrawal would enable the implementation of a more effective policy. Such a policy—lift, arm, train, and strike—involved lifting the arms embargo, arming, and training the Muslims, and using NATO air strikes against Bosnian Serb forces during the transition period. The paper left unclear, however, how the short-term emphasis on reinvigorating UNPROFOR would be linked to a long-term policy based on the UN force's withdrawal from Bosnia.[17]

When the principals met to discuss the NSC paper in May, fighting had resumed in Bosnia and UNPROFOR's continued viability had moved from a largely theoretical question to a real one. Given the many drawbacks of a NATO operation to assist in the UN's departure from Bosnia, the principals decided to make a concerted effort to convince the Europeans to keep their troops in place.[18] Although the U.S. response to developments inside Bosnia was the main issue discussed at the meeting, the principals also examined the longer-term options detailed in the NSC paper. The principals decided that in the event of an UNPROFOR withdrawal, the United States would support a multilateral (but not unilateral) lifting of the arms embargo as well as the limited arming and training of Bosnian forces. However, the principals would not support air strikes during a transition period.[19] When Strobe Talbott read about the Principals Committee's decision to support lift, arm, and train in the summary of conclusions circu-

16. Details of the paper are based on interviews with a senior administration official, October 21, 1997, and an administration official, July 7, 1998.

17. Interview with an administration official, November 3, 1998.

18. See pp. 49–50 above and sources cited there for details.

19. Interview with a senior administration official, October 21, 1997; "Key Meeting/Event Chronology," p. 1.

lated after the meeting, "his hair (what little he had of it) stood right on end."[20] Contrary to the State Department's long-standing preference for containment, this implied that there was a point at which the United States would favor the UN's departure from Bosnia. Once informed by Talbott of the meeting's conclusions, Christopher strongly protested, calling it an "overstatement" to say that the principals had made a commitment on lift, arm, and train (though he agreed they had rejected air strikes) and insisted that the focus of U.S. policy remain on keeping UNPROFOR in place.[21]

"Blue Skies" Thinking

By early June 1995, the official policy of the Clinton administration toward Bosnia remained stuck in essentially the same place it had been since the Bihac debacle the previous November. The foremost objectives of policy continued to be preventing the deployment of American troops to Bosnia, maintaining NATO unity, containing the conflict as much as possible, and awaiting the outcome of European diplomatic efforts. Clearly, Lake had failed to move the administration away from the reactive, muddle-through policy it had been pursuing for more than two years. Every time the principals were confronted with the need to make strategic choices, their inclination was to punt and focus instead on dealing with the latest crisis. Equally evident was the fact that the traditional way of developing policy was not serving the president—and the administration's foreign policy more broadly—very well. Developments on the ground, combined with continuing bickering inside the administration and between Washington and allied capitals, left Clinton feeling like "he had been mouse-trapped."[22]

As U.S. policy was lurching, like a punch-drunk boxer, from one crisis to the next, the president met with his senior advisers on June 14, 1995, to preview an impending meeting with the newly elected French president, Jacques Chirac. According to several accounts, this "pre-brief" quickly

20. Interview with a senior administration official, October 21, 1997.

21. Interview with a senior administration official, October 21, 1997, and an administration official, July 7, 1998. Christopher's surprise reflected the fact that, at least on Bosnia issues, the State Department often ignored decisions summarized in the conclusions circulated to participants following the innumerable PC and DC meetings.

22. Quoted in Elizabeth Drew, *Showdown: The Struggle between the Gingrich Congress and the Clinton White House* (Simon and Schuster, 1996), p. 247.

turned into a debate about Bosnia. The discussion made clear the president's growing frustration with his inability to control developments in Bosnia—or even his own policy. Clinton accurately put his finger on the problem: "We've got no clear mission, no one's in control of events." Vice President Al Gore joined in, seizing an opportunity to make his case for tougher action. "It's the issue from hell," he said. "The Europeans are self-delusional" in rejecting strong NATO action to back up the UN force. NATO was weakened and the United States, as NATO's leader, looked even weaker. "The need for us to protect and preserve the alliance is driving our policy," Gore said. "It is driving us into a brick wall with Congress." As his advisers debated the next steps in what Assistant Secretary of State for European and Canadian Affairs Richard Holbrooke described as "an angry and contentious discussion," Clinton abruptly cut in: "We need to get the policy straight or we're just going to be kicking the can down the road again."[23]

Clinton's evident frustration, which Lake had witnessed building over the past weeks during his morning briefings with the president, provided the national security adviser with the opening he had sought. For some time, he had been meeting informally with his deputy Sandy Berger and his principal Bosnia aides, Vershbow and Drew. They had sought to look beyond "immediate crisis management" toward a more strategic approach to the issue.[24] A key concern was how to gain leverage over the main protagonists—the parties, the allies, and the U.S. government—in order to get the administration out of its policy bind. How could the parties, especially the Bosnian Serbs, be persuaded to come to the negotiating table? How could the allies be convinced to accept the need to use air power in the service of diplomacy? How could they be cajoled into recognizing that UNPROFOR as currently constituted was part of the problem rather than part of the solution? How could Christopher, Perry, and their respective departments be persuaded to support a more forward-leaning and assertive posture? What means, Lake and his aides wondered, could the U.S. government employ to convince these key actors to adopt a new policy and support a new direction?

23. Quoted in Woodward, *The Choice*, p. 255. The Holbrooke quotation is from Holbrooke, *To End a War* (Random House, 1998), p. 67.

24. Interviews with senior administration officials, October 21, 1997, and April 27, 1998. See also Tihomir Loza, "From Hostages to Hostiles: How the West Dropped Its Policy of Neutrality and Took on the Bosnian Serbs," *War Report*, no. 43 (July 1996), p. 17.

Lake's concerns were shared by Madeleine Albright, the administration's leading hawk on the issue of Bosnia. While some of her aides had resigned themselves to never being able to convince the administration to adopt the policies she had long advocated, Albright continued to push for a more assertive strategy whenever the occasion presented itself—sometimes to the chagrin of other principals who either did not share her views or believed that it was impossible to marshal a consensus in their favor.[25] Since early spring 1995, Albright had been discussing various options with her Bosnian counterpart at the United Nations, Ambassador Mohammed Sacirbey. According to Sacirbey, "in our discussions Madeleine and I both came to the conclusion that the UN forces, particularly the British and French, were more and more becoming an impediment to finding a solution." The preferred approach—a sustained NATO bombing campaign— could not be executed so long as UN forces remained vulnerable to being taken hostage. Albright's advice, Sacirbey recounted, was therefore straightforward: "You've got to come down and take the British and French out of the picture. Don't let them say 'Our soldiers are in danger'."[26] U.S. policy, however, was moving in the opposite direction, focused on keeping the UN in Bosnia so as to avoid deploying U.S. troops as part of a NATO evacuation effort.

By June, Albright was ready to press her case at the highest level. The occasion was a foreign policy team meeting with the president on June 21 to discuss both immediate and long-term Bosnia policy issues. The discussion of long-term issues revolved around possible alternatives to the existing U.S. strategy of keeping UNPROFOR in place and trying to isolate the Bosnian Serb leadership in Pale until it accepted the 1994 Contact Group peace plan as the basis for a settlement. Alternative possibilities included taking another look at the Contact Group map (which divided Bosnia between a Bosnian Serb and Bosnian Muslim and Croat parts), and examining possible steps to take if UNPROFOR left, including lift and strike or a unilateral lift if Russia blocked action by the UN Security Council. The participants also raised the key question of whether there was a point at which it would be advisable to shift the U.S. position on UNPROFOR and encourage its withdrawal.[27]

25. Interview with a senior administration official, June 8, 1998.
26. Quoted in Loza, "From Hostages to Hostiles," p. 3.
27. Interview with a senior administration official, March 1, 1999; "Key Meeting/ Events Chronology," p. 2.

Albright came to the meeting with a strongly worded one-and-a-half-page memo entitled "Elements of a New Strategy."[28] In the memo, Albright stressed three points. First, although the administration had painstakingly reestablished the credibility of U.S. foreign policy through recent successes in North Korea and Haiti, the disaster in Bosnia was now "destroying" the administration's credibility. U.S. "reluctance to lead an effort to resolve a military crisis in the heart of Europe has placed at risk our leadership of the post–Cold War world," she wrote. Already, the allies were no longer taking the United States seriously. "Chirac's statement that 'the position of leader of the Free World is vacant' has been chilling my bones for weeks."[29] Second, the time had come to challenge the fundamental assumption of the administration's policy: that UNPROFOR's withdrawal would be disastrous and that the administration should therefore expend every effort to convince the Europeans to stay. In fact, UNPROFOR's presence prevented NATO from doing what was right: lifting the arms embargo and engaging in sustained air strikes against the Bosnian Serbs. Rather than being the problem the United States sought to avoid, Albright maintained, UNPROFOR's withdrawal offered the solution to the administration's predicament. Third, the immediate way ahead was to press Milosevic to recognize Bosnia in return for limited sanctions relief or else face the prospect that by winter there would be no more UNPROFOR and a rearmed Bosnia, thus leaving him with the decision to intervene in defense of the Bosnian Serbs and possibly confront NATO air strikes against Serbia in response.

The president welcomed the memo, saying that he liked the thrust of Albright's argument. So did Lake, who had raised similar concerns with the president prior to the meeting.[30] During the next few weeks, Lake and Albright met occasionally, including once over Chinese food at Albright's house, to discuss possible contours of a new strategy.[31] Most of the details

---

28. Interview with administration officials, July 9, 1998, and August 13, 1998; and "Key Bosnia Meetings/Event Chronology," pp. 2–3. See also Elaine Sciolino, "Madeleine Albright's Audition," *New York Times Magazine*, September 22, 1996, p. 67; and Michael Dobbs, *Madeleine Albright: A Twentieth Century Odyssey* (Henry Holt, 1999), p. 363. Much of the memorandum repeated an earlier plan for U.S. leadership that Albright had sent to the president in August 1993.

29. Dobbs, *Madeleine Albright*, p. 363; and interview with an administration official, July 9, 1998.

30. Interview with a senior administration official, March 1, 1999.

31. Albright's memo became a hot commodity within the administration. Within hours of the foreign policy team meeting, James P. Rubin, Albright's communications

of the emerging policy shift, however, were the products of intense discussions between Lake and members of his NSC staff.

The first of these NSC staff meetings took place in Lake's office on a sunny Saturday morning, June 24. The four-hour meeting included Lake's key aides: Sandy Berger, Sandy Vershbow, Nelson Drew, and Lake's executive assistant, Peter Bass. Lake began by saying that he wanted to engage in a "blue skies discussion on what [the] longer-term strategy would be."[32] He told his colleagues that they had to get away from the day-to-day perspective so common in Bosnia policymaking. Suppose, Lake suggested, they decide how things should be six months from now and then work back to the present to see what changes were needed to get there. "Let's think from the end backward," Lake said. "I don't want to hear about what's next."[33] That meant answering some difficult questions. Should we work to forestall UNPROFOR's departure? What should we do if UNPROFOR does withdraw? Should we push for lifting the arms embargo? If so, how hard? Should we revisit the principals' decision to lift but not strike? How can the diplomatic track be revitalized? What kind of leverage do we have to get the parties—Serbs as well as Muslims—to accept a deal? Should we talk to the Bosnian Serb leadership and relax our insistence that the Contact Group plan be accepted as the basis of negotiations? What would an acceptable diplomatic outcome look like? Are there changes in the Contact Group map or the proposed constitutional arrangements that might make a settlement more likely?

This set of questions kept the participants occupied for a great deal of time. All quickly agreed that the basic bargain of the Contact Group plan—a territorial division according to the 51-49 proportion in favor of the Muslim-Croat Federation—would remain fundamental to any settlement. However, as drawn, the Contact Group map did not provide the Federation with the most defensible or sustainable slice of Bosnia's territory. "[R]ather than drawing the lines in a kind of higgledy-piggledy way, that might make sense in terms of a detailed negotiation and where the current

director, received a call from Sandy Vershbow for a copy, followed by many more requests from people in a variety of different agencies. Interview with an administration official, July 9, 1998.

32. The quotation is drawn from Loza, "From Hostages to Hostiles," p. 17. Details on the meeting are from interviews with senior administration officials, October 21, 1997, and April 27, 1998, as well as Loza, p. 17; Woodward, *The Choice*, pp. 257–58; and Laura Silber and Allan Little, *Yugoslavia: Death of a Nation* (New York: TV Books, distributed by Penguin USA, 1996), p. 351.

33. Quoted in Woodward, *The Choice*, p. 257.

populations are," Lake recalled that the Contact Group map had to be adjusted. More useful would be to do "what we could to have a federation territory that was as consolidated and simplified as possible." A key concern was the eastern enclaves—particularly Srebrenica and Zepa, neither of which was easily defensible. "Already, in June, the fate of Srebrenica seemed pretty gloomy," Vershbow recounted. "So we were already considering that some kind of swap for at least the smaller of the eastern enclaves, in exchange for more territory in central Bosnia, might be one of the things that the Federation might accept as part of a more coherent map."[34]

At the end of the meeting, Lake proposed that Vershbow take his hand at drafting an integrated strategy incorporating the points that had been raised. The strategy paper should focus on the carrots and sticks that would be available to support a new, U.S.-led diplomatic initiative to achieve a political settlement by the end of 1995. It should determine the kind of military and diplomatic leverage the United States could employ vis-à-vis both the allies and the warring parties to get them to come around to the American way of thinking. And it should consider what the United States could do if the diplomatic strategy failed. That afternoon, Vershbow began writing the first of many drafts of what came to be known as the "endgame strategy."

Shortly after this meeting in Lake's office, the national security adviser raised the idea of developing an endgame strategy with Clinton during one of their regular morning briefings. According to Bob Woodward, Lake suggested to the president that he wanted "to try to think this thing through and come back to you with a coherent, comprehensive strategy." Clinton was intrigued, so Lake pressed on. "Mr. President, tell me if you don't want to do this, stop me now because the risks are very clear." Those risks were in fact twofold: another major embarrassment for the president and his administration if they failed; or the deployment of 20,000 American troops if they succeeded in brokering a settlement, a deployment that many would regard as the beginning of a quagmire just as the president was entering his re-election year. Even so Clinton supported the idea, urging Lake to put his thoughts on paper. Woodward summarizes Clinton's quandary: "The current position was untenable. He wanted rethinking. They had to break out of the old mind-set. He hadn't heard anything new . . . and new was what he wanted."[35]

---

34. Quoted in Loza, "From Hostages to Hostiles," p. 17.
35. Quoted in Woodward, *The Choice*, p. 258.

A Policy Review at State[36]

Lake and Albright were not alone in believing that the current policy course was heading the United States—and Bosnia—headlong into disaster. So did many that managed the Bosnia issue on a day-to-day basis at the State Department. Starting in late May, Strobe Talbott began hosting informal meetings at his home to talk about Bosnia policy. Attending were his State Department colleagues Peter Tarnoff (undersecretary for political affairs), Thomas Donilon (Christopher's chief of staff), and James Steinberg (director of policy planning), and the NSC's Sandy Berger. They were sometimes joined by CIA Director John Deutch.[37] The focus of these meetings was to develop a diplomatic plan that could be used to move the process forward. A consensus soon developed among the participants on the need for a higher level of U.S. engagement in Bosnia—diplomatically and possibly militarily—even if this meant a higher degree of political risk.

Steinberg drafted a paper based on these informal discussions in which he proposed a new U.S. diplomatic initiative. Its basic concept was to combine a push for new negotiations on the basis of the Contact Group plan with a fresh attempt to involve Milosevic directly by offering Belgrade the relief from sanctions it had long sought. The paper's core idea was the proposal for an international summit of Presidents Milosevic of Serbia, Franjo Tudjman of Croatia, and Alija Izetbegovic of Bosnia. At the summit, the three countries would recognize one another and agree to a set of principles to encourage direct negotiations between Pale and Sarajevo.

36. Information in this section is based on interviews with a senior administration official, January 11, 1999, and administration officials, July 7, 1998, and August 13, 1998.

37. Absent from these meetings was the person directly responsible for Bosnia policy at State, Richard Holbrooke. It is unclear whether Holbrooke was unaware of the meetings or decided not to attend. However, it does suggest that the displeasure he later expressed about being excluded from the Lake meetings that were going on at the same time may have been misplaced. Holbrooke writes, "Disturbed by this exclusion, I consulted Vernon Jordan," the chief FOB (friend of Bill). "I told Jordan that I was considering departure [from government] before the end of the summer. If Bosnia policy was going to be formulated without my involvement, then there was little reason to stay." According to Holbrooke, Jordan talked to Clinton and Christopher "and the situation eased slightly." Holbrooke, *To End a War*, p. 68. Holbrooke's exclusion from these Bosnia policy brainstorming sessions, however, cannot be blamed on Lake. Attendance at many of Lake's meetings was confined to the NSC staff, while others were conducted by the principals in their principals-only weekly breakfasts. In neither was it necessarily appropriate to invite an assistant secretary of state.

Independent from the Talbott meetings and the Steinberg paper, the State Department's Bosnia point man, Robert Frasure, was also coming to the conclusion that current U.S. policy was going nowhere.[38] Although he personally favored a much more assertive policy, he believed the record demonstrated that the administration was not prepared to go down this path. At the same time, Frasure was convinced that the current policy was beyond redemption and should be ended before 1996 lest the president's opponents be handed a major campaign issue. Frasure sketched out the policy alternatives in what came to be known as the "waterfall memorandum," suggesting that the United States was standing on the edge of two waterfalls and the trick was to make sure that it went down the right one.[39] The wrong waterfall was the one foreshadowed in NATO's OPLAN 40104, which involved the deployment of thousands of American troops in Bosnia to assist in the withdrawal of the UN force. This would either draw the United States in deeper or risk massive casualties and dislocation. The right waterfall was the one that focused on containing the conflict by making sure UNPROFOR stayed; handing off negotiations with Milosevic to the Europeans and their new envoy, former Swedish Prime Minister Carl Bildt; hanging tough against lifting the arms embargo; and approving a modest covert arms program to aid the Bosnians.

The Steinberg and Frasure efforts came together following an internal State Department meeting in late June in Christopher's office on where U.S. policy toward Bosnia should be going. In addition to emphasizing the containment aspects of Frasure's paper, this effort modified Steinberg's diplomatic initiative: mutual recognition would be sought between Serbia and Bosnia only; Milosevic would be the main interlocutor for the negotiations in order to avoid the need to deal with the madmen of Pale; and sanctions could be lifted rather than merely suspended if Milosevic were able to deliver. The new paper also suggested an implementation strategy. Once the Europeans realized that their efforts to get Milosevic on board would fail, they would turn to Washington for new ideas. In return for taking the lead on the new diplomatic initiative, the administration could insist that UNPROFOR stay in order to give the initiative a chance to succeed. In this way, the United States would be able to pre-

38. Interviews with administration officials, July 7, 1998, and August 13, 1998.

39. The Frasure memo is referred to by Christopher as an example of the importance of public service. See Warren Christopher, "Above and Beyond," *Washington Post*, September 13, 1998, p. C7.

vent the disastrous withdrawal of the UN forces while still retaining the diplomatic lead.

Christopher sent a summary of this paper in a "night note" to Clinton in early July.[40] In the note, Christopher expressed his concern about the implications of NATO's plans to assist in UNPROFOR's possible withdrawal, especially the all-or-nothing emphasis on U.S. troop deployments to Bosnia in case the UN requested assistance. He emphasized the need to consider other options involving a reduced U.S. troop commitment, and suggested that a new diplomatic initiative along the lines of the Steinberg-Frasure proposal might be useful.[41] Although Christopher and many others at State had been dismissive of the kind of "blue skies" thinking Lake was encouraging, in his night note the secretary of state had begun to sketch out the core of State's concept of where U.S. policy should be heading in the weeks and months ahead. The concept was developed just in time for a meeting Lake had called to discuss long-term policy for Bosnia.

Debating a Bosnia Endgame

Since Lake first raised the idea of the endgame strategy with Clinton in late June, he had kept the president regularly informed of the progress he was making. He had given Clinton a draft of the strategy before he had shown it to anyone else outside the NSC. Clinton liked it, stressing the need to get the diplomatic process back on track by directly involving the Bosnian Serbs. Once Lake had the president's approval for the basic thrust of the strategy; he told Clinton that he would convene a meeting with the other principals to discuss long-term options. He planned to present his strategy paper and asked Clinton to drop by the meeting in order to emphasize the importance of getting a viable long-term policy.[42]

---

40. Previous secretaries of state, including Cyrus Vance and James Baker, wrote regular short memoranda, called night notes, on key developments about which they wished the president to be informed directly. Christopher used this vehicle of direct communication to the president only sparingly. His notes, which were generally drafted by Steinberg or Donilon, tended to be on major policy issues and less a means to inform the president on issues of concern at that moment. Interview with an administration official, August 13, 1998.

41. According to one source, Clinton read Christopher's note and scribbled "agree" in the margin. The president then passed it on to Lake, who, by all accounts, ignored it. Interviews with administration officials, July 7, 1998, and August 13, 1998; and a senior administration official, October 21, 1997.

42. Woodward, The Choice, pp. 259, 261.

On July 17, Lake, Christopher, Perry, Albright, Shalikashvili, and Berger gathered around the oblong table in the national security adviser's West Wing office for breakfast and another discussion of Bosnia. Lake presented the strategy he and his staff had been working on for close to a month. Its essence was twofold.[43] First, Lake argued that the United States needed to lead a diplomatic effort before the end of the year to get a peace settlement that would preserve Bosnia as a viable, single state composed of two entities. This required a willingness to abandon some long-standing and cherished principles regarding both territorial and constitutional provisions. Second, if this effort failed, the United States should force the issue of an UNPROFOR withdrawal in 1995, prior to the presidential elections. Avoiding a discussion of political calculations, Lake argued that the strategic rationale for doing so was that all sides in Bosnia would have an incentive to try to exploit perceived U.S. vulnerability to outside pressure because of the presidential campaign in 1996 to get their way either diplomatically (by asking for the unattainable) or militarily (by drawing NATO and the United States into the conflict).

Lake then set out what he had in mind for the diplomatic strategy. The key to success would be to gain leverage over the Bosnian Serbs by wielding real carrots and real sticks. Real sticks included: using the recently deployed Rapid Reaction Force to open up a corridor from the Sarajevo airport to the city, as well as to establish UNPROFOR control over the airport; issuing a new NATO ultimatum for reestablishing the heavy weapons–exclusion zone around Sarajevo; encouraging increased covert arms shipments to the Bosnians by third parties;[44] using the congressional resolution mandating a unilateral lifting of the arms embargo to gain added diplomatic leverage; and reconfiguring UNPROFOR in a more defensible posture, possibly by offering U.S. assistance to extract those UN troops still deployed in the eastern enclaves. Lake stressed that additional sticks could be wielded against Milosevic, including terminating sanctions relief

---

43. Details of the strategy in the next few paragraphs are based on interviews with senior administration officials, October 21, 1997, and April 27, 1998. See also Woodward, *The Choice*, p. 259; Mark Matthews, "Peace Bid for Bosnia Is Backed," *Baltimore Sun*, August 15, 1995, p. A1; and Lippman and Devroy, "Clinton's Policy Evolution," p. A1.

44. It was well known that the Iranians and other Islamic countries were supporting the Sarajevo government with military equipment. See, for example, Thomas Lippman and Daniel Williams, "U.S. Is Allowing Iran to Arm Bosnia Muslims," *Washington Post*, April 14, 1995, p. A1.

in case Serbia did not end its military and economic support for the Bosnian Serbs. Moreover, Belgrade should be warned that a resumption in direct support to Pale would result in a tightening of sanctions as well as U.S. or NATO air strikes against key targets, including inside Serbia.

In addition to sticks, Lake maintained that real carrots were necessary to get the allies on board and convince the Bosnian Serbs to negotiate seriously. For example, the Contact Group map could be modified in realistic ways, such as trading the smaller eastern enclaves and the widening of the Posavina corridor linking Bosnian Serb–held territory to the east and west for Federation control of Sarajevo and additional territory in central Bosnia. Constitutional provisions for a unified Bosnia could stress some degree of autonomy for the Bosnian Serbs—possibly including a referendum on secession within two to three years as the Bosnians had agreed to in 1993. Significant international assistance could be provided for a post-settlement, mini-Marshall Plan for the Balkans. And Bosnia might be offered the prospect of associate membership in the European Union. Lake stressed that it would not be easy to get an agreement even with these modifications. The United States would need to take the lead in the negotiation effort, get the allies and Russians on board, and probably engage Pale directly.

Lake stressed that if this last-ditch effort to achieve a settlement failed, then he would favor forcing the issue of UNPROFOR's withdrawal that year. In anticipation of a withdrawal, Lake suggested that Washington press the allies to consolidate UN forces as much as possible on Federation-controlled territory. This would minimize the risk to American forces that would participate in a NATO operation to assist in the UN's departure. Once UNPROFOR had been withdrawn, the goal of U.S. policy should be to assist the Bosnians so that they could recover at least the territory that was allotted to them under the Contact Group plan. This would involve lifting the arms embargo, multilaterally if possible and unilaterally if necessary; arming and training the Bosnians; and conducting air strikes against Serb targets to protect Sarajevo and other strategic areas during the transition period.

Although many of the particulars in Lake's presentation had been discussed previously, this was the first time that they had been pulled together in a comprehensive endgame strategy. Despite the boldness of his presentation, however, much of the subsequent discussion among the principals was as staid and business-as-usual as previous ones on Bosnia. Albright was fully supportive of the effort, including the particulars. Christopher warned that the United States did not have any leverage over the allies or the parties. The risks of failure therefore loomed larger than the possible benefits of trying something new. Lake disagreed, arguing that the United States needed to go for broke, because the risks of not trying a new approach were by now outweighed by the risks of failing if they did try. Lake also rejected Christopher's preference for diplomatic half-measures. He argued that the administration needed to "leap-frog" the obstacles in order to get an integrated approach to the problem.[45]

Notwithstanding this brief exchange of views, it soon became clear that Christopher, Perry, and Shalikashvili showed minimal interest in the ideas Lake had laid before them, preferring instead to return to the immediate issues at hand. Of course, in the aftermath of the Srebrenica debacle, a response was needed to the French proposal that the United States provide helicopters to ferry French troops into Gorazde. And the London conference called by British Prime Minister John Major to chart a new course was only days away.[46] Another reason for their seeming dismissal of the ideas in the endgame strategy was that Christopher and Perry in particular were not enthralled by yet another policy review. As usual, preoccupation with immediate tactical considerations was crowding out consideration of long-term strategy. And past policy reviews had hardly been fruitful.

Toward the end of the meeting, the president entered Lake's office and joined the discussion, just as Lake had arranged. "I don't like where we are now," Clinton said. "This policy is doing enormous damage to the United States and to our standing in the world. We look weak." Without a change, more trouble lay ahead. "[It] can only get worse down the road. The only time we've ever made any progress is when we geared up NATO to pose a real threat to the Serbs." He called on his advisers for new ideas that would get them out of the rut the administration was in, and then left.[47]

With this boost from Clinton, Lake urged his colleagues to begin thinking about Bosnia policy in a longer-term perspective. A new direction was needed. He asked them to study his proposal and suggested that the president would be well served if they could put their own thoughts on paper. Where did they think we should be in six months' time and how could we best get there? The principals left, taking the endgame strategy with them and agreeing to provide the president with their own ideas.

45. Interview with a senior administration official, August 7, 1998.
46. See the discussion on pp. 71–75 above.
47. Woodward, *The Choice*, p. 261.

The President Decides

Following the meeting in Lake's offices on July 17, 1995, an informal interagency group was established to supervise the drafting of the agency strategy papers and to ensure that each retained their distinctiveness vis-à-vis the others. The group was chaired by Sandy Berger and included Sandy Vershbow from the NSC; James Steinberg, Peter Tarnoff, and Bob Frasure from the State Department; Walter Slocombe and Joseph Kruzel from the Defense Department; and David Scheffer from the Washington office of Ambassador Albright. They met almost daily over the next two weeks to ensure that the papers presented the president with real policy options.

The Strategy Papers

By early August a package of some thirty pages, containing a cover memo from Tony Lake to the president and four separate papers (by the U.S. mission to the UN, or USUN, NSC, State, and Defense, respectively), was sent to the president for his consideration at a meeting scheduled for August 7. The papers presented clear, distinctive points of view on where America's Bosnia policy should be headed.[48]

USUN. Albright's paper was an extended version of the "Elements of a New Strategy" memo she had given the president in June. Rather than setting forth a different policy from the endgame strategy, which Albright supported, the paper provided the strategic rationale and political chapeau for that strategy. This is why Lake placed it on top of the group of papers he delivered to the president.

Albright made three points in the paper. First, although the president and his administration had done much to restore confidence in American foreign policy during the past year, notably by securing an agreement to halt North Korea's nuclear program and restoring the democratically elected government of Haiti, all this could be lost if Bosnia policy was not put on the right track. For better or worse, Bosnia's future and the credibility of American foreign policy were inextricably linked. Albright stressed that the latter was possible only if the United States now took the lead to bring the Bosnia issue to a head in 1995.

48. This summary of the four papers is based on nearly all the interviews I conducted, especially with senior administration officials, October 21, 1997, April 27, 1998, June 8, 1998, July 20, 1998, January 11, 1999, and March 1, 1999; and with administration officials, April 3, 1998, July 9, 1998, and July 15, 1998.

Second, it was time to challenge the fundamental assumption of U.S. policy—that UNPROFOR's withdrawal was to be avoided at almost all costs. The allies were going to withdraw their forces; the only remaining question was when, not whether. If American troops were going to be deployed in Bosnia sooner or later, then they should go on U.S. terms rather than on terms set by the allies or the United Nations.

Third, of the many lessons Bosnia taught, one stood above all others: every time the United States and NATO threatened or used force seriously, the Serbs folded. "The essence of any new strategy for Bosnia must recognize the one truth of this sad story. Our only successes have come when the Bosnian Serbs have faced a credible threat of military force. Hence, we must base our plan on using military pressure to convince the Bosnian Serbs to negotiate a suitable peace settlement."[49]

NSC. The endgame strategy was a modification and refinement of the paper Lake had shared with his colleagues three weeks earlier. The strategy set as its basic objective the preservation of a viable Bosnian state along the lines of the Contact Group plan. The only way to achieve that goal was either by getting a political settlement or by establishing a balance of power on the ground that provided the Bosnians with the ability to recover and defend roughly the territory allotted to them under the Contact Group plan. The paper emphasized that a clear indication from Washington that the United States was prepared to support the Bosnians to achieve their goals militarily would provide the best leverage to get the Serbs to negotiate a political settlement. At the same time, Washington would make clear to the Bosnians that its willingness to support this military strategy was conditioned on their evident cooperation and flexibility in reaching such a settlement. The key elements of the diplomatic and military strategies to achieve this objective were similar to the original paper.

To get a political settlement in 1995, the United States would have to take the lead in the negotiations as it had last done in the first half of 1994, when Washington brokered the Federation agreement and Contact Group plan. Success would require increased U.S. flexibility: to encourage Bosnian flexibility on the map (for example, by trading the eastern enclaves and a widening of the Posavina corridor for control of Sarajevo and

---

49. Quoted in Ann Blackman, *Seasons of Her Life: A Biography of Madeleine Korbel Albright* (Scribner, 1998), p. 242.

more defensible territory in central Bosnia), on constitutional issues (for example, by conducting a referendum on secession in two to three years and spelling out the meaning of the "parallel special relationships" of the Bosnian entities with Serbia and Croatia), and on the basis for restarting negotiations (for example, by finessing the issue of Bosnian Serb acceptance of the Contact Group plan as the basis of negotiations); to deal directly with the Pale leadership, which would have to be a party to any negotiation; and to broaden the interaction with Milosevic, who, in his evident desire to see sanctions lifted, ought to be willing to work to achieve a settlement.

If, as seemed likely, a political settlement failed to materialize, then the United States should seek UNPROFOR's withdrawal and put in place a strategy designed to provide the Bosnians with the ability to recover and defend the territory they would gain under a peace settlement. This would require direct U.S. assistance, including lifting the arms embargo, multilaterally if possible, but unilaterally if necessary; providing arms to and training for the Bosnian forces; enforcing the no-fly zone, including by preemptive attacks on air defense systems to ensure the safety of U.S. and possibly other NATO aircraft monitoring the ban; conducting aggressive air strikes to defend Sarajevo and other remaining "safe areas" for up to one year; and encouraging a successor to UNPROFOR, possibly composed of moderate Muslim states.

State Department. Christopher's contribution was based largely on the Steinberg-Frasure paper that had been written some weeks earlier. Its main thrust was an initiative to restart negotiations. Like the endgame strategy, the State paper made a plea for reasserting an American leadership role. Unlike the NSC contribution, however, State focused more on the mechanics of getting negotiations started than on the strategy for reaching an agreement. As for a post-UNPROFOR strategy, the paper stressed the considerable risks—including the absence of congressional and public support—of deploying U.S. troops to assist in the UN's withdrawal and cautioned against pressing the allies to withdraw their forces as both Lake and Albright advocated.

The diplomatic strategy focused on two ideas that were developed as part of the talks hosted by Talbott in June. Specifically, it proposed a summit of the Serbian, Croatian, and Bosnian presidents together with the Contact Group at which the three countries would recognize one another. Principles for negotiating a Bosnian settlement would also be agreed at that summit. Complementing the summit would be a reinvigorated effort to convince Milosevic to deliver the Bosnian Serbs in a Bosnia negotiation in return for sanctions relief. The paper was largely silent on the details of these negotiations, only suggesting that progress might be more likely if the final territorial division coincided with that which the parties possessed at the time of a cessation of hostilities.

As for the military strategy, while the paper made a strong case for keeping UNPROFOR in Bosnia, it recognized that countries contributing troops might wish to pull out. In that case, State favored lifting the arms embargo and providing arms. Any training would have to be conducted outside Bosnia, however. Moreover, consistent with the position Christopher had first adopted in May, State opposed air strikes to support the Bosnians, even during a transitional period.

Defense Department. This paper also rejected the thrust of the endgame strategy, especially the idea that the United States should not just become more engaged in Bosnia, but do so in a manner that would make it more responsible for Bosnia's future. It was not that the Pentagon's leadership rejected any military involvement in Bosnia, although many in the building clearly did. Indeed, Perry had long supported the use of substantial NATO air power for clearly defined purposes. In fact, he had been the primary mover, with General Shalikashvili, in persuading the allies two weeks earlier to make a final stand in Gorazde by threatening "substantial and decisive" air strikes in case of a threat or attack against the UN "safe area."[50] At the same time, Perry and his staff did not believe that U.S. interests were sufficiently engaged to use military power—especially ground troops—to do what some might judge necessary for the cause of justice: namely, to support the Bosnians in their effort to recover all, or even much, lost territory. Instead, Defense's preferred end point would be more or less consistent with the status quo, absent continued violence.

Specifically, the paper argued for acceptance of the de facto partition of Bosnia. UNPROFOR would be withdrawn, the fighting halted, a permanent cessation of hostilities established, and Sarajevo would be demilitarized. As for the map, territory would essentially be divided between the Bosnian Serbs and the Federation along the existing confrontation line. Small modifications to ensure more congruous and defensible lines should be encouraged and these could result in a division "somewhere in between

50. For details, see pp. 69–70 above.

the current territorial division and the Contact Group map, with the final line closer to the former."[51] The Serb areas would be relatively autonomous from the central Bosnian government and would be free, after an agreed interval, to vote to join Serbia. To ensure its viability over the long term, the United States and Europe would provide considerable economic support to the smaller Bosnian state that would remain.

A Crucial Set of Meetings

The president and vice president were scheduled to meet with the principals on August 7, 1995, to discuss the papers and decide what course the United States should follow. Christopher was on his way back from Asia and could not attend the meeting. However, he called Clinton to make his views clear.[52] The secretary of state told the president that while he liked some of the ideas in the endgame strategy, he believed the plan promised more, especially on the military side, than the United States could deliver.[53] He was convinced that the American public would not support the deployment of U.S. troops to Bosnia other than to help enforce an agreement reached by the parties themselves. He was equally firm in his belief that the allies would never support a policy of lift, arm, train, and strike. Moreover, Christopher told the president that he was uneasy about Lake's apparent willingness to strong-arm the Bosnians to accept modifications in the Contact Group map (even though his own department's contribution would be satisfied with less territory for the Bosnians than the endgame strategy foresaw). He strongly believed that the map was one thing the parties themselves would need to negotiate.[54]

Aware of Christopher's warnings to the president, Lake used his private briefing with Clinton before the principals meeting to stress the seriousness of what the president was about to decide. "We're rolling the dice here," he told Clinton. "It's imperative everybody be on board, and while you need to listen to all views, you need to then lay out the marching

51. Interview with a senior administration official, July 20, 1998, reading text of the paper.

52. Interview with a senior administration official, January 11, 1999.

53. Clearly, Christopher remained haunted by the ghost of May 1993, when he had traveled to Europe trying to convince the allies to endorse lift and strike only to return empty-handed to a Washington (and a president) that had apparently abandoned faith in the strategy while he had been away.

54. Interviews with a senior administration official, October 21, 1997, and an administration official, July 7, 1998.

orders. You have to make it clear, and this is dangerous, that you're going to act on this unflinchingly if the worst comes to the worst."[55] In other words, Clinton had to go for the endgame strategy as a whole, realizing that if the diplomatic part failed—which was possible, if not likely—the military part would have to follow. Once embarked on the strategy, the difficult part could not be abandoned, as Christopher appeared to suggest. That would mean a complete loss of U.S. credibility.[56]

The president and vice president entered the Cabinet room on August 7, 1995, and seated themselves in the middle of the long table, across from Lake and the other principals, including Perry, Albright, Deutch, Shalikashvili, and Tarnoff, who was sitting in for Christopher.[57] Lake led off the meeting, going over the major points in the papers.[58] He said everyone agreed that muddling through no longer was a credible option. Instead, they accepted that a last-ditch effort to reach a diplomatic settlement should be made by exploiting NATO's newfound resolve and engaging directly with the Pale leadership. All agreed that U.S. leadership would be indispensable, but they realized that even then the effort might not succeed. Finally, there was consensus that if no settlement could be reached soon, or if UNPROFOR's credibility did not improve, "we should pull the plug on UNPROFOR, lift the arms embargo, and agree on a post-UNPROFOR withdrawal strategy."[59] However, there was no agreement on what the content of such a strategy should be.

Lake then went over the differences dividing the president's major foreign policy advisers. He focused on two key areas. First, they differed on the kind of Bosnia each would settle for. Christopher and Perry argued that the United States should help the Bosnians consolidate the territory they controlled at the time of a cease-fire and perhaps make some marginal territorial additions thereafter. However, to press for appreciably

55. Clinton was well aware of the consequences. "I'm risking my presidency," he replied to Lake's admonition. Quoted in Woodward, *The Choice*, p. 265.

56. Interview with a senior administration official, April 27, 1998.

57. Others at the meeting included Leon Panetta (the president's chief of staff), George Stephanopoulos (the president's senior adviser), Leon Fuerth, Sandy Berger, Sandy Vershbow, and Nelson Drew.

58. Details on this and the subsequent two meetings are based on the extensive discussion in Woodward, *The Choice*, pp. 265–67, as well as interviews with a senior administration official, April 27, 1998, August 7, 1998, and March 1, 1999, and administration officials, July 7, 1998, and August 13, 1998. Unless otherwise noted, all quotations in the text are from Woodward's account.

59. Interview with a senior administration official, March 1, 1999.

more would make agreement far less likely. Albright and Lake, on the other hand, argued that the United States could not depart in any substantial way from the essence of the Contact Group plan of a single Bosnian state, consisting of two entities, each with about fifty percent of the territory, give or take five percentage points.

The second major difference among the principals, Lake pointed out, related to the interests at stake and the risks the United States should be willing to run to safeguard those interests. State and Defense believed that the limited U.S. interests involved did not warrant running the grave military risks that a defense of a unified Bosnia would entail. State believed that U.S. interests would be best served by an end to the violence, and that this should be the primary aim. The Pentagon was most concerned about avoiding a sustained military involvement, and saw in arm, train, and strike the shades of Vietnam. Lake noted that he and Albright had a quite different view. They maintained that the stakes went far beyond the particulars in Bosnia. The issue was not one state or two, three, or none. Rather, the issue was U.S. credibility as a world leader, its credibility in NATO, the United Nations, and at home. That credibility would be enhanced, moreover, if Washington were clearly prepared to go the extra mile to get a settlement. This included adopting a "tough love" approach toward the Bosnians and making clear that U.S. support was conditioned on their adopting a constructive attitude in the talks.[60]

Following Lake's summary, the president, used to a seminar-type style of decisionmaking, wanted to hear what everyone else had to say. Each principal in turn elaborated on his or her perspective, stressing the points he or she most thought Clinton should hear. After they finished, the president indicated support for Albright's argument. "I don't agree with every one of her prescriptions, but I agree with her paper," Clinton said.[61] "We should bust our ass to get a settlement within the next few months," the

60. Perry agreed with this "tough love" approach toward the Bosnians, while Christopher rejected it, arguing that the United States could not pressure the war's victims into signing a deal they would not want to accept on their own. Interview with a senior administration official, August 7, 1998.

61. Quoted in Blackman, *Seasons of Her Life*, p. 242. One of the recommendations Clinton did not like was Albright's proposal to send U.S. military personnel to conduct the training of Bosnian forces inside Bosnia. According to an administration official involved in drafting the paper, this proposal was included in part so that there was something in the paper the president could reject, while still accepting its underlying rationale. Interview with an administration official, July 9, 1998.

president added, indicating that he liked the specifics of Lake's diplomatic approach. "We've got to exhaust every alternative, roll every die, take risks." If the situation were not resolved soon, Clinton feared the decision to engage would be "dropped in during the middle of the campaign."[62]

Much of the discussion that followed focused on two issues. First, there was the question of how to implement the diplomatic game plan. The NSC's approach was for Tony Lake to go to Europe and tell the allies what the president had decided: that the United States was prepared to lead a last-ditch effort to get a settlement this year. Once the Europeans were on board, a senior presidential envoy would lead a diplomatic shuttle to the Balkans to get the negotiations under way. There would also be a secret, high-level approach to the Bosnian Serb leadership in Pale to make clear what was at stake. State's alternative approach was to focus the effort on getting the three regional presidents together, believing that the Europeans would block any significant change in direction. Tarnoff proposed suspending sanctions in exchange for Milosevic's recognition of Bosnia. Then Milosevic and Izetbegovic would meet and agree on a set of principles for negotiating a Bosnian peace, at which point Tudjman would join them and seal both a three-way recognition and the negotiating principles. In the end, the president decided to support the NSC approach. Lake would go see the Europeans. "I agree we make a full court press to seek a diplomatic solution," Clinton said. "How quickly can you get your bags packed?" he asked Lake. "I've got a toothbrush in my office," Lake responded.[63]

The second issue was what the United States should do if the diplomatic push, however determined, failed to end in a settlement. Should the United States seek to end the current impasse in 1995 or wait until 1996 to see how events unfolded? Whereas most participants favored cutting the knot that year, Tarnoff, acting on Christopher's instructions, resisted. He maintained, as the State Department had throughout 1995, that Milosevic could be brought along to deliver an acceptable outcome once he truly believed that sanctions would be lifted. The focus should be on that effort, especially since the risks of getting UNPROFOR out militated against forcing the issue in 1995. Clinton listened carefully to the argument, and then ended the meeting by saying he wanted to sleep on what he had heard. Before leaving, he made clear that they all had to face down

62. Final quotation is from Stephanopoulos, *All Too Human*, p. 383.
63. Stephanopoulos, *All Too Human*, pp. 383–84.

the issue now. Clinton said he liked the combination of carrots and sticks in the endgame strategy and that he would likely go that way.[64]

After the meeting, Clinton called Chirac, Major, and German Chancellor Helmut Kohl to tell them to expect Lake to arrive in the next day or two with a major new initiative on Bosnia. The details of the initiative were set out in a list of talking points—a script, really—that Sandy Vershbow had been drafting for some time. The first and most important point was that the president's national security adviser had come to share with them "the decisions the president has taken."[65] Unlike Christopher in May 1993, Lake would tell the allies what the United States would do, not ask them what they wanted. Lake then planned to get straight to the point. In case the UN force collapsed or withdrew, the points read, "we have decided what we will do in those circumstances." The points detailed the steps the United States would take to support the Bosnian government in its quest to recover and defend at least the territory allocated to it under the Contact Group plan. At each point, Lake would stress that the president felt strongly about the issue, and that the basic decisions had been made.

The next evening, August 8, the same group of people reconvened. The president opened the meeting by saying that he thought the endgame strategy was the right way to go. He wanted Lake to go to Europe and tell the allies exactly what he had decided. He then pulled Lake's talking points from a folder and asked him to go over every point in the presentation— almost ten pages—to see whether everyone agreed. Lake went over the points, emphasizing that the president had decided to make one last-ditch effort to get a political settlement this year and, failing that, to support the Bosnians militarily. At each point, Lake solicited input from the participants and proceeded only when everyone had agreed. Lake went over the carrots he would offer to get the parties to the table and emphasized the sticks, including the threat of significant bombing against the Serbs. However, he made clear that the Bosnians would not get a free ride. "If the Bosnians are the bad guys [during the negotiations], they don't get the strike or the arms," Lake read from his talking points. "They get lift and

64. Confident of the outcome, Lake had told his executive assistant some days earlier to make all the travel arrangements for his trip to London, Paris, and Bonn. Interview with an administration official, November 3, 1998.

65. Interview with a senior administration official, March 1, 1999, reading from notes.

leave," meaning that the United States would support an end to the arms embargo but otherwise abandon Sarajevo.

It took nearly two hours to go through the script. When Lake finished, Clinton suggested they meet again the next morning at 8:00 a.m. "I want to see a new version of your talking points. I want to make sure that everybody else is comfortable with them. If everything is within reach, then Tony can leave at ten. If not, we'll delay his flight. We need to push this. Fortunately we're in a different situation than we were in 1993 and finally we're not asking for something the Europeans won't like. This time we'll be pushing on an open door."[66] Clinton was right on the diplomatic part of the strategy, but not the military part, which the allies had never supported.

When the group reassembled the next morning, August 9, Clinton wondered whether Lake's presentation would not be more powerful if he started off by presenting the carrots, leaving the sticks for the end. Lake did not agree, but he did not object.[67] Clinton indicated that he was now comfortable with the points. Lake wanted to be sure that everyone—including the president—was behind what he would be saying. He wanted no ambiguity. "The line I'm going to take in the meeting with the allies is that this is the U.S. policy, this is what we're prepared to do if there is no settlement. This is what we intend to do. We hope you'll come with us. We won't be so inflexible to refuse changes to our approach but we want to give them an accurate understanding that these are presidential decisions, this is a strategy we're wedded to and now's the time to move on." He would make sure that the allies understood that, if necessary, the United States was willing to go it alone. Clinton responded by saying, "The whole thing sounds pretty good." Back from his trip to Asia, Christopher chimed in, "I'm fully supportive of this." He then added a cautionary note that suggested he really was not: "I agree it may work. It will be too difficult if we actually have to implement the worst-case option, fortifying the Bosnian state. Some of the allies will cringe at that if we're actually arming and training them." Congress and the public would not be supportive either, he warned. But Lake had the president's full backing, and that was all he needed to set off for Europe.[68]

66. Woodward, *The Choice*, pp. 266–67.

67. Interview with a senior administration official, April 27, 1998. After having made his presentations to the allies, Lake admitted that the president had been right.

68. Woodward, *The Choice*, p. 267.

Selling It to the Europeans

That same morning at 10:00 a.m., August 9, Lake set off to Europe accompanied by Sandy Vershbow and Peter Bass from his staff, Peter Tarnoff and Bob Frasure from State, Lieutenant General Wesley Clark from the Joint Staff, and Joe Kruzel from the Office of the Secretary of Defense.[69] The original plan was for the group to travel to London, Paris, and Bonn before returning to London on August 14. En route, however, Lake suggested it might be useful to meet with the Russians and perhaps others. While Bass scrambled to get everyone visas to go to Sochi (a Black Sea resort where Russian Foreign Minister Andrey Kozyrev had his dacha), other cities were added to the itinerary: Rome, to assuage Italian concerns about being excluded from the Contact Group—which the European members had insisted on, rather than Washington; Madrid, since Spain held the six-month EU presidency; and Ankara, which was the closest NATO ally the Bosnian government had.[70]

At each stop, Lake made the same presentation, reading the points the president and his principals had worked out over two days of meetings. As Clinton had suggested, Lake started by laying out the diplomatic initiative the United States had in mind. The initiative comprised seven key points:

—A comprehensive peace settlement based on the core principles of the Contact Group plan, including a united Bosnia;

—Three-way recognition between Croatia, Bosnia, and the Federal Republic of Yugoslavia;

—Consideration of changes in the Contact Group map to take account of recent territorial changes and to ensure viable and defensible borders;

—A framework for the long-term constitutional arrangements of a united Bosnia, including the possible scope of the "parallel special relationship" of the two entities with Croatia and Serbia;

69. Christopher had objected to Lake heading the mission and insisted that a high-level State Department official go as the co-head of what State referred to as the "Lake-Tarnoff" delegation. Interview with a senior administration official, January 11, 1999. See R. W. Apple Jr., "Clinton Sending 2 Foreign Policy Advisors to Europe With New Proposals on Balkans," *New York Times*, August 9, 1995, p. A7; and Drew, *Showdown*, p. 252.

70. Interviews with a senior administration official, April 27, 1998, and an administration official, November 3, 1998.

—Sanctions relief for Yugoslavia, with the suspension of sanctions once an agreement had been signed and complete lifting of sanctions once the agreement had been implemented;

—A plan to resolve the situation in eastern Slavonia, a part of Croatia bordering Serbia; and

—A comprehensive plan for regional economic integration, to be assisted through an international "mini-Marshall" plan.[71]

After detailing the diplomatic initiative, Lake turned to the question of what to do in case the all-out negotiating effort failed and UNPROFOR had to be withdrawn. He pointedly said that the president had decided what the United States would do once the UN had withdrawn:

—Seek to end the arms embargo multilaterally, through a vote by the UN Security Council;

—Provide arms, training, and support to the Bosnians (whether the arms embargo was lifted or not) in order to assist in establishing a balance of power on the ground;

—Enforce the no-fly zone and conduct air strikes for a nine-month transition period in case the Bosnian Serbs attacked; and

—Encourage the presence of a multinational force to assist the Bosnians in defending their territory.

Lake emphasized that U.S. support to the Bosnians was predicated on a constructive and cooperative Bosnian attitude during the negotiations; otherwise the United States would lift the arms embargo and leave. He asked the allies for their support, but again indicated that the president had decided that this was the strategy the United States would implement once UNPROFOR had been withdrawn.

Based on Christopher's experience in May 1993 and his own the following August, Lake had anticipated a difficult set of meetings with the allies—especially in London and Paris. He did encounter some skepticism in Paris, where some officials could not fully believe that this time the United States was really serious.[72] On the whole, however, the meetings

71. Interview with a senior administration official, October 21, 1997. See also Holbrooke, *To End a War*, p. 74; and Matthews, "Peace Bid for Bosnia Is Backed," p. A1.

72. One official from the Quai d'Orsay asked Lake, with reference to the Republican-controlled Congress, "How do we know that the president speaks for the United States?" Lake shot back, "The president makes foreign policy in the United States; I'd be happy to send you a copy of the Constitution." Jean-David Levitte, Lake's counterpart as Chirac's national security adviser, berated his countryman and reassured Lake

went as Vershbow had suggested they would; they were "a piece of cake."[73] The allies were grateful that after years of muddling through, someone had come up with a plan of action. Even if they did not agree with every aspect of the proposed strategy, they were nevertheless pleased to see the United States engaged and willing to take the lead.[74] The trip underscored for Lake what some of the Clinton administration's critics had long argued and many in the administration had apparently forgotten—that American leadership was needed to resolve Europe's most acute problems. Asked along the way how he was going to get the allies on board, Lake had said that the United States was the "big dog" that others followed. After each successful stop in a European capital, the Lake team concluded that "the big dog had barked."[75]

Holbrooke Takes Over

Lake's success in getting the Europeans on board—even the Russians liked the new initiative—convinced key members on his team, including Kruzel, Clark, and Frasure, that he should lead the next phase of the shuttle, meeting with the parties to convince them to engage in a serious negotiating effort.[76] Lake was tempted. He liked negotiations and he had played a leading negotiating role in successful efforts in Haiti and Northern Ireland, but he also knew his place in the policymaking process. His was not to negotiate, to shuttle for weeks on end from one capital to the next in the single-minded pursuit of an agreement. As national security adviser, Lake was uniquely placed to communicate the president's interest in and commitment to a last-ditch effort to negotiate a political settlement. Once this interest and commitment had been made clear, however, others needed to

---

that, of course, France fully understood that the U.S. president was committed and would follow through. Interview with a senior administration official, April 27, 1998. See also Woodward, *The Choice*, p. 268.

73. Interview with a senior administration official, April 27, 1998.

74. London and Paris were notably skeptical about arming and training the Bosnians or encouraging a force composed of moderate Islamic countries to remain once UNPROFOR had been withdrawn. Interview with a senior administration official, April 27, 1998. See also Matthews, "Peace Bid for Bosnia Is Backed," p. A1.

75. Interviews with senior administration officials, October 21, 1997, and April 27, 1998; and an administration official, November 3, 1998. See also Lippman and Devroy, "Clinton's Policy Evolution," p. A1.

76. Interviews with a senior administration official, April 27, 1998, and an administration official, November 3, 1998.

take over, leaving Lake to concentrate on the myriad of other foreign policy issues that needed attention.

During the White House meetings in early August, there had been some discussion of who should take over from Lake and continue on the regional shuttle. Some participants, including Madeleine Albright, with support from Lake, suggested that the best way to underscore the president's commitment was to appoint a White House envoy to the job—someone who worked out of the White House and reported directly to the president. One suggestion was Charles Redman, who as Bosnia envoy in 1994 had successfully brokered the Croat-Muslim Federation agreement and the original Contact Group plan. Christopher objected vigorously. Not only had Redman just arrived in Bonn as Holbrooke's successor as U.S. ambassador to Germany, but the negotiations should be led by the State Department. While Christopher was known to harbor mixed feelings about Holbrooke (in part because they disagreed strongly on the risks worth taking in Bosnia), the secretary of state argued for the appointment of his assistant secretary for European affairs as the Bosnia envoy. Holbrooke possessed the kind of ego, drive, aggressiveness, and bluster necessary to negotiate with intransigent parties such as those in Bosnia. Clinton agreed that he would be the right man.[77]

Holbrooke's selection did raise some eyebrows. He had played no part in the development of the policy, believing that the review was largely "wheel spinning." He maintained that it was one thing to create tough policy on paper and another to implement it.[78] In an interview in the *New York Times* published just two days before he was to meet Lake in London, moreover, Holbrooke had been highly skeptical about the administration's efforts. He referred with disdain to a policy process that was "a gigantic stalemate machine" producing only "a bleating cacophony instead of one voice, creating policies that contain many points of view but no point."[79] In his memoirs, Holbrooke is less critical, explaining his

77. Interviews with senior administration officials, October 21, 1997, and April 27, 1998. See also Woodward, *The Choice*, p. 268.

78. Interview with an administration official, August 13, 1998.

79. Tim Weiner, "Clinton's Balkan Envoy Finds Himself Shut Out," *New York Times*, August 12, 1995, p. 5. Weiner's story ended by intimating that Holbrooke had had enough and that he was contemplating a return to Wall Street sooner rather than later. This caught the Lake team, reading the story while in Rome, by complete surprise. After all, Holbrooke was to take over the effort in two days' time. Some on the team wondered whether he was really the right man to take on this crucial effort if his heart was not in it. Interview with a senior administration official, October 21, 1997.

non-involvement in part because of family commitments (he was vaca-tioning in Colorado at the time) and in part "because participating might have reduced my negotiating flexibility later."[80] Of course, Holbrooke's selection as negotiator was not decided until the very end of the review on August 8.

Lake was well aware of Holbrooke's views, and he worried about how much Holbrooke "was prepared to throw himself into this."[81] When Lake returned to London to meet with Holbrooke on August 14, Sandy Berger called, warning that Holbrooke remained highly skeptical about the ef-fort. Apparently, Holbrooke was worried that Lake's success in Europe meant that he would be blamed for any failure. Berger urged Lake to talk to Holbrooke and make sure that he was on board.[82] When they met at the American embassy, Lake pulled Holbrooke aside in a small room to stress the importance of the next phase. He assured him that this was something Holbrooke could pull off. "This is the kind of thing we dreamed of doing together thirty years ago when we started out in Vietnam," Lake said, reminding Holbrooke of their time in Saigon. "I'm going to be with you all the way. And if this thing fails, it's my ass [on the line] more than yours."[83] They were then joined by the rest of the team and discussed the points—drawn from Lake's presentation—which Holbrooke would make to the parties. Holbrooke resisted pushing the Bosnians to give up Gorazde after what had happened in Srebrenica and Zepa. Lake readily agreed. The suggestion had originally been included only because the Pentagon did not want to have to defend Gorazde if called upon to implement a peace agreement.[84]

Having agreed on what Holbrooke would say, Lake, Vershbow, and Bass returned to Washington. Holbrooke headed to the Balkans with his interagency team consisting of General Clark, Colonel Nelson Drew, Bob Frasure, and Joe Kruzel. Five days later, on August 19, on a dirt road down Mount Igman overlooking the besieged city of Sarajevo, an acci-dent would take the lives of Drew, Frasure, and Kruzel—giving the search for peace in Bosnia new meaning to many in Washington.

80. Holbrooke, *To End a War*, p. 74.

81. Cited in Roger Cohen, *Hearts Grown Brutal: Sagas of Sarajevo* (Random House, 1998), p. 448.

82. Interview with a senior administration official, April 27, 1998.

83. Quoted in Holbrooke, *To End a War*, p. 74.

84. Interview with a senior administration official, October 21, 1997. See also Holbrooke, *To End a War*, p. 74; and Woodward, *The Choice*, p. 268.

CHAPTER FOUR

The Road to Dayton

ON NOVEMBER 21, 1995, the presidents of Serbia, Croatia, and Bosnia-Herzegovina gathered with representatives from the Contact Group countries in the auditorium of a U.S. Air Force base in Dayton, Ohio. There, they initialed a peace agreement ending the war in Bosnia after three-and-a-half years of the worst violence that Europe had witnessed since the end of World War II. The road from London, where National Security Adviser Anthony Lake handed over the negotiations baton to Richard Holbrooke on August 14, to the initialing ceremony in Dayton was a long one. Along the way, there was the Croatian military offensive that for the first time turned the military tide against the Serbs; there were the tragic deaths of three U.S. officials on Mount Igman that gave the negotiators a renewed determination to succeed in their efforts; there was a NATO bombardment, which boosted the diplomatic efforts; there were the hard-won negotiating successes in Geneva and New York that cemented the basic principles of a final settlement; there were the three weeks of emotionally draining "proximity talks" at Wright-Patterson Air Force base that finally produced agreement. And through it all, there was Richard Holbrooke, the negotiator, who through sheer energy and skillful exploitation of rapidly changing circumstances on the ground was able to finalize an agreement ending the war and charting a course for peace.

The course of events during these turbulent three months is now well known, not least because its main protagonist has authored its history in brilliant and fascinating detail.[1] Others, too, have delved into this remark-

1. Richard Holbrooke, *To End a War* (Random House, 1998). Michael Kelly, "The Negotiator," *The New Yorker*, November 6, 1995, pp. 81–92; and Roger Cohen, "Taming the Bullies of Bosnia," *New York Times Magazine*, December 17, 1995, pp. 58–61.

able period and written revealing accounts of their own.[2] Rather than recounting those developments here, this chapter focuses on two aspects. First, the circumstances that helped make a deal possible are examined, including the Croatian military offensive of August-September, the decision by Serbian president Slobodan Milosevic to seize control of the negotiations from the Pale Serbs, and the NATO bombing campaign of early September. Together, these three developments fundamentally altered the strategic context for the negotiations, most importantly by placing the Bosnian Serbs on the defensive for the first time.

Second, the key issues that preoccupied policymakers in Washington are considered. These issues proved to be determinative for the implementation of the Dayton Accords. They included clarifying the mandate and mission of the NATO-led Implementation Force (IFOR), especially what it would and would not do in support of non-military implementation efforts; the exit strategy for IFOR, especially the notion that basic military tasks could be accomplished and military stabilization achieved within twelve months; and the authority, responsibility, and capability of the person in charge of coordinating implementation of the civilian aspects of the Accords.[3]

2. Among the most useful are: Anthony Borden and Drago Hedl, "Twenty-One Days at Dayton: A Special Report," *War Report,* no. 39 (March 1996); Carl Bildt, *Peace Journey: The Struggle for Peace in Bosnia* (London: Weidenfeld and Nicolsen, 1998), pp. 73-119; James Gow, *Triumph of the Lack of Will: International Diplomacy and the Yugoslav Wars* (Columbia University Press, 1997), pp. 276–97; *Deutsche Aussenpolitik 1995: Auf dem Weg zu einer Friedensregelung für Bosnien und Herzegowina: 53 Telegramme aus Dayton* (Bonn, Germany: Auswärtiges Amt, August 1998); Susan Rosegrant, *Getting to Dayton: Negotiating an End to the War in Bosnia,* Harvard University Kennedy School of Government Case Program, C125-96-1356.0 (Cambridge, Mass.: Kennedy School of Government, 1996); and Laura Silber and Allan Little, *Yugoslavia: Death of a Nation* (New York: TV Books, distributed by Penguin USA, 1996), pp. 364–79.

3. Of course, there were other issues that preoccupied policymakers in Washington. A key issue, particularly for the Pentagon, concerned the possible inclusion of Russian military forces in IFOR, especially the command-and-control arrangements between Russian, U.S., and NATO forces. On this issue, see Ashton B. Carter and William J. Perry, *Preventive Defense: A New Security Strategy for America* (Brookings, 1999), pp. 33–46. Other important issues to be resolved included the timing and circumstances for suspending and lifting sanctions on Belgrade and Pale; the nature and extent of economic assistance to be provided to Bosnia; and obtaining congressional support for the deployment of U.S. forces as part of the NATO-led force.

A Changing Strategic Landscape

The tragic accident on Mount Igman proved to have a galvanizing effect on peace. For Holbrooke and his newly constituted team, the accident would have meaning only if and when they succeeded in negotiating an end to the war and the peace for which Robert Frasure, Joseph Kruzel, and Nelson Drew each, in his own way, had worked so hard.[4] This determination to make the U.S. initiative succeed also permeated the remarkable meeting President Clinton and his principal foreign policy advisers convened with the new negotiating team in the anteroom of the chapel at Fort Myer following the memorial service for the three peacemakers who had lost their lives. At that meeting, Clinton gave Holbrooke and his team their marching orders—to go back into the region and leave no stone unturned in the search for peace. From that moment on, there was a palpable sense of mission, in which failure was not really an option.

Turning this desire into a reality required more than just hard work and dedication. It also needed a change in the strategic landscape in Bosnia—a change that was occurring without any direct coordination in Washington or by the Holbrooke team when the U.S. negotiators returned to the region in late August. Three events, in particular, were responsible for bringing about this change. First, there was the military ground offensive: first by the Croatian army that swept through the Krajina; then by the Bosnian army that attacked its way out from the Bihac pocket; and finally by the Croatian and Bosnian forces together. Second, Milosevic secured the agreement from the Bosnian Serb military and political leadership—including from "president" Radovan Karadzic and the military commander, General Ratko Mladic—to represent the Serb side in the peace negotiations. Third, in response to yet another shelling of Sarajevo, which left thirty-eight dead in the town's marketplace, NATO launched the most sustained bombing campaign in its history, suspending operations only after the siege of Sarajevo had been lifted and hundreds of heavy weapons had been withdrawn outside the twenty-kilometer exclusion zone around the city.

4. After the Mount Igman tragedy, Holbrooke's negotiating team consisted of Brigadier General Donald Kerrick (National Security Council), Christopher Hill (State Department), James Pardew (Office of the Secretary of Defense), Lieutenant General Wesley Clark (Joint Chiefs of Staff), and Roberts Owen, a lawyer who consulted for the State Department.

The confluence of these three factors had a decisive impact on the circumstances within which the U.S. peace initiative was launched. Yet even though they proved essential to the success in Dayton, each development occurred independently from the U.S. negotiating effort itself.

The Western Offensive

The Croat offensive against the Serb-held Krajina in early August 1995 did not catch Washington by surprise.[5] Croatian President Franjo Tudjman had long made his intentions clear, declaring as early as January 1995 that he wanted the UN forces to leave so Croatia could re-establish control over all areas in Croatia, including those held by the Krajina Serbs. Intervention by Vice President Al Gore had succeeded in heading off the use of force in March 1995, but it was clear to everyone that this only temporarily postponed the reassertion of Croatian control. Indeed, in May the Croatian army forcefully ousted the Serbs from western Slavonia, the most vulnerable of the Serb-held areas in Croatia. Then on July 22, Tudjman and Bosnian President Alija Izetbegovic met in Split. They agreed to defend the Bihac pocket jointly against the combined assault of Bosnian and Croatian Serb forces, which in the preceding days had sought to cut the pocket in half. The next day, Croatian forces moved into Bosnia, pushing north up the Livno valley, saving Bihac and cutting off Knin, the Krajina Serb "capital," from the rest of Krajina.

Washington was supportive of Croatian assistance in defending the Bihac pocket, and it may even have engineered the Tudjman-Izetbegovic meeting.[6] But the Clinton administration was split on what to do about a likely follow-on attack on the Krajina, which officials realized was Tudjman's real aim.[7] On the one hand, some top officials (among them Anthony Lake, Madeleine Albright, and Richard Holbrooke) believed that a suc-

---

5. Interview with a senior administration official, May 20, 1999. See also Silber and Little, *Yugoslavia*, pp. 353–63.

6. Interview with senior administration officials, October 21, 1997, and May 20, 1999. See also Silber and Little, *Yugoslavia*, p. 353; and Stephen Engelberg, "U.S. Took a Calculated Risk in Not Curbing Croat Attack," *New York Times*, August 13, 1995, p. 11.

7. As the U.S. Ambassador to Croatia, Peter Galbraith, said after Croatia's defense minister informed him of Zagreb's decision to engage in "direct military action" in support of Bihac, "I never imagined it would be a limited action, but that it would be part of an overall action to take the entire Krajina." Quoted in Silber and Little, *Yugoslavia*, p. 353.

Figure 3. *Croatian and Bosnian Offensives of August to October 1995*

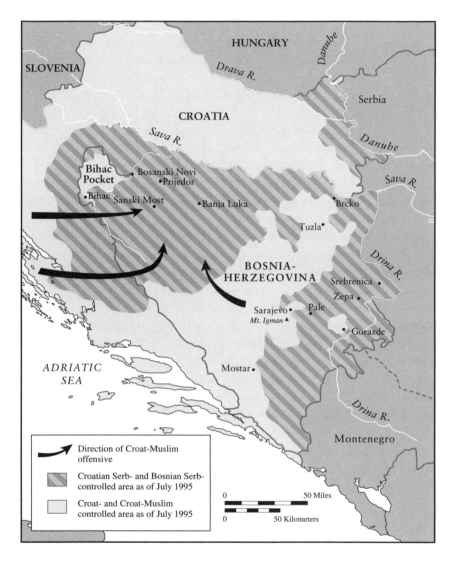

cessful offensive against the Serbs would be a welcome blow against those most responsible for the wars in the former Yugoslavia. It might also save Bihac and could even open new opportunities for peace negotiations. As Robert Frasure reportedly said after the start of the offensive, "We thought we needed a fundamental reshuffling of the deck."[8] On the other hand, the Pentagon and intelligence community feared that Zagreb was too optimistic in its assessment that it could achieve victory in the Krajina in just four to eight days. If the offensive ground to a halt, chances were that Milosevic could not resist the pressure to intervene, thus escalating the entire conflict. Moreover, even without further escalation, the fighting was likely to be brutal and set off a whole new flow of refugees.[9] Given this split at the top, the Clinton administration decided on a middle course, sending neither a green nor a red light, but what one official characterized as "an amber light tinted green."[10]

The yellow-light approach consisted of trying to dissuade Zagreb from opening up a new offensive, but without the forcefulness the administration had used earlier in the year. Instead of involving the vice president, Ambassador Peter Galbraith was instructed to deliver a *démarche* to President Tudjman indicating that Washington was "concerned that you are preparing for an offensive in sector South and North," the UN designation for southern and northern Krajina. Unlike previous instances, however, Galbraith's *démarche* did not mention any sanctions.[11] When the Croatian ambassador to the United States visited officials at the State Department and White House to gauge Washington's likely reaction, he received the same message each time: an offensive of this kind would not be viewed favorably.[12] At the same time, it was clear to both Washington and Zagreb that the United States would not stand in Croatia's way if and when it resorted to the use of force.

On August 4, 1995, the Croatian offensive began in earnest. Within days it had achieved its objective of taking control of the entire Krajina.

8. Interview with a senior administration official, May 20, 1999.

9. Engelberg, "U.S. Took Calculated Risk in Not Curbing Croat Attack," p. 11; and Holbrooke, *To End a War*, pp. 72–73. According to Holbrooke, as late as February 1995, Defense Secretary William Perry and General John Shalikashvili had successfully used the pessimistic argument to dissuade Croatia from launching an offensive at the time (Ibid., p. 62n).

10. Quoted in Engelberg, "U.S. Took Calculated Risk in Not Curbing Croat Attack," p. 11.

11. Interview with a senior administration official, May 20, 1999. Quotation is in Silber and Little, *Yugoslavia*, p. 356. See also Engelberg, "U.S. Took Calculated Risk in Not Curbing Croat Attack," p. 11.

12. However, according to one administration official who was present at the meeting, Bob Frasure had refused to repeat the standard line, saying instead that Croatia should do what it had to do. Interview with an administration official, July 15, 1998.

Rather than resisting the Croatian attack, the Krajina Serb armed forces fled without a fight, leaving close to 200,000 Serbs with little choice but to flee or face the Croatian military's wrath.[13] Those who feared that Milosevic would intervene to protect his dream of a "Greater Serbia" were proven wrong. Milosevic wanted the sanctions lifted, and he was willing to sacrifice most Serb territorial gains to end his isolation from the international community. This was an important indicator of Milosevic's intentions, and it was one the Croatians had counted on before launching their offensive.[14]

The Croatian military successes had an immediate impact on the situation in Bosnia. The military balance of power changed abruptly against the Serbs, who just weeks before had defiantly taken control of the UN-declared "safe areas" around Srebrenica and Zepa, and threatened to take over the remaining areas around Gorazde, Bihac, Sarajevo, and Tuzla. Within days of the Croatian offensive, the Bosnian army's V Corps broke out of the Bihac pocket, attacking to the south and east. For the first time in the war, the possibility emerged that Bosnian military action might begin to reverse the tide that had been running against the Bosnian Muslims and Croats for more than three years.

The Croatian and Bosnian successes confirmed for Washington that its yellow light approach had been right. According to Secretary of State Warren Christopher, once the offensive "became a fact of life, we sought to use it to our advantage."[15] President Clinton similarly expressed the hope on August 7 that the offensive "will turn out to be something that will give us an avenue to a quicker diplomatic resolution."[16] The question became how to exploit the changing military balance to achieve a viable settlement. Holbrooke argued forcefully to the president and his advisers in late August that "the Croatian offensive was valuable to the negotiat-

13. See Raymond Bonner, "War Crimes Panel Finds Croat Troops 'Cleansed' the Serbs," New York Times, March 21, 1999, p. A1.

14. According to one senior administration official, it was clear, at least in retrospect, that Belgrade and Zagreb had "cut a deal" that enabled Croatia to retake the Krajina (though not eastern Slavonia) without having to fear Milosevic's intervention. Silber and Little similarly argue that the offensive was "executed not so much on the assumption, as on the certainty, that Milosevic would do nothing." Interview with a senior administration official, July 20, 1998; and Silber and Little, Yugoslavia, p. 361.

15. Quoted in Tom Lippman and Ann Devroy, "Clinton's Policy Evolution: June Decision Led to Diplomatic Gambles," Washington Post, September 11, 1995, p. A1.

16. Cited in International Institute of Strategic Studies, "A Fragile Peace for Bosnia," in Strategic Survey: 1995/96 (Oxford University Press, 1996), p. 132.

ing process. The time would come when a cease-fire was desirable, but right now the trend on the battlefield was, for the first time, favoring the Bosnians. Unless given specific instructions to the contrary . . . we would not seek a cease-fire yet." To Holbrooke's relief, "no one took issue with this."[17]

By mid-September, the military efforts in western Bosnia were fully coordinated. Bosnian and Croatian forces were supporting each other in a large-scale offensive designed to exploit Serb weaknesses that had resulted from NATO's broad-scale bombing attacks, then entering their third week and further discussed below. As the reality on the ground approached the desired negotiated outcome of a 50-50 territorial split, Washington increasingly feared that a continuation of the offensive threatened the prospects for a successful settlement, a concern communicated both publicly and privately to Croatian officials.[18]

Holbrooke disagreed with the predominant sentiment in Washington. Not having been instructed to urge an end to the military action, he privately assured Tudjman and others at every turn that he believed the territorial gains were helpful to his negotiating effort. In a memo to Christopher, dated September 20, 1995, Holbrooke explained his position: "[T]he map negotiation, which always seemed to me to be our most daunting challenge, is taking place right now on the battlefield, and so far, in a manner beneficial to the map. In only a few weeks, the famous 70 percent-30 percent division of the country has gone to around 50-50, obviously making our task easier."[19] With a final territorial settlement in mind, Holbrooke urged the Croatians and Bosnians to continue the offensive, although he and his team decided to draw the line at Banja Luka.[20] Holbrooke told Tudjman and Izetbegovic that the city was "unquestionably within the Serb portion of Bosnia," so even if it were captured it would have to be

---

17. Holbrooke, *To End a War*, p. 86.

18. See the statements quoted in Holbrooke, *To End a War*, pp. 158–59.

19. Quoted in Holbrooke, *To End a War*, p. 167–68.

20. Holbrooke and Galbraith met with Tudjman on September 17 to tell him not to take Banja Luka. The other members of the team met at the same time with Croatian Defense Minister Gojko Susak, who proudly displayed maps depicting the Croat gains. Susak showed the Americans the key mountain near Banja Luka that his forces would take within twenty-four hours, enabling the capture of the major Serb-held city within forty-eight hours. When informed by the Americans that the United States wanted the offensive halted before it reached the city, Susak was both astonished and disappointed, but Banja Luka was not taken. Interview with an administration official, April 1, 1998. See also Holbrooke, *To End a War*, p. 160.

handed back to the Serbs at the negotiating table. Moreover, there was the humanitarian concern about directing an offensive against a city swollen with refugees from the Krajina offensive. To Holbrooke, the latter decided the case: "I did not think the United States should contribute to the creation of new refugees and more human suffering in order to take a city that would have to be returned later."[21] Tudjman and Izetbegovic agreed not to attack Banja Luka, and Holbrooke announced this fact to the press on September 19.[22]

In announcing the two presidents' decision publicly, Holbrooke did not reveal what he had urged them privately, namely that "[n]othing we said today should be construed to mean that we want you to stop the rest of the offensive, other than Banja Luka. Speed is important. We can't say so publicly, but please take Sanski Most, Prijedor, and Bosanski Novi. And do it quickly, before the Serbs regroup!"[23] The importance of the three towns reflected moral rather than strategic considerations; each had been at the center of the Serb "ethnic cleansing" campaign. Whether the continued offensive was in fact critical to the eventual territorial negotiations is questionable. Indeed, by the time Holbrooke persuaded Tudjman and Izetbegovic to take these towns, various sources had estimated that the offensive had succeeded in whittling Serb territorial holdings down to less than the 49 percent foreseen in the Contact Group plan.[24] Moreover, when the offensive was finally halted, only Sanski Most, not Prijedor or Bosanski Novi, was under Federation control—a territorial division that would be

21. Holbrooke, *To End a War*, pp. 160, 166; quotation is from p. 166. Left unsaid in the conversations with the Croatians was the U.S. team's belief that at some point Milosevic would have to act militarily. Whether Banja Luka would be that point remained unknown, but the risk was nevertheless real. Moreover, if Banja Luka fell, the road to the Posavina corridor and, through it, the way to the Drina would be wide open. In other words, taking Banja Luka constituted a military solution that went counter to Holbrooke's mandate, which was to negotiate a political settlement. Yet it was the prospect that the former might have succeeded—thereby permanently erasing the gains of ethnic cleansing—that left some (including Holbrooke) to wonder both at the time and ever since whether halting the offensive was the right decision. Interviews with an administration official, April 1, 1998, and a senior administration official, May 20, 1999; Holbrooke, *To End a War*, pp. 166–67; and Rosegrant, *Getting to Dayton*, p. 31.

22. Stephen Kinzer, "Bosnia Vows Not to Attack Serb Town," *New York Times*, September 20, 1995, p. A14.

23. Cited in Holbrooke, *To End a War*, p. 166.

24. Interview with an administration official, July 7, 1998.

Figure 4. *Cease-fire Lines, October 1995*

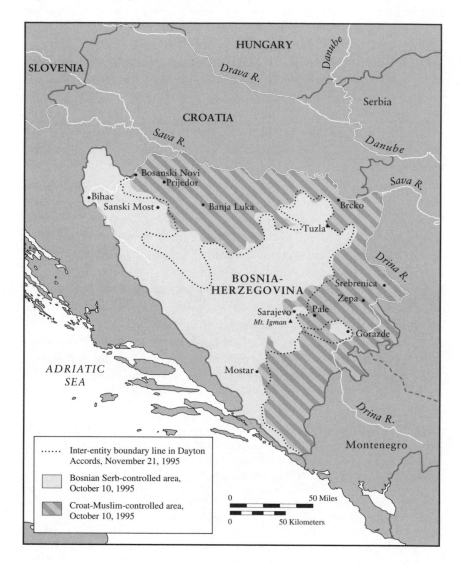

codified in the Dayton map, which placed the latter two towns in the Bosnian Serb Republic.

By early October it was clear that the offensive had achieved its strategic purpose and that any continued fighting would be counterproductive, not least because the Croats had stopped attacking, leaving the Bosnian Serb forces to concentrate on defeating the Muslim forces. A cease-fire was finally, though reluctantly, agreed to by President Izetbegovic on October 5, and announced publicly by President Clinton in the White House briefing room hours later.[25] By the time it went into effect on October 10, virtually every territorial issue that needed to be negotiated, including, in particular, the overall division, had effectively been decided. What remained were red-button issues: the status of Sarajevo, which remained divided between the Bosnian Serbs and the Federation; Gorazde, including access from Federation territory to the town surrounded by Bosnian Serb forces; the Posavina pocket, the area where the Bosnian Croat leader, Kresimir Zubak, hailed from; and the width of the Posavina corridor connecting western and eastern parts of Bosnian Serb territory, including the status of the crucial town of Brcko. These issues would take days of negotiation at Dayton and one of them—Brcko's status—would be deferred rather than resolved. But the overriding territorial issue—who would get what overall share of Bosnian territory—had been settled even before the negotiations actually began.

The Patriarch Paper

The second factor to alter the strategic negotiating environment was the Serb decision to offer an interlocutor—President Milosevic—eager to reach a settlement. Up to this point, a central dilemma confronting the United States had been with whom to negotiate on the Serb side. Washington regarded the Pale leadership as the aggressors in the war and, apart from occasional exceptions in late 1994 and early 1995, had decided not to deal with "the madmen of Pale" directly. Instead, the preferred diplomatic conduit had been Belgrade and Serbia's president, Slobodan Milosevic. At the same time, a full year of often-intense diplomatic effort had failed to secure Milosevic's cooperation in getting the Pale Serbs to end the conflict through negotiations. It was for that reason that President Clinton favored a direct approach to the Bosnian Serbs, believing that diplomatic progress was impossible without having them at the bargaining table.[26] The NSC's endgame strategy paper endorsed such an approach, and Clinton and his advisers had agreed during the meeting in early August at which the strategy was approved that the United States should relax the stricture against talking to Pale. At the same time, they acknowl-

---

25. "Remarks by the President Regarding Bosnian Cease-fire" (White House, Office of the Press Secretary, October 5, 1995).

26. Interview with a senior administration official, October 21, 1997. See also Bob Woodward, *The Choice* (Simon and Schuster, 1996), p. 259.

edged that there was no reason to rush the issue, especially since Karadzic and Mladic, the two most notorious Bosnian Serb leaders, had in July 1995 been indicted for war crimes by the International Criminal Tribunal for the former Yugoslavia in The Hague. The first regional shuttle would therefore bypass Pale and involve only the presidents of Serbia, Croatia, and Bosnia.[27]

Holbrooke had no intention of ever dealing with Pale directly. In his first meeting with Milosevic on August 17, Holbrooke told him, "You must speak for Pale. We won't deal with them ever again."[28] Apparently, Milosevic saw no reason to disappoint Holbrooke. On the weekend of August 26–27, the Serb President summoned the Bosnian Serb leadership to Belgrade, including Karadzic, Mladic, "assembly speaker" Momcilo Krajisnik, and "foreign minister" Aleksa Buha. Joining them was the Montenegrin president, Momir Bulatovic, and Patriarch Pavle, the head of the Serbian Orthodox Church, who was a close sympathizer of the Pale leadership. The ostensible purpose of the meeting was to forge a united Serb front in preparation for the coming peace negotiations, but Milosevic's real aim was to put himself in charge of the Serb side so he could ensure that an agreement would in fact be reached and sanctions lifted.[29]

Using Patriarch Pavle as his lever over the Pale leadership, Milosevic secured an agreement that effectively put him in charge of the Serb negotiating team. According to the document that came to be known as the "Patriarch paper," a six-member delegation of the Federal Republic of Yugoslavia, headed by Milosevic, would be responsible to "conduct negotiations on the overall peace process for Bosnia-Herzegovina" and was "authorized to sign on behalf of the Serb Republic the part of the peace plan that refers to the Serb Republic." The three Bosnian Serb members were Karadzic, Mladic, and Krajisnik. Filling out the delegation were the presidents of Serbia and Montenegro, Milosevic and Bulatovic, respectively, and the Yugoslav foreign minister, Milan Milutinovic. Since the document made clear that everyone, including the Bosnian Serbs, would

27. Interview with an administration official, July 7, 1998.

28. Holbrooke, *To End a War*, p. 5. In an earlier article about the start of his Bosnia negotiations, Holbrooke had gone further, claiming that "Warren Christopher and I had concluded that we should negotiate only with Milosevic, holding him accountable for the actions of the Bosnian Serbs." See Richard Holbrooke, "The Road to Sarajevo," *The New Yorker*, October 21 and 28, 1996, p. 88.

29. Silber and Little, *Yugoslavia*, pp. 365–66; and Kevin Fedarko, "Louder than Words," *Time*, September 11, 1995, pp. 50–57.

be bound by the delegation's decisions and that Milosevic would have the tie-breaking vote, Milosevic (who controlled both Bulatovic and Milutinovic) in effect gained exclusive and legal authority for the peace negotiations.[30]

Although cautiously welcoming the document as a "procedural breakthrough" when Milosevic presented him with the paper on August 30, Holbrooke immediately realized its critical importance. "We knew that we had entered the realm of serious negotiation[s]."[31] For months, Frasure and other members of the Contact Group had tried to convince the Serb president to deliver the Bosnian Serbs to the negotiating table. Now, with the Patriarch paper in hand, Pale need not even show up for an agreement to be concluded.[32] Henceforth, Milosevic's word concerning the negotiations would not just be final, it would be the only word that mattered.[33] Since Milosevic was most interested in getting an agreement—any agreement—so that sanctions would be lifted, the burden for achieving a final settlement now shifted from the Serb side to the Croatian and, especially, the Bosnian sides. As a result, the dynamics of the negotiations underwent a tremendous shift.

Operation Deliberate Force

The final factor to fundamentally alter the strategic landscape was the initiation of the bombing campaign that NATO had agreed to in late July

30. For the text of the agreement, see "Milosevic, Karadzic Agree on Unified Peace Policy," Belgrade Radio Beograd Network, August 30, 1995, reprinted in *Foreign Broadcasting Information Service*, August 30, 1995. In a secret clause of the agreement, Milosevic agreed to secure the minimal Bosnian Serb territorial demands, including widening of the Posavina corridor at Brcko, access to the Adriatic, and the division of Sarajevo and contiguous territory for the Bosnian Serb Republic. At Dayton, Milosevic reneged on all but the last of these demands. See Silber and Little, *Yugoslavia*, p. 380, n3.

31. Quoted in Silber and Little, *Yugoslavia*, p. 366. See also Holbrooke, *To End a War*, p. 105–06; and Rosegrant, *Getting to Dayton*, p. 20.

32. This was affirmed in the Dayton Accords. The preamble to the General Framework Agreement reads that the Patriarch paper "authorized the delegation of the Federal Republic of Yugoslavia to sign, on behalf of the Republika Srpska [the Bosnian Serb Republic], the parts of the peace plan concerning it, with the obligation to implement the agreement that is reached strictly and consequently." See "The General Framework Agreement for Peace in Bosnia and Herzegovina," www.ohr.int/gfa/gfa-frm.htm, accessed October 1999.

33. Meeting in Geneva two weeks later to sign the first agreement on basic principles for a peace settlement, the parties and negotiators were seated at a round table that had been specially constructed to prevent the Bosnian Serb representatives even

following the London conference.[34] Richard Holbrooke addressed the possibility of NATO air strikes in an interview on NBC's "Meet the Press" on August 27, just before returning to the region to resume the negotiating shuttle. Reiterating the policy approved by the president almost three weeks earlier, Holbrooke warned that "if this peace initiative does not get moving, dramatically moving, in the next week or two, the consequences will be very adverse to the Serbian goals. One way or another NATO will be heavily involved, and the Serbs don't want that."[35] The next day, an artillery shell landed on the Sarajevo marketplace during the morning rush, leaving thirty-eight dead and eighty-five wounded. Within twelve hours of the attack, UN investigators had determined that the origin of the shell was Serb, thus providing the basis for commencing the NATO air campaign.

At 11:00 p.m., August 28, 1995, Lieutenant General Rupert Smith, the head of the UN Protection Force in Bosnia, and Admiral Leighton "Snuffy" Smith, commander of NATO's Allied Forces Southern Europe (AFSOUTH) agreed to turn their "keys" ordering NATO bombing to begin.[36] No pub-

---

from taking a seat. The table had room for no more than nine people: the representatives from the five Contact Group nations; the EU representative to the talks, Carl Bildt; and the Serbian, Croatian, and Bosnian Foreign Ministers. See Holbrooke, *To End a War*, p. 138.

34. For details on the London conference and NATO's planning for an air campaign, see pp. 73–79 above.

35. Cited in Holbrooke, *To End a War*, p. 90. Holbrooke's comments, which received a lot of press attention, were echoed by other administration officials the same day. A prescient story in the *New York Times* quoted a State Department official saying that the time was running out on the Serbs, explaining that the United States and its NATO allies had been holding off on air attacks in response to Serb shelling and sniper attacks in Gorazde and Sarajevo earlier in August only in order to give the peace talks a chance to succeed. A senior White House official, restating agreed U.S. policy, warned the Bosnian Serbs that failure to follow through on the negotiations would lead to a lifting of the arms embargo and prolonged NATO airstrikes designed to "level the playing field." Steven Greenhouse, "U.S. Officials Say Bosnian Serbs Face NATO Attack if Talks Stall," *New York Times*, August 28, 1995, p. A1.

36. Rick Atkinson, "Air Assault Set Stage for Broader Role," *Washington Post*, November 15, 1995, p. A1. The Commander of the UN Peace Force, General Bernard Janvier, who held the UN key, had delegated authority to his British subordinate in order to attend his son's wedding in Provence. Ironically, the U.S. and NATO officials had earlier sought to devolve the UN key to General Smith, believing that the British officer would be more likely to agree to air strikes than his French counterpart. However, both the UN secretary general and the French president had vigorously objected, leaving the key in Janvier's hands.

lic announcement of the decision was made in order to give UN forces, including some eighty British military observers still in Gorazde, time to seek safer ground and avoid a repeat of the hostage drama that had followed the limited use of NATO air power the previous May. In the early morning hours of August 30, NATO aircraft commenced Operation Deliberate Force.[37] When the operation ended on September 14, a total of 3,515 aircraft sorties had been flown, delivering 1,026 high explosive ammunitions against 338 aim points on 48 Bosnian Serb targets.[38] Though modest in comparison to the use of air power during the Gulf War, in which a similar size attack would occur in a single day, this was the largest NATO military action in its almost fifty-year history.

The relevance of the bombing operation was almost immediately called into question when on September 1, General Janvier requested a tempo-

---

37. It should be noted that the decision to launch air strikes rested solely with "the Commander in Chief of Allied Forces Southern Europe and the Force Commander, UN Peace Forces," as NATO's Secretary General Willy Claes noted in his statement announcing the commencement of the operation. See "Statement by Secretary General of NATO," *NATO Press Release* (95)73, August 30, 1995. This contradicts Richard Holbrooke's detailed account of the decision, which credits "four factors: the sense that we had reached the absolute end of the line . . .; the grim, emotional reaction of Washington after losing three close and trusted colleagues on Mount Igman; the President's own determination; and the strong recommendation of our negotiating team." Holbrooke, *To End a War*, pp. 95–105; quotation is on p. 103. Holbrooke also credits Claes and UN special representative Kofi Annan with taking the reins in their own hands and authorizing their respective military commanders to begin bombing. However, the decision to launch air strikes in this particular circumstance (namely, in case of a threat to or attack on a UN-declared "safe area") had *already* been predelegated to the respective NATO and UN commanders as a result of the London conference decisions on July 21; NATO's subsequent decision of August 2; and the memorandum of understanding signed by Admiral Smith and General Janvier on August 10. (See the discussion at pp. 76–79 above.) To be sure, there were a lot of consultations and telephoning back and forth in the hours before the bombing occurred, all of which is described in full detail by Holbrooke. Such material, as Mark Danner has noted, is "obviously irresistible to the memoirist, but one that gives an emphasis that is not entirely true to the facts." See Mark Danner, "'Operation Storm,'" *New York Review of Books*, vol. 45, October 22, 1998, p. 78. The fact is that the decision to launch the air campaign resided with the military commanders on the ground, and they made it the moment the one salient fact—whether the artillery shell had come from a Serb tube or not—had been established. Interview with a senior NATO official, August 7, 1998.

38. Robert C. Owen, "Summary," in Owen, Study Director, *Deliberate Force: A Case Study in Effective Air Campaigning*, Final Report of the Air University Balkans Air Campaign Study, School of Advanced Airpower Studies (Maxwell Air Force Base, Ala.: SAAS, 1998), Chapter 12, p. 14.

rary halt in the bombing and Admiral Smith concurred. The suspension enabled Janvier to meet with Mladic, who for fourteen hours engaged the UN general in a harangue against NATO—only to produce a vague, albeit written, assurance that Bosnian Serb forces would halt their attacks on Sarajevo and remove weapons outside the twenty-kilometer exclusion zone once Bosnian government forces were similarly restricted. NATO officials and much of official Washington were deeply upset by the bombing halt, fearing that once suspended, air strikes would be difficult to resume. Although Holbrooke had originally supported a pause to give Janvier a chance to negotiate with Mladic, he shared Washington's and Brussels's dismay at Mladic's offer and, particularly, its public endorsement by Janvier and Smith.[39] Fortunately, the NATO countries agreed with this assessment when the issue was discussed in the North Atlantic Council on September 2. In a nine-hour meeting, the biggest issue confronting the allies was not whether Mladic's offer was sufficient (which it was not) nor what NATO should demand in return for ending the bombing, but whether the alliance should give the Serbs forty-eight or seventy-two hours to comply. In the end, NATO rejected Mladic's offer and made three specific demands:

—No Bosnian Serb attacks on Sarajevo or other "safe areas";

—Bosnian Serb withdrawal of heavy weapons from the twenty-kilometer total exclusion zone around Sarajevo without delay;

—Complete freedom of movement for UN forces and personnel and nongovernmental organizations (NGOs) and unrestricted use of Sarajevo airport.

While the NAC informally agreed to give Mladic until 11 p.m. on September 4 to agree to the demands, its public statement merely warned that the "NATO military commanders are authorized to resume air strikes at any moment in conformity with the Council's [earlier] decisions."[40]

When it became clear that the Bosnian Serbs had no intention of meeting the NATO demands—and following intense pressure on the UN and NATO military commanders from Washington and Brussels through both civilian and military channels—bombing resumed on the morning of September 5. It took another nine days of sustained bombing—including the

39. Holbrooke, *To End a War*, pp. 113, 119–20.

40. "Statement by the Secretary General Following Council Meeting," *NATO Press Release* (95)76, September 2, 1995. For developments leading up to this decision, see Owen, "Summary," Chapter 12, p. 22; Rick Atkinson, "In Almost Losing Its Resolve, NATO Alliance Found Itself," *Washington Post,* November 16, 1995, pp. A1, A32; and Holbrooke, *To End a War*, pp. 112–13, 118–20, 127–28, and 131–32.

use of cruise missiles against air defense targets near Banja Luka and the entry of Croatian forces into Bosnia on September 9 alongside the Bosnian Muslim and Bosnian-Croat troops—to turn the tide. By the time Holbrooke and his team arrived in Belgrade on September 13, the Bosnian Serbs were finally ready to deal.[41] Milosevic had brought Mladic and Karadzic to Belgrade, and he urged Holbrooke to negotiate with them directly. It was evident that the Serb president wanted to end the bombing and get on with the peace negotiations (which four days earlier had resulted in the successful signing of the first basic principles agreement in Geneva). The talks with the two indicted war criminals were uncomfortable for the Americans, but after many hours of negotiations they produced an agreement in which the Bosnian Serbs acceded to NATO's and the UN's demands within an agreed timeframe.[42] That same day NATO suspended the bombing operation for seventy-two hours. When it was clear that the Serbs intended to fulfill the terms of the agreement, the suspension was extended for another seventy-two hours to enable the removal of all heavy weapons under the UN's supervision. On September 20, Admiral Smith

41. In a meeting with President Clinton on September 11, Christopher (with support from Lake, Albright, and Holbrooke) strongly objected to a suggestion by William Perry to call a unilateral halt to the bombing, arguing that, "We must carry on the bombing until it has achieved real effectiveness. . . . The Serbs must be impressed with our willingness to bomb on a continuous basis." The Vice Chairman of the Joint Chiefs of Staff, Admiral William Owens, chimed in, immediately saying that NATO would be running out of targets within the authorized categories (the Option 1 and 2 targets) within the next few days. Owens noted that NATO could attack the targets it had already hit, but this would have diminished value and put NATO pilots at unnecessary risk. Alternatively, NATO could escalate by attacking Option 3 targets—which involved a theater-wide air campaign. This, however, required approval by the North Atlantic Council and the UN Security Council, which seemed highly unlikely. Based on this discussion, Christopher ordered Holbrooke back to the region four days earlier than originally planned in order to secure Serb agreement to the NATO conditions before the bombing campaign might have to be shut down. As it turned out, those actually responsible for planning and conducting the air campaign did not equate running out of targets to hit with a need to end the operation. In addition to the options mentioned by Admiral Owens, NATO planners also had the option of attacking aim points within targets that remained undestroyed or, as General George Joulwan, the NATO commander, suggested, to add new Option 1 and 2 targets to the list. See Holbrooke, *To End a War*, pp. 145–47 (the Christopher quotation is on p. 145); Owen, "Summary," Chapter 12, p. 24; and Donald L. Dittmer and Stephen P. Dawkins, *Deliberate Force: NATO's First Extended Air Operation* (Alexandria, Va.: Center for Naval Analysis, July 1998), p. 40.

42. Holbrooke, *To End a War*, pp. 142–52.

and General Janvier announced that the Bosnian Serbs—having withdrawn nearly 240 heavy weapons from Sarajevo, most of which were immediately moved west to counter the Croatian-Bosnian offensive—had complied with all the conditions and that there was therefore no need to resume the air strikes.[43] After nearly three-and-a-half years, the siege of Sarajevo that had dominated television screens around the world had finally ended.

A Settlement Becomes Possible

When the Clinton administration embarked on its last-ditch effort to secure a negotiated peace settlement, few believed that the effort was likely to succeed. Indeed, to some officials, the negotiating component of the endgame strategy provided a convenient—and politically necessary—cover for the strategy's real purpose, which was to implement the post-UNPROFOR withdrawal strategy designed both to punish the Serbs and to level the playing field by assisting the Bosnians militarily. It was only on that basis that a negotiated settlement would prove possible or viable. However, within the space of a single month, this assessment had fundamentally changed. After the NATO bombing had resumed in early September, the administration's operating assumption was that negotiations would ultimately succeed rather than fail.[44] Of course, this assumption was grounded in the realization that success was not automatic, if only because the parties' behavior in the past did not bode well for achieving an agreement all sides would accept. Indeed, it would take two more months of arduous and creative negotiations to arrive at a successful conclusion.

However, there is little doubt that by mid-September 1995, the combination of the successful ground offensive in western Bosnia, Milosevic's seizure of control from Pale, and the sustained NATO bombing campaign

---

43. Even this decision was marred by disagreement between NATO (which wanted to declare the air campaign "indefinitely suspended") and the United Nations (which wanted to announce that it was "terminated"). After a day-long back and forth, it was agreed that Smith and Janvier would state that "the resumption of air strikes is currently not necessary." Atkinson, "In Almost Losing Its Resolve, NATO Alliance Found Itself," p. A32. For further details on the events from September 14–20, see Dick Leurdijk, *The United Nations and NATO in Former Yugoslavia, 1991–1996: Limits to Diplomacy and Force* (The Hague: Netherlands Atlantic Commission, Netherlands Institute of International Relations, Clingendael, 1996), pp. 80–82.

44. Indicative of the changing assessment was the nature of the concerns dominating interagency meetings, from principals meetings on down. Rather than being preoccupied with day-to-day developments in the Balkans, the focus of these efforts was on how to implement whatever agreement was going to be reached.

had fundamentally transformed the strategic landscape in Bosnia. Together, these changes radically altered the context within which negotiations took place.[45] Whereas the Serbs had from the very beginning been the main obstacle to a peace settlement—with Belgrade, Pale, or both rejecting every peace proposal, from Vance-Owen to the Contact Group plan—they now were eager to get an agreement. For Milosevic, a peace agreement meant the end to sanctions and the possible reintegration of Serbia into the community of nations. This had been his motivation for over a year, but the Croatian offensive and its attendant refugees, combined with the NATO bombing campaign, had given new urgency to get an agreement in place.[46] As for the Bosnian Serbs, the combination of the ground offensive and NATO bombing had resulted in major military and territorial losses, including almost 20 percent of the Bosnian territory it had controlled since the summer of 1992.[47] Fearing the loss of even more territory, the Bosnian Serb leadership was ready to settle as well—as their unilateral acceptance of NATO's conditions on September 14 indicated. And even if they had not been ready to accept the peace agreement being offered, Milosevic was. By way of the Patriarch paper, he effectively deprived the Pale leadership of a voice at the negotiating table.

45. For an argument along similar lines, see James Goodby, *Europe Undivided: The New Logic of Peace in U.S.-Russian Relations* (Washington, D.C.: U.S. Institute of Peace Press, 1998), pp. 130–31.

46. As one of Holbrooke's team members, Christopher Hill, observed before the bombing, Milosevic "always had a rather cocky view of the negotiations, sort of like he's doing us a favor," but after the bombing, "we found him . . . totally engaged—[with an] attitude of let's talk seriously." Quoted in Owen, "Summary," Chapter 12, p. 22.

47. The NATO bombing campaign had targeted the Bosnian Serb communications system, which military planners knew was its Achilles' heel. Lacking manpower, the Bosnian Serb army had been able to hold on to almost 70 percent of Bosnian territory for three years by using their communications system to rapidly reinforce troops in the east and west whenever they were challenged as well as to attack areas with massed formations where and when necessary. During the summer of 1995, General Mladic had moved many of his forces east in order to take over the three enclaves (Srebrenica, Zepa, and Gorazde). When the bombing started, these forces remained pinned down in the east and were thus unable to defend against the Bosnian and Croatian offensives in the west. Thus, while not coordinated, the ground offensive and NATO bombing had a synergistic military and strategic impact. This became evident only after the bombing was halted and Mladic was able to use the weapons and forces withdrawn from around Sarajevo to counter the offensive in the west. Interviews with a senior NATO official, August 7, 1998, and an administration official, July 7, 1998.

The NATO bombing and the Croatian-Bosnian ground offensive in the west settled a crucial question that the international community had been arguing over for many years: whether the use of military force against the Bosnian Serbs could effect a favorable political outcome. Led by a U.S. military still very much under the influence of the former JCS chairman, General Colin Powell, the anti-interventionist camp had argued that nothing less than a full-scale involvement of tens, if not hundreds, of thousands of troops designed to achieve a military victory could guarantee to bring the Serbs to heel while avoiding the risk of getting stuck in a Vietnam-like quagmire. Others, including key Clinton administration officials such as Madeleine Albright, Richard Holbrooke, and Alexander (Sandy) Vershbow[48] believed that the use of air power was desirable not only to punish the Bosnian Serbs for their barbarous behavior but also to force the Serbs to come to the negotiating table—to use air power in the service of diplomacy. This view finally prevailed in the endgame strategy, in which the threat of air strikes in support of a rearming Bosnian military was to act as the quintessential stick to get the Serbs to the table.[49]

In short, by mid-September 1995 the negotiating dynamic had radically changed. Most importantly, there had been a crucial switch in which side posed the greatest obstacle to reaching a settlement. Instead of the Serbs who had long refused to deal, the main obstacle now was the Bosnians. This change put a United States acting as mediator in a much better position to reach a deal. Rather than having to pressure the Serbs,

48. While these critical players used every opportunity to make the case for employing air power in the service of diplomacy, others who shared their views (Vice President Gore, Tony Lake, and Bill Perry) did not consistently press the case. For Gore's views, see Elizabeth Drew, *On the Edge: The Clinton Presidency* (Simon and Schuster, 1994), pp. 145ff. For Lake's view, see Ibid., p. 142ff. and pp. 82–85 above. For Perry's view, see Jim Hoagland, "A Better Battlefield for Bosnia," *Washington Post*, October 1, 1995, p. C7, as well as interviews with an administration official, April 1, 1998, and a senior administration official, July 20, 1998.

49. In this respect, Holbrooke's claims—that "in none of the discussions prior to our mission had we considered bombing as part of the negotiating strategy" and that "Lake himself never mentioned it during his trip to Europe, and in private he had shown great ambivalence toward it"—are wrong. Bombing was central to Lake's strategy and concept and formed the crux of his presentation in Europe. Holbrooke knew this to be the case, for Lake provided him in London with his talking points for use with the parties. Holbrooke, *To End a War*, p. 104; and interview with a senior administration official, October 21, 1997. See also Danner, "'Operation Storm,'" p. 78, who agrees that, on this point, Holbrooke "is simply not credible."

over whom prior to the military interventions the United States had had almost no leverage, Washington now could focus on pressuring the Bosnians, over whom the United States had tremendous leverage because Washington was their last best friend. Given these negotiating conditions, concluding a final agreement was not only possible but likely, even though the specific details and the relative balance of gains between the parties still required very intense and difficult negotiations.

Holbrooke's detailed account of the talks leading up to Dayton confirms as much.[50] Milosevic was willing to compromise without much ado, acceding to a united Bosnia here and a single Sarajevo within Federation territory there. But the Bosnians were another matter. They were deeply split internally and agonized over the minutest detail at each and every turn. And, yet, Sarajevo really had no choice. Either the Bosnians could accept the deal on the table or they would be on their own. Holbrooke and other U.S. officials made it clear—repeatedly and openly at Dayton— that this was it as far as the United States was concerned.[51] Failure to get an agreement then and there would mean that Washington would wash its hands of the conflict. With the United States threatening to walk away and having earlier made clear that there would be no military or other U.S. assistance if Sarajevo caused the negotiations to fail, Izetbegovic knew that the only thing he could do was to sign the agreement.[52] This he did, albeit with evident reluctance, on November 21, by signing his name next to those of Milosevic and Tudjman.

The Dayton Peace Accords consisted of the General Framework Agreement for Peace in Bosnia and Herzegovina and eleven annexes setting forth obligations by the parties and the international community to implement the agreement.[53] The more than fifty pages of detailed text in the annexes contained provisions dealing with military aspects of the peace

50. Holbrooke, *To End a War*, especially pp. 142–52, 169–84, and 231–312.

51. Ibid., especially pp. 273–74 and 282.

52. It was not until the final hour, on November 21, that Izetbegovic acted on this conclusion. Three days earlier, Holbrooke still wondered whether the Bosnians would. "There is a sense here that peace is probably inevitable because of the dangers if we fail. That may be true, as far as it goes. But the critical question—will the Bosnians grasp an imperfect peace or let the war resume—remains unresolved. . . . They have let other opportunities for peace slip away before. It could happen again." Holbrooke, *To End a War*, p. 288.

53. "The General Framework Agreement for Peace in Bosnia and Herzegovnia."

settlement, regional stabilization, elections, human rights, refugees and displaced persons, and even a new constitution. In addition, the annexes described the role and responsibility of international military and civilian agencies to assist in the implementation of the Accords' provisions. The essence of the Accords was contained in the Contact Group plan, and reaffirmed in agreements on basic principles the parties had negotiated in September 1995. These included the following provisions:

—Bosnia and Herzegovina will continue to exist as a single state within its current, internationally recognized boundaries;

—Bosnia will consist of two entities, the Muslim-Croat Federation and Republika Srpska, which respectively occupy 51 and 49 percent of Bosnia;

—The central government will be composed of a popularly elected three-member presidency and parliamentary assembly, which will reflect the multiethnic character of Bosnia and guarantee minority rights;

—The central government will have authority over foreign relations and trade, customs, monetary policy, immigration, international communications, and inter-entity transportation;

—All powers not specified as belonging to the central government will be retained by the entities, including authority over defense and fiscal policy as well as the right to establish "parallel special relationships" with neighboring countries so long as these are consistent with Bosnia's sovereignty and territorial integrity;

—Refugees and internally displaced people have the right to return to their homes or to be compensated for their loss of property.

At Dayton, the negotiators recognized that the effectiveness of these provisions for resolving the underlying conflict in Bosnia would depend crucially on the agreement's implementation, including what the international community would be willing to do to enforce the Accords' provisions. As Holbrooke noted in his remarks at the conclusion of the initialing ceremony, "ahead lies an equally daunting task: implementation. On every page of the many complicated documents and annexes initialed here today lie challenges to both sides to set aside their enmities, their differences, which are still raw with open wounds. On paper we have peace. To make it work is our next and greatest challenge."[54] For this reason, in the weeks and months leading up to Dayton, Washington was primarily preoccupied with the details of how the agreement under negotiation would be implemented.

54. Quoted in Holbrooke, *To End a War*, p. 312.

Key Decisions on the Road to Dayton

A large measure of the success in Dayton is attributable to the decision by Christopher, Lake, and others to give Holbrooke and his team wide latitude in conducting the regional shuttle and proximity talks. As Warren Christopher recounts, to "maximize U.S. negotiating flexibility, I felt that Holbrooke and his team had to be allowed to shape the specifics of an agreement. . . . I trusted the Holbrooke team to stay within the red lines of our policy, such as preserving the territorial integrity of Bosnia and adhering to the 51-49 percent territorial breakdown between the Muslim–Croat Federation and the Serbs."[55] There were a number of reasons for this decision. First, Christopher had learned the importance of giving negotiators flexibility from his own experience fifteen years earlier when, as deputy secretary of state, he strove valiantly to secure the release of U.S. hostages in Teheran. Moreover, it was clear that Holbrooke was not the kind of person whose actions were easy to control from a distance, and Holbrooke would have effectively resisted Washington's interference in his efforts.[56] Finally, as long as Holbrooke was getting the job done, there was little incentive in Washington to try to guide or control his actions. In the end, what Washington desired most was to see an end to the conflict in Bosnia; the details of the settlement achieving that goal were distinctly secondary and best left to those most immediately engaged in reaching it.

Yet there were some issues in the lead-up to Dayton that could not be left to Holbrooke. These had less to do with the structure of the agreement than with the international community's responsibility for assisting in its implementation. Three such issues stood out in Washington. The first two concerned the international military presence that would be deployed to help enforce compliance with any agreement. Since the United States would be contributing a large share of the total number of troops, the mandate and mission of this force was inevitably of key interest to the Clinton administration. Equally important was the question of how long

55. Warren Christopher, *In the Stream of History: Shaping Foreign Policy for a New Era* (Stanford University Press, 1998), pp. 349–50.

56. Holbrooke's own experience as a junior member of the U.S. delegation during Paris peace negotiations with the North Vietnamese reinforced his desire for team unity, negotiating flexibility, and independence. Referring to the Paris experience, Holbrooke writes, "I would not tolerate similar internal divisions within our team, and the negotiating flexibility we needed could come only with the full backing of all the key members of the Principals' Committee." Holbrooke, *To End a War*, p. 83.

the force would have to remain deployed in Bosnia. A third critical issue concerned the authority, responsibility, and capability of the person and organization responsible for overseeing the implementation of the non-military aspects of the eventual peace settlement. As Holbrooke shuttled back and forth in the region and, later, among the delegations in Dayton, Washington turned to the task of deciding these issues in a manner that would enhance the likelihood that whatever agreement emerged from his efforts would in fact be implemented.

Whereas the locus of activity in the months leading up to the new U.S. initiative had been the Principals Committee and the informal meetings Tony Lake had convened in his West Wing office, much of the interagency work on the implementation was conducted by the Deputies Committee. Chaired by Deputy National Security Adviser Samuel R. (Sandy) Berger, the Deputies Committee brought together representatives from the State Department (Deputy Secretary Strobe Talbott, Undersecretary for Political Affairs Peter Tarnoff, and Policy Planning Chief James Steinberg), the Office of the Secretary of Defense (Deputy Secretary John White and Under-secretary for Policy Walter Slocombe), the Joint Chiefs of Staff (Admiral William Owens), the Central Intelligence Agency (Deputy Director George Tenet and Vice Admiral Dennis Blair), as well as representatives from the Office of the Vice President, U.S. Mission to the United Nations, and (when appropriate) the Treasury Department, the Agency for International Development, and the Office of Management and Budget. These officials and their key staff met two or more times a week to flesh out the details of many fundamental issues before sending their recommendations up to the principals for approval. The vast majority of their time was devoted to sorting out U.S. policy on the three issues discussed below.[57]

The Mandate and Mission of IFOR

Even before Tony Lake returned from his August trip to Europe to inform the allies about the new U.S. initiative, the deputies had assigned the Joint Chiefs of Staff the task of thinking about the military implications of successful negotiations, including the nature and purpose of an international military presence to assist in the implementation of a peace

---

57. Much of the information in this section draws on the author's own experience as a member of the National Security Council staff. Where possible, the information has been supplemented by interviews and published sources.

settlement. It was immediately clear that this question would require many long hours of debate. The fact that the first version of the JCS concept paper to circulate among other agencies was the seventeenth revision of that paper underscored that even within the Pentagon there were large differences concerning the basic contours of the problem. Repeated requests by the State Department and NSC to see a copy of the JCS paper were rebuffed with the argument that the paper had not yet been cleared internally. The lack of clearance reflected basic differences between JCS (which wanted a large force deployed to ensure a robust enforcement capability) and the Office of the Secretary of Defense (which wanted to minimize both the size and nature of American military involvement). In a classic bureaucratic maneuver, the paper was released for interagency review only when the NSC's Richard Clarke, the Senior Director for Global Affairs, called a meeting of the Peacekeeping Core Group with the sole purpose of discussing the JCS paper. The paper was distributed just one hour before the meeting took place.

By the end of August, the deputies had agreed on a basic concept for what was then called the Peace Implementation Force (PIF).[58] Thinking about the force was heavily influenced by two considerations. First, the deputies wanted at all costs to avoid a repeat of the UN's experience in Bosnia, a deployment of military forces in a situation where there was no peace to keep nor forces capable or authorized to act under robust rules of engagement. Second, reflecting the thinking behind the endgame strategy, the agreed-upon concept was consistent with the notion that the United States would send troops to Bosnia both to help enforce a peace settlement and to assist the Bosnians should the settlement fail. Much of the focus was therefore on ways the United States could help the Federation, while still retaining the ability to enforce an agreement signed by all parties.

With these considerations in mind, the concept endorsed by the deputies consisted of a NATO-led force, operating under a unified NATO command (no "dual keys"), and with robust rules of engagement. Its objective

---

58. The force was referred to as the PIF throughout August and September and only formally became known as the Implementation Force (or IFOR) following the informal NATO Defense Ministers meeting hosted by Secretary Perry in Williamsburg, Virginia, on October 4–5, 1995. Other contenders for the name included the State Department's proposal for the "Bosnia Settlement Force" (which was rejected because its partial acronym, "BS Force," did not imbue much confidence) and OSD's preferred acronym, "NIFOR," for NATO Implementation Force (which proved to be too much of a mouthful).

would be to implement the military aspects of a peace agreement: primarily marking boundaries and enforcing compliance with the cessation of hostilities, the separation of forces, and the withdrawal of forces to agreed territories. IFOR would be deployed mainly in Federation territory and would respond forcefully to isolated violations or a deterioration in the security environment. The deputies proposed that if the peace were to break down completely as a result of large-scale violations, IFOR should respond asymmetrically, depending on the cause of the breakdown. If the Bosnians were at fault, IFOR should be withdrawn and any military assistance to them ended. However, if the Bosnian Serbs were to blame, IFOR would enforce the terms of the settlement with all forces at its disposal, including the use of NATO air power.

Once Washington had settled on the basic concept for the force, attention turned to Brussels, where NATO authorities would have to turn the concept into reality. Preoccupied with the conduct of the bombing campaign, the North Atlantic Council proved unable to approve political guidance and assign NATO military authorities the task of developing a concept of operation for the NATO-led Implementation Force until late September. Drawing on the detailed planning for a NATO operation to assist in the withdrawal of the UN force in Bosnia contained in OPLAN 40104, General George Joulwan and his staff finalized a basic concept of operations by early October, which the NAC approved on October 11.

The plans drawn up by NATO bore a strong resemblance to those agreed in Washington a month earlier.[59] As explained by Defense Secretary William Perry and General John Shalikashvili in testimony before the Senate, the operation would be led by a NATO force, under NATO command, with NATO rules of engagement. Its main task would be to oversee the separation of forces and to monitor a "narrow zone of separation" between Federation and Bosnian Serb territory. It would "deploy and operate predominantly in Federation territory, but [would] be prepared to operate throughout Bosnia." Finally, the "IFOR mission will not include

59. The similarity should not be surprising. Given the dominance of U.S. military personnel at the top and within the NATO military structure, every detail of force planning is shared between Washington and Mons, Belgium (where Supreme Headquarters Allied Powers in Europe, or SHAPE, is located). Indeed, JCS representatives would often refuse to clear cables containing instructions from Washington to the U.S. mission at NATO until it had first been checked with the U.S. military representatives in Brussels. A similar process was followed in the drafting of the JCS concept paper in August, which in being cleared by SHAPE both reflected and influenced thinking at NATO.

reconstruction, resettlement, humanitarian relief, election monitoring, and other non-security efforts that will need to be undertaken in Bosnia."[60]

Although NATO approved the basic structure of IFOR by mid-October, many critical details still remained to be decided. Concerned that if decisions about these details were left solely in the hands of military authorities, the overall mandate would be exceedingly narrow in scope, the NSC staff drew up a series of questions designed to ensure that IFOR's role in the implementation of a peace agreement was considered to the fullest possible extent. Originally drafted by John Feeley, who had replaced Nelson Drew on Sandy Vershbow's staff, the list was narrowed to thirty-two precise questions, ranging from the timing of IFOR's deployment, the area of its likely operation, and the nature of its exit strategy to IFOR's role in responding to humanitarian atrocities, arresting war criminals, and in assisting civilian agencies that would be engaged in implementing non-military aspects of a peace agreement. The list was circulated by Sandy Berger to his colleagues on the Deputies Committee in mid-October who, in a series of meetings during the remainder of the month, answered most of them. The deputies agreed, *inter alia*, that IFOR's primary objective was the implementation of the military aspects of the peace agreement. It would therefore have no responsibility for basic policing functions. It would assist civilian agencies in the conduct of their duties so long as this did not interfere with its main mission. It would create a secure environment for elections, but would not be responsible for security during the elections themselves. It would not assist in the resettlement of refugees. It would not hunt for war criminals, although IFOR could apprehend those indicted if the opportunity for doing so presented itself during the course of performing its mission.

By late October only eight issues remained unresolved.[61] These included whether IFOR should be regularly deployed, or even stationed, in Bosnian

---

60. Joint Statement by William J. Perry, secretary of defense, and General John M. Shalikashvili, chairman of the Joint Chiefs of Staff, *Situation in Bosnia*, Hearings before the Senate Committee on Armed Services, 104 Cong. 1 sess., June 7, 1995 (Government Printing Office, 1996), pp. 206–07, quotations on p. 206.

61. Holbrooke lists eleven issues, but some of these had been resolved prior to the October 25 and 27 Principals Committee meetings he mentions. Two of the issues on Holbrooke's list—the location of IFOR's headquarters (which it was agreed would be in Sarajevo) and IFOR's role in arresting war criminals—had been agreed by the deputies. A third, IFOR's role in eastern Slavonia, although originally part of the NSC's list of thirty-two questions, was discussed and decided separately. See Holbrooke, *To End a War*, pp. 220–21 and 216.

Serb territory; whether IFOR should patrol Bosnia's international boundaries, as Izetbegovic had requested; whether the parties should be required to store their heavy weapons in cantonment sites separate from deployed forces and, if so, whether IFOR should be obligated to enforce this provision; whether IFOR should respond to "over the horizon" attacks on international agencies or gross human rights violations; and whether the United States should take a leading role in developing a robust international policing component that would be backed by IFOR in case of major civil unrest. Some of these issues were decided by the principals without much rancor or debate, including agreement that as a force designed to enforce and keep a peace signed onto by all parties, IFOR would deploy and possibly even be stationed in Bosnian Serb territory as well as along the borders. But other issues could not be so easily resolved, because they went to the heart of the disagreement within the Clinton administration about IFOR's basic role in the implementation of a peace settlement.

The debate about IFOR's role was driven to a considerable extent by political considerations of what the Congress and the public were likely to support a year before presidential elections. It was also characterized by typical bureaucratic politics, pitting a Pentagon bent on minimizing the military's involvement against a State Department that looked to the military to force—or enforce—what its diplomacy could not achieve alone.[62] But there were also real differences of perspective, of which two stood out. First, many in Washington believed that the immediate objective was to end the war and reduce the likelihood of it restarting. Since a resumption of hostilities was less likely if an internal military balance of forces existed, IFOR's main purpose was to provide a period of tranquility to enable Federation forces to rearm sufficiently to defend their territory against a possible Bosnian Serb attack. A narrow IFOR mission would suffice for this limited purpose. In contrast, others believed that the immediate objective was to build a lasting peace in Bosnia, one that required not just an end to the war, but the construction of a multi-ethnic, demo-

---

62. This classic State-Defense battle regarding the use of force in conflicts other than war had been played out for years, most memorably when George Shultz and Caspar Weinberger respectively headed these departments. See especially George P. Shultz, *Turmoil and Triumph: My Years as Secretary of State* (Charles Scribner's, 1993), pp. 648–53; Caspar Weinberger, *Fighting for Peace: Seven Critical Years in the Pentagon* (Warner Books, 1990), pp. 159–60 and 433–45; and Christopher Gacek, *The Logic of Force: The Dilemma of Limited War in American Foreign Policy* (Columbia University Press, 1994), pp. 262–72.

cratic, and prosperous state. This, of course, required a much broader peace-building role.

Second, there was the question of who should bear primary responsibility for implementing whatever agreement was reached. Some argued that the stability of any peace depended on the parties to the agreement being willing, able, and responsible for implementing that agreement. As Tony Lake, one of the strongest proponents of this perspective, argued some months after the Dayton Accords had been concluded, assigning too large a role to the international community for rebuilding war-torn societies would create "unreasonable expectations [on the part of the parties] that the hard work will be done for them not by them." The role of the international community should be limited to providing "governments and people the breathing room they must have to tackle their own problems."[63] Others maintained, however, that the deep splits in Bosnian society caused by the brutal years of conflict would require many years of effort to overcome. Without a significant international contribution to this effort—including the evident willingness to use a big stick to keep the parties in line—peace would not be achievable. This implied that IFOR, as the largest and most capable international organization in Bosnia, would have to bear the largest burden in securing the implementation of a peace agreement.

Thus by the end of October, there were two schools of thought within the administration regarding what and how much IFOR should do.[64] As Holbrooke recounts, the "minimalists," who were found primarily in the Pentagon, but who were supported by Tony Lake and others in the White House, believed that the military should be assigned precise tasks limited to the military aspects of any agreement: force protection, enforcement of the cease-fire, force separation, and monitoring compliance with the military provisions of the agreement. Fearing both "mission creep" if IFOR were drawn into performing non-military tasks associated with nation building and likely congressional (and public) opposition to any military operation involving U.S. troops that went beyond the immediate military

63. He went on to say, "This 'tough love' policy may sound harsh. . . . But consider the alternative: self-defeating efforts to take on responsibilities that are not ours—to create unsustainable dependencies instead of giving nations a chance to act independently." See Anthony Lake, "Defining Missions, Setting Deadlines: Meeting New Security Challenges in the Post–Cold War World," Speech delivered at George Washington University, March 6, 1996.

64. Holbrooke, *To End a War*, pp. 216–20.

tasks at hand, the Pentagon, with White House support, argued forcefully for a narrow IFOR implementation role. On the other side of this debate stood the "maximalists," who were led by Holbrooke and his team of negotiators. They argued for a broader IFOR mission, which would include such non-military tasks as keeping roads open to ensure freedom of movement, providing security during the election process, arresting war criminals, forcefully responding to human rights violations, and protecting refugees as they returned to their former homes. As Holbrooke writes, "[w]ithout the backing of IFOR, the civilian parts of an agreement—the test of true peace—could not be carried out. And if the civilian provisions of a peace agreement were not carried out, then withdrawal of NATO forces would be more difficult." This, Holbrooke maintained, "could create a self-defeating cycle: the narrower the military mission, the longer they would have to stay."[65]

These differences came to a head in heated exchanges at two Principals Committee meetings in late October, just days before talks at Dayton commenced.[66] The meetings were called to resolve the issues outstanding from the original thirty-two questions the NSC had tabled and the deputies had debated in previous weeks. Pitted on one side of the debate was Richard Holbrooke, the chief maximalist, who argued vigorously for as expansive a role for IFOR as possible. As it turned out, Holbrooke stood alone in the maximalist camp—not because others disagreed with his basic argument that the success of any peace agreement required a proactive role by the most capable international organization present in Bosnia, but because the political climate at that time could not support such a role, especially if it came to be known that the administration had adopted this position over the military's objection.[67] Undaunted, he pressed his case with his

---

65. Holbrooke, *To End a War*, p. 219.

66. The meetings are described in Holbrooke, *To End a War*, pp. 221–23.

67. In retrospect, Holbrooke recognizes this political reality, arguing with respect to the military that the administration "had to have their backing to get congressional and public support for the mission, which meant that they had the upper hand in the debate over what their mission would be." Holbrooke, *To End a War*, p. 219. At the time, however, Holbrooke vigorously and loudly rejected this argument. While in Christopher's limousine on the way to the White House for the final meeting on this issue, Holbrooke got into a shouting match with Robert Gallucci (who had just been appointed as the State Department point person for implementing a peace agreement) over what State's position in the meeting should be. With Christopher watching in quiet astonishment, Holbrooke shouted that opposing a broad IFOR mission would doom any peace in Bosnia. Gallucci, while agreeing with Holbrooke in principle, coun-

usual forcefulness and intensity, so much so that General Shalikashvili, normally the mildest and most pleasant of persons, got visibly angry, cut Holbrooke off, and made clear that there were certain things IFOR should not, would not, and could not do.[68]

When calm returned, Shalikashvili proposed that the issues be settled by making sure that IFOR would have broad authority to assist in civilian implementation, even if its obligation was limited to the military aspects of the agreement.[69] The distinction was important to the military. If IFOR would be required to undertake the broader implementation tasks then it would have to deploy the forces necessary to make sure these tasks could in fact be implemented. Since some of the tasks—protecting returning refugees, providing security at hundreds if not thousands of polling places, hunting down indicted war criminals—were manpower-intensive, being obligated to undertake them would have exploded the force requirement well above the 60,000 troops then contemplated.[70] However, if IFOR possessed the authority rather than the obligation to assist in implementing non-military tasks, the commander on the ground could decide to allocate forces if and when they were available to do so. It was recognized that as implementation of the military aspects of an agreement proceeded along the tight timetable contained in the draft agreement, more and more forces would become available to undertake non-military tasks. For that reason, the principals readily agreed to Shalikashvili's proposal as providing them with the best of both possible worlds.

In the end, both Annex-1A of the Dayton Accords (which detailed the military aspects of the agreement, including IFOR's role) and NATO's

---

tered that Shalikashvili would never accept an expansive IFOR mandate. Therefore Christopher should not put the president in the politically untenable position of having to overrule the military. Instead, Gallucci, who had talked about this with General Wesley Clark, the person responsible for drafting the military annex of the peace agreement, argued that the best that could be hoped for would be a permissive mission statement—one that provided IFOR with the authority to act proactively without obligating it to do so. Holbrooke strenuously disagreed. The shouting match continued for some time, even in the small anteroom outside the White House Situation Room where everyone gathering for the meeting could not help but overhear what was being said. Interview with a senior administration official, July 8, 1998.

68. Interview with a senior administration official, April 27, 1998. See also Holbrooke, *To End a War*, p. 222. Holbrooke writes that despite its importance the debate "was never personal or tense."

69. Holbrooke, *To End a War*, p. 222.

70. Interview with a senior administration official, May 18, 1999.

OPLAN 40105 setting forth Operation Joint Endeavor followed the U.S. decisions made in late October. The focus of IFOR's mission was to implement the military aspects of the agreement. In particular, these centered on monitoring and enforcing the parties' compliance with the cessation of hostilities, withdrawal of forces to respective territories, redeployment of forces and heavy weapons to designated cantonment sites and barracks, and establishment of zones of separation. In addition, IFOR was assigned key supporting tasks to be implemented within its given capabilities and consistent with its ability to implement the military tasks. These tasks included providing assistance to the United Nations High Commissioner for Refugees and other international organizations in their humanitarian missions; in the observation, security, and prevention of interference with the movement of civilian populations; and in the creation of secure conditions for the conduct by others of tasks associated with the peace settlement, including holding free and fair elections.[71] However, as General Shalikashvili repeatedly emphasized, IFOR would have the authority—but not the responsibility—for these supporting tasks: "IFOR will not be responsible for the conduct of humanitarian operations. It will not be a police force. It will not conduct nation building. It will not have the mission of disarming, and it will not move refugees."[72]

The combination of a large, NATO-led force operating under robust rules of engagement and a limited mission focused on implementing the military aspects of the Dayton Accords according to a precise timeline set forth in the agreement ensured that IFOR would successfully implement the mission that it was assigned. The ability to claim success was especially important in view of the fact that the United States had insisted on a mission of limited duration—one year—after which the U.S. and NATO troops would be withdrawn. Not everyone believed that the United States could accomplish its objective within this short period of time. Indeed, those who had argued that the U.S. objective was not simply to end the war but to build a stable and self-sustaining peace were, of course, right to argue that this could not be accomplished in twelve months. Yet just as IFOR's narrow mission was framed around more limited objectives, so

71. This summary is taken from "Summary of OPLAN 40105 (Joint Endeavor)—SACEUR Operation Plan for the Implementation of the Peace Agreement in the Former Yugoslavia" (Brussels: Supreme Headquarters Allied Powers Europe, December 1995).

72. Statement by Shalikashvili, *Situation in Bosnia*, Senate hearings, October 17, 1995, p. 332.

the one-year deadline was constructed on the basis of an exit strategy that had a more limited purpose than advocates of a durable peace in Bosnia had in mind.

The Exit Strategy and the One-Year Deadline

Aside from the issue of what U.S. and allied troops would do once they entered Bosnia, no question was of more interest to Washington than how long they would stay. From the outset, deliberations about the military aspects of implementation assumed that U.S. and other forces would remain in Bosnia for about a year and could be gone by the end of 1996. This assumption was driven in part by political considerations and in part by a particular conception of what an acceptable end state might look like by the time American troops were to depart. Although the twelve-month deadline was largely artificial, these considerations did provide it with a certain military and strategic logic.

Without a doubt political considerations played a significant part in the decision to limit the military operation to one year, a decision that the Atlantic alliance codified in adopting the political guidance for a possible NATO operation in Bosnia in late September 1995. With presidential elections only one year away, the prospect of an open-ended and undefined military operation was not acceptable to President Clinton and his political advisers, and no one suggested that it should be. Quite apart from the president's own political fortunes, however, the administration's experience in Somalia and Haiti had underscored the critical, political importance of a clear "exit strategy" tied to a definitive end date. Indeed, presidential policy guidance on U.S. participation in military operations of this kind predicated the decision to do so on the clear identification of a definite endpoint.[73] From a strictly strategic and military point of view, such an insistence was, of course, questionable. Advertising the date certain on which troops will leave provides recalcitrant parties an incentive to hold back until after the forces have departed.[74] At the same time, a clear and easily communicated exit strategy tied to a date certain for the withdrawal of U.S. forces was believed to be crucial to convincing a skep-

---

73. See *The Clinton Administration's Policy on Reforming Multilateral Peace Operations* (Department of State, May 1994), p. 5; and *A National Security Strategy of Engagement and Enlargement* (White House, February 1995), p. 13.

74. For an excellent critique of exit strategies, see Gideon Rose, "The Exit Strategy Delusion," *Foreign Affairs*, vol. 77 (January/February 1998), pp. 56–67.

tical, increasingly inward-looking Congress and public that the deployment of American forces abroad was worthwhile. Few within the Clinton administration—and none at senior levels—therefore questioned the need to set a firm exit date on the military operation.

What made a twelve-month deadline acceptable, however, was the conviction of many in the administration that the major objectives of the deployment could be accomplished within this time frame.[75] First, the basic military aspects of a peace agreement would have to be implemented, which appeared to be possible given that the detailed implementation time lines incorporated in the Dayton Accords called for the completion of all major military steps within 120 days after the agreement entered into force. These tasks included monitoring and, where necessary, enforcing the parties' compliance with key provisions detailed in Annex-1A of the Accords, including maintaining the cessation of hostilities, separating forces along a zone of separation, withdrawing forces from territories to be exchanged between the entities, deploying heavy weapons and forces to cantonment and barrack areas and demobilizing the remainder, ensuring the withdrawal of all foreign forces, and providing for the exchange of prisoners. The U.S. military had little doubt that all these tasks could be completed in six months, and it offered to do so in twelve just to be on the safe side.[76]

Second, the administration concluded that stability in Bosnia would depend on an internal balance of power among the remaining military forces rather than on a long-term, foreign military presence. As President Clinton assured the Congress, "We believe that establishing a stable military balance within Bosnia by the time IFOR leaves is important to preventing the war from resuming and to facilitate IFOR's departure."[77] The administration's preferred means for doing so was by reducing what Secretary Perry identified as the "primary threat to stability and security"[78]— the Bosnian Serbs' preponderance in heavy weapons—through arms

---

75. When asked by Senator John Warner (R-Va.) whether IFOR would be able to complete its mission within its twelve-month timetable, General Shalikashvili responded, "It is inconceivable for me to think that the tasks that I showed you here will not be completed in one year. And so for me there is no doubt that by the time we leave in 12 months, our mission will be completed." See Statement by Shalikashvili, *Situation in Bosnia*, p. 354.

76. Interview with a senior administration official, May 18, 1999.

77. Letter from President Bill Clinton to Senate Majority Leader Bob Dole, December 10, 1995.

78. Statement by Shalikashvili, *Situation in Bosnia*, p. 207.

control. At the same time, it recognized that some military assistance to the Federation, in terms of both training and additional equipment, would be necessary. As a result, Washington was committed to leading an international effort, separate from IFOR, to provide such assistance as was necessary to effect a more stable balance of military power. As Clinton explained, "The United States will take a leadership role in coordinating an international effort to ensure that the Bosnian Federation receives the assistance necessary to achieve an adequate military balance when IFOR leaves."[79]

The administration believed that whether through arms control, a buildup of Federation forces, or both, a military balance of forces could be established within one year, at which point stability could be assured internally rather than with forces drawn from the outside. To be sure, even a balance of power was no guarantee that conflict would not resume. However, the one-year time frame was judged to be sufficient to give the parties an incentive to continue resolving their differences without resort to arms. As Holbrooke told Congress following Dayton's completion, "We think a year is sufficient. If a year does not work, two, three or five years will not do either."[80] In that case, moreover, the changing balance of forces would at the very least ensure that the Bosnian forces could hold their own.

Within this limited perspective, a one-year deadline for the military operation made both political and strategic sense. But as Holbrooke and others have noted, both the decision on setting the deadline and its public announcement preceded the talks that would lead to the final agreement that the military forces were supposed to implement.[81] This meant either

79. Letter from President Bill Clinton to Senate Majority Leader Bob Dole, December 12, 1995. See also Statements by Perry and Shalikashvili, *Situation in Bosnia*, p. 398. The "equip-and-train" program, as the effort came to be called, acquired two additional purposes, quite separate from the original goal of establishing an internal balance of forces. First, the promise of such a program proved to be crucial to convincing the Bosnians to sign on to the Accords. That is, without "equip-and-train" there would have been no Dayton. (On this point, see Holbrooke, *To End a War*, p. 286.) Second, the program was used as a way to force the Bosnian government to cut its military and intelligence ties with Iran and to expel Mujahedin and other foreign forces from Bosnia. With Congress conditioning both military and economic assistance on Bosnian compliance with these demands, Izetbegovic had little choice but to end his close ties with fundamentalist influences from abroad.

80. Statement of Richard C. Holbrooke, *Situation in Bosnia*, p. 344.

81. Holbrooke, *To End a War*, p. 211.

that the agreement that was to be negotiated would have little, if any, influence on determining the objectives for which troops were to be deployed or that the deadline might have to be revisited in light of the specifics agreed to as part of the negotiations. Yet following Dayton, the twelve-month deadline stood unchanged. This left the administration open to justifiable criticism that either the deadline was not serious and would be abandoned following the presidential elections or it was a fatal flaw in U.S. policy that, if followed through, would lead to the unraveling of a peace the administration had so successfully negotiated.[82]

Following Dayton, the deadline for the U.S. troop presence in Bosnia was defended by everyone in the administration, from the president on down.[83] However, once Dayton was completed, the more limited strategic rationale that had formed the foundation for the one-year time frame—that peace depended upon a balance of power and the Bosnians' capacity for self-defense—was soon replaced by a more expansive U.S. objective, which was not just a stable military balance but a self-sustaining peace. As the president said on a December 1995 visit to Germany, "What the military is supposed to do is . . . maintain a secure environment so there can be free movement throughout the country, so the refugees can go home and the reconstruction can begin and the elections can be held. It is believed by all of our planners, and agreed to by the people who signed the peace treaty that that should be done in about a year."[84]

Within days, this objective was translated into securing the "full implementation of Dayton." Yet the Accords incorporated rather than resolved the differences among the parties—some of whom had only reluctantly signed on and others of whom had been barred from participating in the negotiations themselves. This was a far more ambitious undertaking than the original objective that had formed the basis of the one-year deadline. Dayton's full implementation would require a major exertion of effort by

82. For an insightful critique along these lines, see Stephen John Stedman, "'The Exit Is the Strategy': IFOR in Bosnia," Background paper prepared for the fifth session of the Henry A. Kissinger Study Group on Exit Strategies and American Foreign Policy, Council on Foreign Relations, July 9, 1996.

83. See, for example, "Address to the Nation on Implementation of the Peace Agreement in Bosnia-Herzegovina" (White House, Office of the Press Secretary, November 27, 1995); and Statements by Perry, Shalikashvili, and Richard Holbrooke, secretary of state for European and Canadian Affairs, *Situation in Bosnia*, Senate hearings, December 6, 1995, pp. 327, 344.

84. "Remarks by President Clinton and Chancellor Helmut Kohl in Photo Opportunity" (Baumholder, Germany: White House, Office of the Press Secretary, December 2, 1995), p. 3.

the international community, an effort that with the best of intentions and fullest possible cooperation would, as subsequent experience was to show, have been difficult to achieve in three or four years, let alone in one. Moreover, given that IFOR would have a limited role in this broader implementation effort, the onus of success fell largely on the civilian agencies that would assist in the construction of the new Bosnia—a multi-ethnic, democratic, and economically prosperous state, as Dayton's most passionate advocates would have it. Unfortunately, the care and interest shown in Washington in constructing the mandate and mission of IFOR was not matched by similar rigor when it came to deciding the critical issue of how the civilian implementation effort would be organized. As a result, the prospects of being able to adhere to the one-year deadline were doomed from the very start.

Organizing the Civilian Implementation Effort

In sharp contrast to the frequent high-level meetings designed to go over the details of how the military implementation effort should be structured, the issue of how to organize the civilian effort received only cursory attention in Washington before its negotiation in Dayton. The outcome of these negotiations was accepted with very little debate among U.S. policymakers. A senior official, known as the High Representative or "HiRep," was to be appointed to coordinate rather than direct the divergent and sometimes competing efforts of multiple international agencies and non-governmental organizations. In retrospect, it is clear that, given the scope of the civilian implementation tasks agreed at Dayton, the HiRep's weak mandate was a mistake, one that was recognized and rectified only much later.[85] In view of the crucial importance of civilian implementation efforts to the overall success of the Bosnia operation, it is instructive to review how this came about.

Negotiations about civilian implementation structures were deeply influenced, if not actually determined, by two crucial assumptions of U.S.

---

85. In December 1996, the Peace Implementation Council, or PIC (the ad hoc body set up at Dayton to oversee the civilian implementation effort) agreed that the High Representative's coordinating structure should be "reinforced," a decision that was finally implemented following the PIC ministerial meeting the following May. (See discussion below.) See also "Bosnia and Herzegovina 1997: Making Peace Work," Conclusions of the Peace Implementation Council, London, December 4–5, 1996; and "Political Declaration of the Ministerial Meeting of the PIC Steering Board," Sintra, Portugal, May 30, 1997. Both documents can be accessed at www.ohr.int/pic.htm, accessed October 1999.

Madrid

policy. The first reflected congressional and perceived public sentiment against the United Nations, as well as a growing disagreement between its secretary general and the administration. Accordingly, U.S. officials insisted that the UN could not have the leading role in the civilian or military effort that it had had in Somalia and Bosnia or even in Haiti. Second, the military operation had to be under sole NATO command, completely separate from, and certainly not subordinate to, the civilian implementation effort. A single chain of military command should lead from the soldier on the ground straight to the Supreme Allied Commander Europe (SACEUR), General George Joulwan, who would report to the North Atlantic Council only.

It is important to underscore that although these assumptions of U.S. policy toward the Bosnia operation were challenged at the working level by people who had worked in the United Nations and had experience in conducting complex peace operations like Haiti and Somalia, they were never openly debated at high levels in Washington.[86] As a result, the assumptions that the UN should have no role and that NATO's actions should be unencumbered were accepted almost as matters of faith, and remained unchallenged when decisions were being made on how to structure the civilian effort. Yet as subsequent developments made clear, these assumptions had a profound impact on the international community's ability to implement the Dayton Accords, suggesting that a more intensive examination of the underlying rationale of the assumptions might have been desirable.

The rejection of a UN role and the sharp separation between the military and civilian implementation efforts were to a significant extent driven by a misreading of the previous UN and NATO experiences in Bosnia,

---

86. Officials made two arguments: first, whatever its weakness, the United Nations had important expertise and capabilities that could be brought to bear in Bosnia; and, second, unity of military and civilian command over a major operation of this kind was absolutely crucial to the success of the operation. For bureaucratic reasons, none of these arguments ever reached senior officials. The decisionmaking process concerning Bosnia, including a possible deployment of a new peace operation, was staffed by officials drawn from the European affairs and NATO worlds (State's Bureau of European Affairs, the NSC's European Affairs Directorate, Defense's Balkan Task Force and European/NATO offices) rather than the world of the United Nations and peacekeeping (State's international organizations bureau, the NSC's global issues directorate, and Defense's peacekeeping offices). The experiences and perspectives of the latter were therefore never incorporated into the advice to senior officials provided by the former.

especially the infamous "dual key" arrangement under which both UN and NATO officials had to approve the use of air power and the targets that could be attacked. Since Washington blamed the United Nations—in particular, its chief representatives, Secretary General Boutros Boutros-Ghali and his special representative Yasushi Akashi—for failing to authorize the forceful use of air strikes against Bosnian Serb targets in 1994 and 1995, excluding the UN from a decisionmaking role was judged to be *correctly* crucial to the success of any future operation.[87] If only for political reasons, then, a continuation of a significant UN role in Bosnia—let alone any involvement in the military aspects of implementation—was simply unacceptable to Washington. For essentially similar reasons, the U.S. and allied militaries voiced vehement opposition to any suggestion, emanating most strongly from Paris, that there be some kind of political control over the military operation other than the political guidance provided by the North Atlantic Council.[88] IFOR's success, General Joulwan repeatedly stressed, would depend on a clear mission, unity of command, robust rules of engagement, and timely political decisions on which to base military action.

With no UN role and with a NATO military operation defined largely without reference to civilian implementation requirements, the nature and scope of how to structure the civilian effort was quite uncertain. By September 1995, senior U.S. officials understood that there would be a number of critical activities in the civilian area that needed to be coordinated to ensure success. These included continued negotiations with the parties, monitoring of human rights, humanitarian efforts, economic reconstruction, war crimes and other law enforcement provisions, refugee resettlement, and elections and institution building efforts. For some of these issues, an international presence already existed in situ, including the United Nations High Commissioner for Refugees, which led the humanitarian

87. See also Michael C. Williams, *Civil-Military Relations and Peacekeeping*, Adelphi Paper No. 321 (Oxford University Press for the International Institute for Strategic Studies, 1998), p. 58. Of course, while UN officials clearly opposed the use of force for purposes other than self-defense for fear that this would bring the lightly armed UN peace operation in conflict with the parties, this sentiment reflected rather than drove allied assessments (especially British and French views.) After all, these allies had insisted on a UN voice in the operational decision to launch air strikes as the price for agreeing to support NATO air strikes in the first place.

88. Holbrooke recounts receiving numerous telephone calls from General Joulwan in Dayton making clear that the general "would never accept" any kind of relationship in-country between IFOR and the HiRep. See Holbrooke, *To End a War*, p. 276.

and refugee efforts; the International Criminal Tribunal for the former Yugoslavia (ICTY) which addressed war crimes issues; and the International Committee of the Red Cross (ICRC) which dealt with missing persons and prisoners of war. For others, there were logical candidates: the Organization for Security and Cooperation in Europe (OSCE) for arms control and confidence building efforts; and the European Union (EU) and International Bank for Reconstruction and Development (IBRD or World Bank) for reconstruction. In some areas, such as elections and police/law enforcement, logical candidates either did not exist or those that did, such as the UN, were unacceptable. The OSCE was assigned the task of conducting elections, even though it had no experience in undertaking a task of this magnitude. Lacking an acceptable alternative, the UN was given the responsibility for setting up a police monitoring force.

Aside from identifying international organizations that could take the lead in critical implementation areas, the question of overall coordination and direction needed to be decided. With the rejection of the UN as an umbrella organization, the question of who would appoint and/or authorize a coordinating body was raised. The answer formulated by the drafters of Dayton was to derive both from the actual settlement. Under the accords, a High Representative would be responsible for coordinating the civilian implementation effort. This effort would be overseen by the Peace Implementation Council—a large, unwieldy body of key countries and international organizations—whose steering committee, consisting of the Group of Seven countries plus Russia, would both appoint and be chaired by the HiRep. This entire edifice would be blessed, as opposed to authorized, by the UN Security Council. As Pauline Neville-Jones, the British negotiator at Dayton, noted, the HiRep "is not fully answerable to any body of uncontested international authority and operates in uncomfortable and unconvincing limbo."[89]

More important than the source of the High Representative's formal authority was the question of that person's role in the implementation process. Here, U.S. policy went through an interesting evolution, one that reflected weariness in Washington about the capacity and resolve of its

89. She went on to say that it "is hard to see how this ad hoc arrangement, which has managed rather than innovated policy . . . can really be regarded as a satisfactory alternative to the UNSC." Pauline Neville-Jones, "Dayton, IFOR, and Alliance Relations in Bosnia," *Survival*, vol. 38 (Winter 1996–97), pp. 51–52. Neville-Jones and her European colleagues at Dayton had all wanted a stronger UN role in the implementation process, and they pushed for this role, but to no avail.

European allies to bring peace to Bosnia. In October, Holbrooke assigned the task of negotiating the annex on civilian implementation (as well as the one on policing) to Robert Gallucci, who upon conclusion of the Dayton negotiations would become the special assistant to the president and secretary of state for implementation.[90] Working with a staff drawn largely from his previous assignment as U.S. negotiator of the U.S.-Korean nuclear framework agreement, Gallucci developed a draft annex that contained a strong mandate for the HiRep, providing that person with direct authority over the international organizations that would contribute to the implementation effort. The strength of the mandate was predicated on Gallucci's belief that the High Representative would be an American.[91] When he briefed the annex to the Contact Group partners the weekend prior to the commencement of the proximity talks in Dayton, Gallucci received enthusiastic backing for a strong mandate. At the same time, the Europeans made clear that if Washington expected them to pay the lion's share of reconstruction and other economic assistance, the civilian coordinating effort would have to be in Europe's hands.[92] Once it was clear that a European rather than an American would be the first HiRep, Gallucci and the other American negotiators worked hard to *limit* the authority and responsibility of the High Representative, for fear that a powerful person whom Washington could not control might fumble the implementation effort or, worse still, interfere with the military effort. As Neville-Jones recalls, "the U.S. negotiating tactic seemed to be to concede to this office [the HiRep] as little authority as possible, either over the agencies engaged in civilian implementation or in relation to the military commander."[93]

90. Gallucci was appointed in September at the behest of both Talbott and Christopher, but apparently over the opposition of Holbrooke. However, since Holbrooke planned to depart government early in 1996, it was not unreasonable to bring someone on board during the negotiations of the agreement whose implementation he would subsequently be asked to oversee. Interview with a senior administration official, July 8, 1998.

91. Holbrooke had not told Gallucci that at a Contact Group meeting in mid-October, he had acceded to the European insistence that Carl Bildt would be appointed as the first HiRep. See interview with a senior administration official, July 8, 1998, and Holbrooke, *To End a War*, p. 209.

92. Neville-Jones notes that this was one of the few firm instructions from the EU Council of Ministers that the Europeans brought to Dayton. See Neville-Jones, "Dayton, IFOR, and Alliance Relations in Bosnia," p. 50.

93. See Neville-Jones, "Dayton, IFOR, and Alliance Relations in Bosnia," p. 53. Also, interview with a senior administration official, July 8, 1998. In his first public remarks on Dayton's implementation after leaving government, Holbrooke, while prais-

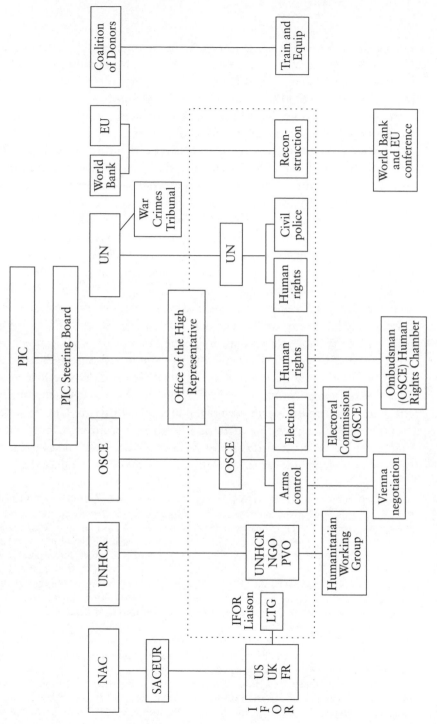

Figure 5. *Civilian Implementation Structure under the Dayton Accords*

The structure for the civilian implementation effort that was finally agreed at Dayton is perhaps as unwieldy as it possibly could be.[94] In addition to creating the clear and unbridgeable separation between military and civilian implementation efforts, the civilian efforts were themselves subdivided among multiple international organizations and agencies, each of which derived its authority from a different body—be it the United Nations, European Union, World Bank, or OSCE. Without a coherent implementation plan that would draw these various activities together or the resources necessary to attract a staff capable of putting such a plan in place, the HiRep's limited authority to coordinate rather than guide or direct left much of the civilian effort in disarray. Although good organization is no guarantee for sound policy and practice, bad organization almost assures unsound policy and practice.

Dayton: To End a War or Build a Peace?

Along the road to Dayton, two critical questions were raised but not answered. The first concerned the overarching objective of U.S. engagement in Bosnia. Most of official Washington tended to view American engagement as serving the limited, even if highly desirable, purpose of ending the war that had raged in Bosnia for more than three years. The continuing violence posed moral, political, and strategic challenges to the United States. Morally, the death of so many innocents in the heart of Europe was a calamity. Politically, the war's continuation called the credibility of the Clinton administration's foreign policy into question. Strategically, the inability to end the war and the constant squabbling with European allies

---

ing the U.S.-led military implementation effort, blamed the Europeans for having insisted on "a messy, ineffective arrangement" on the civilian side that "created multiple chains of command and little enforcement authority." Holbrooke was rightly taken to task by Pauline Neville-Jones for this misrepresentation of what happened at Dayton, and in his memoirs he does not blame the Europeans for this arrangement and even approvingly quotes Neville-Jones's criticism. See Richard Holbrooke, "Backsliding in Bosnia," *Time*, May 20, 1996, p. 38; Pauline Neville-Jones, "Don't Blame the Europeans," *Financial Times*, May 17, 1996, p. 13; and Holbrooke, *To End a War*, pp. 319, 276.

94. See Annex 10, "Agreement of Civilian Implementation," especially Article 2, of the Dayton Accords, which limits the HiRep's mandate to coordinating "activities of the civilian organizations and agencies in Bosnia" and calls on that person to "respect their autonomy within their spheres of operation." Accords can be accessed at www.ohr.int/gfa/gfa-an10.htm, accessed October 1999.

on how to proceed threatened to undermine NATO, the most successful peacetime alliance in history. Each of the challenges could be met by successful U.S. leadership to end the war.

However, as negotiations proceeded and a peace agreement appeared within reach, the objective of U.S. engagement began to expand, first among the negotiators and later among Washington officialdom as a whole. In addition to ending the war, the goal of engagement became to build a viable, lasting peace in a united Bosnia. This change was in part due to the unmistakable calculation that a long-term end to the war required that Bosnia become a society at peace with itself. In other words, to ensure that hostilities would not resume required a peace that was self-sustaining— not only because of the military balance of forces on the ground but also because of political reconciliation among the former warring parties. In part, however, the change in objectives was also due to the natural inclination of negotiators to try to achieve as much as possible while negotiations were still ongoing in the reasonable belief that this might well be the last chance to get the parties to sign on. Whatever the reason, it was clear that building a peace would require a far greater effort in terms of time and resources than the more limited goal of ending the war. At Dayton's conclusion on November 21, 1995, Washington had yet to make the decision whether it was prepared to provide the time and resources necessary for that broader task.

A second question raised along the road to Dayton concerned the issue of implementation. The proof of Dayton would come not on the day the agreement was initialed or signed but in the months that followed, when its many detailed provisions needed to be implemented. Mirroring the uncertainty concerning the objectives of U.S. engagement in Bosnia was the issue of how much the international community ought to do to make sure the parties to Dayton in fact implemented the provisions to which they had assented. Ideally, a peace agreement's implementation is self-sustaining, meaning that the parties fulfill its terms because doing so is as much in their self-interest as was their original decision to sign the agreement.[95] In practice, however, parties seldom cooperate to that extent, since

---

95. See the analysis of Barry M. Blechman, William J. Durch, Wendy Eaton, and Tami Stukey, in *Effective Transitions from Peace Operations to Sustainable Peace*, Final Report, prepared for the Office of the Assistant Secretary of Defense, Peacekeeping and Humanitarian Affairs (Washington, D.C.: DFI International, September 1997), pp. 20–23.

either their agreement was coerced or implementation itself is a way to continue the original conflict by non-violent means. In the case of Dayton, both reasons existed. All three warring parties were to a considerable extent coerced into signing the agreement by their respective patrons: Milosevic for the Serbs, Tudjman for the Croats, and the United States for the Bosnians. Moreover, since the Accords did not resolve the underlying differences among the parties—namely, whether Bosnia should be de facto partitioned or reintegrated—implementation offered the parties a way to continue their basic conflict.

As a result, the implementation of Dayton has from day one suffered from what might be called an "enforcement gap."[96] Under the accords, enforcement of the agreement's provisions is the responsibility of the parties, and the international community's role is only to assist them in this effort. However, in the absence of consensus among the parties on the core issues, many matters integral to the Dayton process—such as the return of refugees, municipal governance, central institutions, and the status of Brcko and Mostar—will continue to be disputed as matters vital to national survival by each party. These issues are both decisive and divisive, since their outcome will indicate whether Bosnia is destined for reunification or de facto partition. As a result, responsibility for securing the implementation of the accords has naturally fallen on the international community rather than the parties. Whence the enforcement gap at the heart of Dayton: although effective implementation of the Accords demands enforcement on the part of the international civilian and military presence in Bosnia, the international community has been either unable or unwilling to take the measures necessary to secure full compliance with Dayton's terms. On November 21, 1995, Washington had yet to consider how these issues would be resolved.

[handwritten marginal note: Only progress is IC-driven]

[handwritten note: because there is no effective Bosnian gov't, and no incentive (self-interest) to form one.]

---

96. The paragraph that follows draws from Ivo H. Daalder, "Bosnia after SFOR: Options for Continued U.S. Engagement," *Survival*, vol. 39 (Winter 1997–98), pp. 7–8.

CHAPTER FIVE

Conclusions
and Implications

THE STORY OF HOW THE Clinton administration finally decided to become fully engaged in Bosnia raises at least four important questions. First, why did the administration decide to take the lead in seeking an end to the war in August 1995 when it had studiously avoided making this commitment since entering into office in January 1993? Second, how did the endgame strategy, which of all the options on the table entailed the greatest risks and potential costs for the United States, become U.S. policy? Third, what was the goal of U.S. involvement in Bosnia: was it to end the war or to build a multiethnic, democratic, and economically prosperous Bosnia? Finally, what were the foreign policy consequences of deciding to become involved, including for the future U.S. role in Bosnia and for America's Europe policy more broadly? The answers to these questions have important implications for American foreign policy—including the process by which it is made and the manner in which it is implemented.

The Decision to Engage

For well over two years, the Clinton administration refused to become fully engaged in Bosnia, instead leaving the policy initiative to the European allies and the United Nations. But by August 1995 the administration decided that the time had come to change course by taking the reins of Bosnia policy firmly into its own hands. The reason for this reversal can be found in the specific policy context the administration faced in the summer of 1995. By then, it was evident that its long-standing preference for containment and disengagement, last reaffirmed in late 1994, was no longer sustainable. While President Bill Clinton's principal national security advisers did not agree on much regarding U.S. policy toward Bosnia, they had reached a consensus by August 1995 that the risks of taking the lead—while considerable—were nonetheless less than the risks posed by any alternative course. A policy of engagement could no longer be avoided.

Of course, the Clinton administration had been there before: in February 1993, when it rejected the preferred European approach to settling the conflict; in April 1993, when the failure of diplomacy suggested the need for concerted military pressure against the Bosnian Serbs; and in November 1994, when the Europeans placed the onus for military pressure squarely on U.S. willingness to take risks similar to those being taken by their troops on the ground. At each of these critical policy junctures, however, the administration had pulled back and deferred to European wishes—including in 1994 by halting pressure for continued NATO bombing. What was different about the summer of 1995? The answer can be found in the confluence of four developments: the expected collapse of UNPROFOR following the humiliation of the hostage crisis; the threat that Bosnia posed to the vitality, if not continued viability, of NATO; the prospect of having to deploy U.S. troops both to rescue UN forces and to sustain the alliance's credibility; and congressional pressure to lift the arms embargo against Bosnia. Undergirding all of these was the president's reelection campaign, then only months away.

The U.S. policy of studied disengagement began to unravel unmistakably in late May when, following two days of pinprick air strikes, allied troops in blue helmets were taken hostage by the Bosnian Serbs. Pictures of this humiliation galvanized the Elysée and Downing Street to bolster UNPROFOR's capacity for action with the deployment of a 10,000-strong Rapid Reaction Force (RRF). However, this reinforcement came too late to alter the indelible image of incompetence and weakness the UN had gained in the eyes of the warring parties in Bosnia, as well as of Washington. As President Clinton exclaimed to his staff just before a meeting with French President Jacques Chirac to discuss the details of U.S. support for the RRF, "I never would have put force on the ground in such a situation. The rules of engagement are crazy!"[1] While the RRF was deployed to give UNPROFOR more spine in standing up to those who violated the plethora of UN Security Council resolutions, few in Washington believed that the

---

1. Quoted in Bob Woodward, *The Choice* (Simon and Schuster, 1996), p. 255.

additional forces would make much of a difference. As long as the RRF operated under UN rules of engagement—which, under the dictates of the UN secretary general and his chief civilian and military representatives in the Balkans, put the safety of UN personnel ahead of the mission they were to perform—the force was certain to fail in its assigned tasks. Indeed, those rules did not prevent the horrors of Srebrenica, which, after they became manifest, led to the total collapse of UNPROFOR's credibility in Bosnia and around the world.

The second factor contributing to the U.S. decision to engage in Bosnia was the need to defend NATO's credibility. For over three years, the issue of what to do in Bosnia divided the allies and strained transatlantic relations. The issue dominated every NATO meeting, but none concluded with a clear consensus on how to proceed. Over time, NATO's failure to end a brutal war on its doorstep had a profound impact on both the alliance's viability and the credibility of the United States. Whereas in November 1994, the priority Washington placed on NATO meant that efforts to resolve the Bosnian conflict had to take second place to maintaining alliance unity, by the summer of 1995 it was clear that the two issues were inextricably linked. It was only by resolving the Bosnia issue that NATO's continued viability could be assured. By this time, it was not only U.S. leadership of NATO that was being called into question by Chirac and others but also the alliance's preeminent role in managing European security. If only for that reason, the United States strongly pushed its allies to accept the more forceful use of NATO air power during the London conference in late July. It also explains why the allies agreed to go along.

With the collapse of the UN's credibility in Bosnia and NATO's future very much in doubt, the Clinton administration faced the unwelcome prospect that summer of having to deploy up to 25,000 American soldiers to fulfill its commitment to the allies to assist in the UNPROFOR's withdrawal if so requested. Few in official Washington relished the possibility of having to put American forces into the Bosnian maelstrom. What concerned top officials equally as much, however, was the fact that a key assumption of U.S. policy—that troops would be deployed only to help implement a peace agreement—could be changed as a result of a decision made by others rather than after full deliberation in Washington. Thus while some officials maintained that the prospect of U.S. troops in Bosnia required an all-out effort to convince UNPROFOR to stay, however ineffective and incredible its presence had become, others argued that if American forces had to go in, they should do so on U.S. terms, and at a time and for reasons of Washington's choosing. This latter argument, which the president found persuasive, suggested the need for the United States to become more rather than less engaged.

A final factor influencing the decision to become more fully engaged in Bosnia concerned the changing domestic context within which America's Bosnia policy was being framed. In the preceding three years, the debate in the country about U.S. policy toward Bosnia had oscillated between arguments for both engagement and disengagement. There were those who were appalled by Washington's inaction in the face of what they believed to be a genocidal policy pursued by the Bosnian Serbs. Although few argued for dispatching American ground forces, many did favor air strikes to support the Muslim forces and, at the very least, lifting the arms embargo that deprived the Bosnian government of its inherent right of self-defense. In contrast, others made an equally strong argument that this was a civil war among people who had fought each other for many years and that any outside interference risked getting the United States stuck in a Vietnam-like quagmire. Whatever the merits of intervention, moreover, this group argued that Bosnia was essentially a European problem that the Europeans themselves should resolve.

Whereas these arguments went back and forth for many months and years, by July 1995 those arguing in favor of doing something were clearly ascendant. Bolstered by the horrifying stories emerging from Srebrenica, the U.S. Congress challenged the Clinton administration to change course by voting overwhelmingly to lift the arms embargo against Bosnia. The administration had long opposed a unilateral lift. It feared the precedent this would set in the UN Security Council, thus allowing Russia and perhaps France to abandon the critically important sanctions regime against Iraq. It also believed that such a step would precipitate the withdrawal of allied forces and force a choice between assisting the allies' departure by deploying thousands of U.S. troops on the ground or abandoning a solemn commitment to NATO. Faced with the fact that Congress had passed the original bill in both houses with majorities sufficient to override a presidential veto, the Clinton administration had to provide Congress with a credible alternative course if its inevitable veto was going to be sustained.

These four factors—the UN's loss of credibility, the threat to NATO, the prospect of U.S. troop deployments, and the congressional vote on lifting the arms embargo—came together during the summer of 1995 in the political context of a pending presidential campaign. This campaign was likely to pit Clinton against Senate majority leader Robert Dole (R-Kans.), a long-standing and vociferous critic of the president's Bosnia policy. It would be wrong to suggest that the prospect of elections alone drove the administration to act, but it is clear that Bosnia represented a significant political problem for the president. Given the high stakes of the election campaign, Clinton's political fortunes could not be held hostage to events in the Balkans. The president therefore had a powerful incentive to reduce Bosnia's potential to disrupt the campaign. That, however, was easier said than done. It was clear that the politically most expedient course—washing America's hands of the problem and blaming others, notably the Europeans and the United Nations, for the mess—might backfire, either because the war (and the televised images that inevitably accompanied it) would intensify, or because the allies would insist that Washington fulfill its commitment to assist in the UN's withdrawal. Yet the alternative to taking a leadership role in Bosnia posed equally grave risks, especially since success implied spending lots of money and deploying tens of thousands of American troops. In the end, the president opted for engagement. "If we let this moment slip away," he told his foreign policy advisers in early August 1995, "we are history."[2]

The Endgame Strategy

The confluence of these four factors, combined with the president's looming reelection campaign, explains *why* the Clinton administration decided to engage in Bosnia in August 1995; the policymaking process explains *how* the endgame strategy became the administration's preferred policy for doing so. The strategy was adopted as a result of a two-step process. The policy context forced the administration to consider an alternative to its policy of non-engagement. The sense that existing policy was boxing the president in led Clinton to demand a new direction, thus providing an opportunity—a policy window—for advocates of engagement (especially Madeleine Albright and Anthony Lake) once again to make their case. Being able to make the case for change was one thing; getting the preferred policy position adopted was quite another. Although Albright's voice was heard and her plea for U.S. leadership was accepted, it was Lake who exploited the opportunity by moving rapidly to ensure his views of what needed to be done would become the president's. Adopting the role of

2. Quoted in George Stephanopoulos, *All Too Human: A Political Education* (Little, Brown, 1999), p. 383.

Tony Lake as the hero of the book.

policy entrepreneur, Lake exploited his position as the manager of the foreign policy process to enhance the likelihood that his preferred views would become America's Bosnia policy.[3]

The Window Opens

Policy windows open infrequently. The start of an administration generally provides such an occasion, and so do major crises. Before the summer of 1995, the Bosnia policy window had opened only twice: first when the Clinton administration came to office in January 1993, and then again in August of that year, when the president responded to pictures of the horrible suffering by demanding that his senior advisers take a fresh look at what could be done militarily to alleviate the misery. As recounted in chapter 1, both occasions produced new policy initiatives that ultimately failed. At each juncture, the United States was not yet prepared to take on the necessary leadership role, fearing that the Bosnia cauldron would become Washington's sole responsibility.

The summer of 1995 provided a third opportunity to reconsider the Clinton administration's Bosnia policy. Sensing that the prevailing policy course was leading his administration headlong into disaster, the president used the occasion of a session with his senior advisers prior to his meeting on Bosnia issues with French President Chirac on June 14 to throw the policy window wide open. After listening with mounting frustration to his aides debating the merits and demerits of the French initiative to strengthen the UN presence in Bosnia, Clinton sharply interjected, "We need to get the policy straight or we're just going to be kicking the can down the road again. Right now we've got a situation, we've got no clear mission, no one's in control of events."[4] It is not often that presidents call for a wholesale review of policy, but when they do, it presents an opportunity for those who want to change policy. Of Clinton's four principal foreign policy advisers, two (Albright and Lake) grasped the opportunity with vigor, while the other two (Warren Christopher and William Perry) resisted.

Albright was the first to respond to Clinton's admonition. A week after his call for a new direction, the president met with Albright and his other

3. On the concept of policy windows and policy entrepreneurs, see John W. Kingdon, *Agendas, Alternatives, and Public Policy* (Little, Brown, 1984), chapter 8. I thank James M. Goldgeier for drawing my attention to the usefulness of these concepts in helping to explain the policy process in this instance.

4. Quoted in Woodward, *The Choice*, p. 255.

advisers to discuss the immediate issue of assistance to the RRF as well as longer-term strategy for Bosnia. At this meeting, Albright brought to the table a short, passionately argued memo that made the case for effective military action. In a thinly veiled appeal to the president's political interests, she maintained that America's inability to address the Bosnia issue put at risk the credibility of the administration's entire foreign policy. The time for action had come. Albright proposed that the allies should acknowledge the UN would need to withdraw before winter, and they should be persuaded to support both a multilateral lift of the arms embargo and NATO air strikes once UNPROFOR had departed. The president, though intrigued by the proposal and appreciative of the forcefulness of her argument, was unsure how the allies could be persuaded to take these steps. Albright's missive was important for underscoring the urgent need for changing policy direction, even if it lacked specifics on how to chart a new course.

The second person to respond to the president's call for a new policy direction was Clinton's national security adviser. In contrast to what Lake called Albright's idea to "just go in and blast them, [he] was looking for a more focused way to use force."[5] Lake turned to his senior European aide, Alexander Vershbow, and asked him to think about how policy might change. Vershbow resurrected some of the ideas that he and Colonel Nelson Drew had developed during the Bosnia policy review earlier that year on what the United States and its allies might do once UNPROFOR had withdrawn. Such a post-withdrawal strategy would aim to establish a new military balance on the ground in Bosnia by lifting the arms embargo, providing training and arms to the Bosnians, and conducting air strikes during the transition period. Vershbow also considered what types of carrots and sticks the United States might wield to convince the parties to negotiate a peace settlement—including ways in which territorial boundaries and constitutional principles might be changed from earlier plans drawn up by the Contact Group. These and other issues were first discussed in detail by Lake and his key staffers during a long meeting on a Saturday morning in late June 1995. This and subsequent meetings laid the basis for the endgame strategy, which the president finally endorsed in early August.

---

5. Quoted in Ann Blackman, *Seasons of Her Life: A Biography of Madeleine Korbel Albright* (Scribner, 1998), p. 243.

In contrast to Albright and Lake, the secretaries of state and defense ✳
remained passive in the face of Clinton's demand for new ideas on Bosnia
policy. From the available evidence, it is not clear whether Christopher, or
Richard Holbrooke for that matter, realized that the president had opened
the policy window in that Oval Office meeting prior to Chirac's visit on
June 14. As Holbrooke recounts, he and Christopher were struck during
the meeting not by Clinton's search for new ideas, but by their impression
that the president might not have understood the nature and extent of the
U.S. commitment to assisting the UN to withdraw from Bosnia if so requested.[6] Yet even if Christopher had noticed the president opening the
policy window, it was unlikely that he would have jumped through it.
Ever since his disastrous European trip of May 1993, Christopher's fundamental approach to Bosnia had been to contain the potential disruption
the issue could cause for American foreign policy generally. He was distinctly wary of proposals to use significant force, believing that the Europeans would never buy into them and that congressional and public support
for an increased American military engagement in Bosnia would be exceedingly difficult to obtain. For Christopher, the aim of America's Bosnia
policy after May 1993 was to contain the conflict and keep the diplomatic
ball firmly in the Europeans' court.

Like Christopher, William Perry did not immediately jump through the
policy window opened by the president in June, although he proved to be
pivotal in pushing for a more forceful policy a month later. The delay was
partly due to the fact that Perry was not present at the meeting and he
therefore may not have realized that the policy window was open. Another reason was that while Perry strongly favored the robust use of air
power and had said so publicly as early as 1994, neither his immediate
staff nor the U.S. military supported him on this score.[7] In certain situa-

6. See Richard Holbrooke, *To End a War* (Random House, 1998), p. 67. See also
the discussion on pp. 58–61 above.

7. Interviews with an administration official, April 1, 1998, and a senior administration official, July 20, 1998. During a meeting of NATO Defense Ministers in Seville,
Spain, on September 29, 1994, Perry had argued, "When we go in, I want to go in
with compelling force. Force not necessarily just proportionate to the act at stake, but
enough to make it clear that there is a heavy price to pay for violating the rules that
NATO has established. . . . Some of us, like myself, have been pushing for much more
robust use of NATO air power, and I hope we can agree on a set of conditions under
which that more robust use will take place." Cited in Richard Curtiss, "Leadership Is
Key to Bosnia Solution," *Washington Report on Middle Eastern Affairs* (November/
December 1994), p. 65.

✳ Is this because of personalities or institutional?

tions, like the Bihac crisis in November 1994, Perry was willing to override these objections and make the case for a major air campaign. But under ordinary circumstance, Bosnia was not an issue over which Perry was willing to make waves within the Pentagon or among the NATO allies. In comparison to the myriad of other issues he had to deal with as secretary of defense, Bosnia was a minor one.

Perry's unwillingness to buck his own department changed in July, when the first reports of the horrors of Srebrenica filtered in. In a principals meeting on July 14, Perry passionately argued for pushing the allies to agree to threaten a major NATO air campaign in order to save Gorazde and, possibly, other UN-declared "safe areas." With General John Shalikashvili's support, he also argued that Washington needed to convince the allies to agree to massive air strikes if Gorazde was threatened or attacked, to modify the dual-key arrangement for deciding on NATO air strikes, and to accept the risk of hostages in case air strikes were launched. These propositions were endorsed by the president and then effectively sold to the allies at the London conference held on July 21, 1995, which laid the foundation for the NATO air campaign in late August and September.

These divergent responses to the president's call for a rethinking of U.S. policy toward Bosnia posed a dilemma for Anthony Lake, the manager of the foreign policymaking process. Only Albright clearly favored a different policy course, although her brief memo was clearer on suggesting the need for a forceful response than on how to obtain support for her position, both within the U.S. bureaucracy and among the allies. Moreover, from Lake's perspective, Albright's opinion was less important than that of Christopher, Perry, or Shalikashvili. In the words of one of her sympathetic biographers, "Albright was in the enviable position of being able to voice her opinion forcefully and unequivocally without being responsible for the decision's consequences."[8] Both Christopher and Perry feared that the allies might respond to a renewed push to use force by pulling out their troops, thus likely triggering a request for U.S. military assistance in the withdrawal operation. Faced with these differing opinions, Lake could have done what he did in the past: call a meeting of the principals; discuss alternative policy options; accept that a change in direction did not have sufficient support; and tell the president that the status quo remained the only feasible course of action. He could have, but he did not.

8. Blackman, *Seasons of Her Life*, p. 243.

The Policy Entrepreneur : Lake

Rather than repeating the failed approach of conducting a formal policy review to narrow the differences among the Clinton administration's key foreign policy players on Bosnia, the national security adviser used his position as manager of the policy process to break the policy deadlock. He abandoned his role as the honest broker and opted to become the policy entrepreneur. Lake not only developed his own policy, but also structured the decisionmaking process in such a way as to enhance the likelihood of his position on Bosnia becoming U.S. policy. At the same time, Lake made sure to avoid the closed and secretive policymaking process that had characterized the efforts of many of his predecessors. There would be no secret missions conducted without the knowledge of the secretary of state, as Henry A. Kissinger had done while traveling to China; and no public grandstanding to underscore policy differences with other principals, as Zbigniew Brzezinski had done over Soviet policy by hoisting a Kalashnikov rifle over his head at the Khyber Pass.

In adopting the role of policy entrepreneur, Lake put in place a policy process that was both closed and open. It was closed in two important respects. First, the national security adviser encouraged the president to conclude that the course of action being pursued by the United States was heading nowhere. Exploiting Clinton's evident desire to get out of the box that two-and-a-half years of muddling through had created, Lake decided that the time was ripe to propose a change in direction and to do so before others in the administration had a chance to explain why this would not work. This was the second respect in which the policy process was closed. As soon as the basic outline of what would become the endgame strategy had been developed in discussions among Lake, Samuel R. (Sandy) Berger, Vershbow, and others on the NSC staff, Lake broached his ideas with Clinton. The national security adviser wanted to the get the president on board *before* talking it through with his counterparts in other agencies, knowing that once Clinton had endorsed the thrust of his approach, competing policy preferences were unlikely to sway the president. To make sure this was the case, Lake first presented a fully developed strategy paper to his colleagues at a meeting in his office in mid-July, which Clinton briefly joined to underscore his support for Lake's approach.

Once the president was on board, however, Lake opened up the policy process, providing each of his colleagues with the opportunity to weigh in with their own thoughts, perspectives, and ideas. Indeed, after having given them his ideas, Lake requested that Christopher, Perry, Shalikashvili, and Albright each come up with their own strategy. All did, albeit some more reluctantly than others. The four resulting strategy papers were vetted by a group of advisers from all concerned agencies to make sure that every option had been considered. The specifics of the papers and the general issue of long-term Bosnia strategy were discussed by the principals and their deputies at innumerable meetings during the second half of July and the first week of August 1995. Most importantly, the final version of the four papers was presented to the president on August 4 and then discussed in well over seven hours of meetings over three days with Clinton, Vice President Al Gore, and the other members of the president's foreign policy team. Objections to the endgame strategy could be and were raised by those engaged in the discussion. While the decision to go ahead was ultimately the president's alone, Lake's talking points for explaining the new approach to the European allies were endorsed by all concerned.

In the end, Lake succeeded in being the true policy entrepreneur: his approach became policy with the full backing not only of the president but of all senior advisers engaged in the formulation of U.S. policy toward Bosnia. To be sure, the way Lake circumvented the policy process was unorthodox. In general, those who are responsible for managing the interagency process should be careful not to undermine that process by exploiting the power gained by their proximity to the president to push their own agenda. Yet this instance was different. Not only had Lake for years sought to employ the traditional interagency process to achieve an administration consensus on Bosnia policy to little avail, but he was directly responding to a request by the president for new ideas. In this sense, Lake sought to meet Clinton's expressed needs rather than to subvert the president's will.

Finally, Lake drew clear lines between his role as advocate in the policy formulation stage, his role as honest broker in the policy decision stage, and his role as enabler during the policy implementation stage. Indeed, while he was sorely tempted to take on the role of negotiator and deprive Richard Holbrooke of that honor, he did not do so in the belief that such operational involvement in policy was inappropriate for a national security adviser. In short, Lake pushed the envelope to get a new policy in place, but once he succeeded in this he reverted to his more traditional role as honest broker.

The Purpose of Engagement

Just as the president and his advisers agreed to move forward on the endgame strategy in early August 1995, the Croatian military was wrapping up its military operation and retaking control of the Krajina region that had been in Serb hands since 1991. Operation Storm, as the offensive was dubbed, provided an important boost to the diplomatic track of the new U.S. strategy, not least because it temporarily put the Serbs on the defensive. Even so, when Lake and his entourage traveled to Europe on August 9, few gave the diplomatic track much chance of success. Instead, it was generally assumed that a concerted diplomatic effort led by the United States was necessary to convince the allies to back Washington's preferred military strategy. That strategy aimed at establishing a military balance on the ground by lifting the arms embargo, arming and training Bosnian forces, and conducting air strikes for a nine-to-twelve month transition period.

By mid-September, assessments of the likelihood that diplomacy might succeed had shifted dramatically. In particular, the strategic climate for negotiations had changed significantly as a result of three key factors: the Croatian-Bosnian offensive, which had reduced Bosnian Serb territorial holdings to less than 50 percent; Milosevic's decision to seize control of the peace negotiations, which effectively sidelined the Pale leadership as a factor in the negotiations; and NATO's bombing campaign, which had destroyed the Bosnian Serbs' perceived invincibility. As a result, a peace agreement became not just possible, but likely.

As prospects for a negotiated settlement increased, questions were raised about the underlying purpose of America's engagement in Bosnia. Two perspectives were discernible. Many in Washington believed that the principal aim of U.S. policy was to end the war in Bosnia and reestablish America's leadership position in Europe and thereby remove Bosnia as a possible issue in the pending presidential election campaign. To them, ending the violence was seen as more important than determining the specific nature of a solution to the conflict. A quite different perspective existed among those responsible for negotiating the terms of a final settlement. In addition to ending the violence, the negotiators sought to build a viable and lasting peace within the basic contours of a single, if divided, Bosnia.

The different perspectives on the essential aims of America's Bosnia policy in the latter half of 1995 had a profound impact on both the nature

[handwritten margin notes: 1, 2, 3, ∴]

[handwritten at bottom: 4. change in French Admin: Chirac]

of the agreement that emerged from the negotiations and the extent of the U.S. commitment to assist in its implementation. As Holbrooke recalls, the negotiators' strategy was to achieve as much as possible in the Dayton Accords: "What was not negotiated at Dayton would not be negotiated later. We recognized that implementation would be at least as difficult as the negotiations themselves, but we rejected the minimalist theory that we should negotiate only those matters on which implementation would be relatively easy."[9] However, since many in Washington viewed the purpose of negotiations in narrower terms—that is, to end the violence rather than build a peace—decisions on how to implement an agreement were made from this more limited perspective. As a result, officials in Washington decided to reject a broad, maximalist mandate for the NATO-led Implementation Force and they insisted a one-year deadline would be sufficient time to establish a self-sustaining balance of military forces inside Bosnia. These positions went counter to the negotiators' perspective and, in effect, repudiated Holbrooke's stated requirements.

The actual negotiations in Dayton did not resolve the contradiction between the minimalist and maximalist views, but instead incorporated it. Whereas the provisions of the Accords were highly ambitious and designed to build a lasting peace, the means for implementing them were severely limited in both scope and authority. Thus, from the outset, Dayton's implementation suffered from an "enforcement gap." The minimalist international means and mandate available to assist in implementation were insufficient to enforce full compliance with the Accords' maximalist provisions.

There are at least two reasons why this enforcement gap emerged during the policy deliberations leading up to Dayton. First, with the exception of issues related to IFOR, Washington essentially ignored the details of the negotiations, so long as the outcome was an agreement that ended the war. The negotiators therefore had a virtually free rein in deciding many of the specific terms. Always eager to maximize his flexibility and control over the negotiations, Holbrooke took full advantage of this apparent disinterest by structuring a bureaucratic process for drafting an agreement that left nearly all of Washington officialdom in the dark about the details of what would be included in the draft until just days before talks commenced in Dayton.[10]

9. Holbrooke, *To End a War*, p. 205.

10. A group of mostly young lawyers drawn from various State Department agencies and working under the supervision of Holbrooke's deputy, John Kornblum, was

Second, with the sole and important exception of IFOR's mission and mandate, little thought was given to the difficult task of implementing the highly ambitious provisions of the Accords. The power of the Office of the High Representative was strictly curtailed, budgetary resources for assisting in implementation were not identified, and little attention was paid to how the activities of the myriad of agencies involved in the civilian implementation effort would be organized and coordinated. Moreover, although Holbrooke was the architect of the Dayton Accords, he did not � change his plans to step down from office and return to private practice as of February 1996, thus leaving to others the difficult task of implementing the agreement he had crafted. What is more, before leaving office, he did nothing to ensure that someone of his stature or capability would carry on the arduous process of turning a paper agreement into reality. Holbrooke actively sought to undermine the authority and confidence of Robert Gallucci, who had been chosen by Christopher, Strobe Talbott, and Lake to lead the implementation effort, and instead promoted his deputy, John Kornblum. Yet whereas Gallucci (who had led the challenging and ultimately successful negotiations with North Korea over its nuclear weapons program) enjoyed the full confidence of senior officials throughout the U.S. government and possessed the weight necessary to pull off this immense task, Kornblum proved to have neither.

The enforcement gap inherent in the Dayton Accords was not immediately apparent to the agreement's proponents in the Clinton administration. Notwithstanding the disconnect between ends and means, the Accords succeeded in meeting the primary objectives of those who had championed U.S. engagement in Bosnia for many months. For much of the Washington policy community, Dayton signified an end to the war and, even though its implementation required the deployment of as many as 20,000 American troops, the Accords effectively removed Bosnia as an issue in the 1996 elections. To those responsible for its negotiation, Dayton provided a detailed blueprint for building a lasting peace in a more prosper-

Dayton + 1 year = December 1996, after elections

---

tasked with drafting a final agreement starting in late August and early September 1995. With the exception of Annex-1A dealing with IFOR (which fell under the purview of the Joint Chiefs of Staff and was discussed in intimate detail within the interagency process) and the question of when sanctions would be lifted (which was addressed by an interagency working group headed by Leon Fuerth, the vice president's national security adviser), the group's products were not reviewed by other agencies in the U.S. government, including the White House, until a few days before the opening of the proximity talks at Dayton. See Holbrooke, *To End a War*, pp. 170–72.

✱ *disconnect between negotiators and implementers*

ous, democratic, and multiethnic Bosnia. In this sense, Dayton represented a classic bureaucratic compromise that served the interests of two very different views of the reasons for the U.S. decision to engage in Bosnia.

Although these two visions of Bosnia could to some extent coexist within Washington policymaking circles as long as peace (or the absence of violence) was maintained, the contradiction between them became more evident as the deadline for IFOR's presence in Bosnia approached in the waning months of 1996. There were those who believed that, in ending the war, the United States had essentially achieved its principal objective. It was important to maintain deadlines, Clinton's national security adviser argued, if only to "serve notice that our only goal is to give governments and people the breathing room they must have to tackle their own problems." To remain engaged for the long term, Lake suggested, would result in "self-defeating efforts to take on responsibilities that are not ours—to create unsustainable dependencies instead of giving nations a chance to act independently. It is a dangerous hubris to believe we can build other nations. But where our own interests are engaged, we can help nations build themselves—and give them time to make a start at it."[11] In contrast, those committed to building a lasting peace in Bosnia viewed deadlines as both artificial and detrimental to meeting key objectives. Deadlines, Holbrooke maintained, "left the impression that the Serbs might be able to outwait the enforcing powers, thus encouraging delaying tactics. By laying out self-imposed time limits, the United States only weakened itself."[12]

Proponents of the two different goals did battle inside the Washington bureaucracy throughout 1996. The issue remained unresolved even after Clinton, having been safely reelected, decided to extend the deadline for troop withdrawal for an additional eighteen months, albeit for a smaller U.S. and NATO troop presence in Bosnia. The mandate of the renamed Stabilization Force (SFOR) remained limited, however, to ensuring continued compliance with the military aspects of Dayton and providing a secure environment so that others could proceed with rebuilding the essential economic, political, and social fabric of a lasting peace.[13]

11. Anthony Lake, "Defining Missions, Setting Deadlines: Meeting New Security Challenges in the Post–Cold War World," Address at George Washington University, March 6, 1996.

12. Holbrooke, *To End a War*, p. 362.

13. See "Remarks by the President in Press Availability" (White House, Office of the Press Secretary, November 15, 1996).

The decision to extend the international security presence in Bosnia without changing either its mandate or its stated goals ensured that the division on U.S. policy toward Bosnia would persist into the second Clinton administration. A discussion on how to balance the means and ends of the policy ensued at the highest levels of government in the first months of 1997, pitting the new secretary of state, Madeleine Albright, against the new secretary of defense, William Cohen. Albright argued that the enforcement gap at the heart of Dayton should be closed by augmenting the means used to ensure Dayton's full implementation. She therefore pressed for an expanded role for U.S. and NATO troops in support of civilian implementation, including arresting indicted war criminals and providing security for returning refugees. In contrast, Cohen, who had been a leading skeptic on Bosnia while still in the Senate, asserted that U.S. interests extended only to ensuring that hostilities would not resume. He favored closing the gap by downgrading the ambitiousness of the ends being sought. Cohen therefore repeatedly and publicly emphasized that the June 1998 deadline for the departure of U.S. troops was firm, and placed the onus for peace and stability in Bosnia squarely on the local leaders: "The parties will have to make that determination," he emphasized. Is peace "something they wish to pursue or do they want to go back to slaughtering each other?"[14]

The differences between Albright and Cohen were addressed in a meeting mediated by the new national security adviser, Sandy Berger, in mid-May 1997. In a detailed examination of the mission and obligations of the U.S. and NATO forces in Bosnia, top officials discussed what NATO troops would and would not do to support the civilian implementation effort. As a result of this discussion, it was decided to shift the emphasis from maintaining a troop presence in Bosnia to ensure hostilities would not resume to a more proactive stance in support of specific civilian tasks. These included providing a secure environment for refugees to return to; supporting separate military efforts to arrest indicted war criminals; forcing the demilitarization of paramilitary police forces; providing security to the International Police Task Force in vetting local police officers; and shutting down media broadcasts that undermined the international community's broader efforts to implement the Dayton Accords.[15]

14. Cited in Charles Aldinger, "Cohen Sets Time Limit on Mission in Bosnia," *Washington Times*, March 5, 1997, p. A13.

15. Madeleine Albright, "Remarks at the Annual Fleet Week Gala," Intrepid Sea-Air-Space Museum, New York, May 22, 1997; and Samuel R. Berger, "The Road

The logic of this shift in emphasis became apparent in December 1997, when President Clinton announced that the United States would remain militarily engaged alongside its NATO allies for as long as it would take for peace to become self-sustaining. There would be no more deadlines, only clear benchmarks to measure progress in meeting the goal of a lasting peace in Bosnia.[16] These benchmarks included a durable cease-fire, reconfiguration of police forces, effective judicial and election reform, free market reform, return of displaced persons, and cooperation with the war crimes tribunal.[17]

Thus two years after the Dayton Accords entered into force, President Clinton finally endorsed the view of those within his administration who argued that the fundamental goal of U.S. engagement in Bosnia would be to build a lasting peace. Yet even then the full extent of what the international community—notably the security presence—would be willing to do to bring about peace remained uncertain. Clearly, while SFOR took on a more proactive posture in 1997, its actions still fell short of the maximalist means that were necessary to achieve maximalist ends. For example, SFOR did not have a mandate to track down and arrest war criminals nor would it provide protection to individuals who might decide to return to minority areas, which helps explain why repatriation of displaced persons to minority areas has fallen woefully short of expectations.[18] Moreover, as the costs of the Kosovo peacekeeping mission next door have risen, NATO's commitment to Bosnia has declined. Thus the decision to cut SFOR's size by more than a third, to some 20,000 troops, suggests that its ability to act proactively in accordance with the precepts of the maximalists is likely to wane.[19]

Forward in Bosnia," address at Georgetown University, September 23, 1997. See also Steven Erlanger, "How Bosnia Set Stage for Albright-Cohen Conflict," *New York Times*, June 12, 1997, pp. A1, A12; Steven Erlanger, "NATO at Crossroads in Bosnia: Serb Power Struggle Is Seen as 'Defining Moment,'" *New York Times*, August 31, 1997, p. 12; and Lee Hockstadter, "Troops Seize Bosnian Serb TV Towers," *Washington Post*, October 2, 1997, pp. A1, A19.

16. "Statement by the President on Bosnia" (White House, Office of the Press Secretary, December 18, 1997).

17. "Continuation of Need for U.S. Armed Forces in Bosnia and Herzegovina–Message from the President of the United States," H. Doc. 105-223, 105 Cong. 2 sess., March 4, 1998 (Government Printing Office, 1998), p. 7.

18. The point is implicitly conceded by Richard Holbrooke in "Battles after the War," *New York Times*, September 14, 1999, p. A23.

19. "Final Communiqué: Meeting of the North Atlantic Council in Defence Ministers Session Held in Brussels." Press Release M-NAC-D(99)156 (Brussels: NATO headquarters, December 2, 1999), Para. 9.

The Meaning of Dayton

The Clinton administration's success in Dayton has had important implications for American foreign policy. Three areas, in particular, stand out. First, the way Dayton was negotiated placed primary responsibility for Bosnia's future on U.S. shoulders. As a result, the United States will be engaged—including with ground forces—for many more years to come. The only question is what purpose this long-term engagement will serve: to ensure violence does not return or to build a multiethnic, democratic, and prosperous Bosnia. Second, U.S. policy toward Bosnia in 1995 had a major impact on how the Clinton administration and others viewed the relationship between force and diplomacy, as became evident in its approach to the Iraq and Kosovo crises during its second term. Although it became a strong proponent of coercive diplomacy, the failure of this strategy in both of these cases suggests the need to reassess the way it should be employed in the future. Finally, ending the Bosnian war proved to be crucial for getting the Clinton administration's policy toward Europe back on track. Within a few years after Dayton, Clinton's vision of a Europe that is undivided, peaceful, and democratic was well on the way to becoming a reality.

Dayton and the Future of Bosnia

Although Bosnia's future fate ultimately lies in the hands of its citizens and their leaders, a major consequence of the manner in which peace was negotiated was to place much of the responsibility for turning this war-ravaged country into a stable and secure nation in U.S. hands. Dayton inaugurated a new and quite distinct approach to resolving violent conflicts. In the past, the success or failure of peace negotiations hinged on whether a particular conflict was ripe for resolution. The ripeness of a negotiating process depends upon a number of factors, the most important of which is a shared perception among the parties to the conflict that a negotiated agreement is desirable.[20] Dayton differed from this traditional negotiating method by substituting American leadership and bluster for the parties' commitment to search for a negotiated solution. This approach not only had profound implications for the stability of the agreement that was reached, but also for making implementation dependent upon the willingness of the international community, and especially the United States, to lead that effort.

20. Richard N. Haass, *Conflicts Unending: The United States and Regional Disputes* (Yale University Press, 1990), pp. 27–29.

The Dayton Accords represented a solution to the Bosnian conflict that was largely imposed on rather than reached by the parties. One party—the Bosnian Serbs—was all but absent from the actual negotiations.[21] And neither they nor the Bosnian Croats actually initialed the final Dayton Accords (although both did sign the agreement when it was presented for signature in Paris on December 14, 1995). Given the specific nature of the Bosnian conflict, it was necessary to include Slobodan Milosevic and Franjo Tudjman as key participants in the negotiations. With their close ties to the Bosnian Serbs and Croats respectively, both presidents needed to be guarantors of any deal that was to be reached. However, being included in negotiations and being guarantors of the outcome is quite different from the surrogate role the Serb and Croat presidents performed all through the Dayton talks. That role was dictated not by the specific nature of the Bosnian conflict, but by the desire to reach a peace agreement quickly. Since the parties to the conflict remained far apart, reliance on Milosevic and Tudjman as negotiating surrogates considerably eased the effort to reach an agreement.

The consequences of the Dayton approach to negotiating a peace agreement have been threefold. First, the fundamental issue that divided the parties before Dayton—whether Bosnia's future lies in reintegration or further separation—was never settled during the negotiations. Rather than resolving this issue, Dayton incorporated it, as is evident from Bosnia's complex constitutional arrangements. Although it was designed to preserve Bosnia as a multiethnic state, the Dayton constitution prescribed an extreme degree of decentralization. The two constituent entities of Bosnia were granted wide-ranging powers, including over defense, fiscal policy, and relations with neighboring states. Most importantly, by granting the entities the sole right to raise and maintain armed forces, the central government was deprived of a key attribute of sovereignty—the right to prepare for self-defense. By incorporating rather than resolving the fundamental disagreement among the parties about Bosnia's future, Dayton assured that its implementation would become little more than the continuation of conflict by other means.

Second, because the parties cannot be relied upon to ensure compliance with the provisions of the Dayton Accords, the alternative has been to look toward Zagreb and Belgrade to make sure that implementation pro-

---

21. In Dayton, Milosevic did not actually inform the Bosnian Serb delegation of the territorial compromises he had reached until the last day of the negotiations! See Holbrooke, *To End a War*, p. 310.

ceeds apace. For well over two years after Dayton was signed, successive U.S. envoys traveled not just to Bosnia, but also to Serbia and Croatia to try to overcome obstacles to implementation. Not only did such reliance further weaken any incentive for the parties to ensure Dayton's implementation, it has also had the perverse effect of limiting Washington's willingness to criticize developments inside Serbia and Croatia for fear that this could undermine the much-sought cooperation of their leaders in securing Dayton's future. Milosevic, the oft-repeated saying went, was not only the arsonist of the Balkans, but also its indispensable fireman. By assigning the Serb president this crucial role, however, the United States had less of an incentive to oppose Milosevic's actions in other areas—be it in the suppression of a vocal opposition movement at home or in undermining aspirations for autonomy in Kosovo, Montenegro, and other parts of the former Yugoslavia.

Third, the central U.S. role in forging the Dayton agreement places a premium on American involvement in its implementation and helps to explain why either pulling out or handing over much of the responsibility for enforcement to others has not been a real option. However, while a long-term U.S. and international presence in Bosnia will be necessary, its purpose is not preordained.[22] A limited purpose for the presence would be to ensure that hostilities do not resume, while leaving Bosnia's future political development largely up to the parties. Over time, the people of Bosnia may work out a *modus vivendi* that would enable them to live and prosper alongside each other. For this limited purpose, the international presence could be quite modest—perhaps no more than ten thousand troops that could be rapidly reinforced with forces stationed outside the country.

Alternatively, the purpose of remaining engaged in Bosnia can be more expansive: to forge a stable and multiethnic Bosnia through active intervention in the country's affairs. But that would require an investment that is far larger than the United States and its allies have so far been willing to make in Bosnia. It would likely involve a mandate for the international military and civilian presence that was akin to the one that has been granted by the international community in Kosovo. There, NATO troops are actively engaged in providing for public security, arresting those suspected of war crimes, and affording protection to returning refugees, as well as ethnic minorities who fear being attacked by those returning. It is the kind

22. For a more elaborate argument along these lines, see Ivo H. Daalder and Michael B. G. Froman, "Dayton: Incomplete Peace," *Foreign Affairs,* vol. 78 (November/December 1999), pp. 106–13.

of mandate that NATO and the United States have always refused to consider for Bosnia. As for the civilian presence, the UN mission in Kosovo effectively rules the territory as an international protectorate and it can, at least in theory, encourage its political and economic development in a stabilizing, possibly even democratic direction. Although the authority of the High Representative in Bosnia has been enhanced over the years, it still falls far short of what his counterpart in Kosovo has enjoyed from the outset.

In short, the United States and its allies confront an important choice in Bosnia. They can adopt the Kosovo model in an attempt to forge a more stable and secure Bosnia by becoming directly responsible for nearly every aspect of Bosnia's political, economic, and societal development and do so at costs that will far exceed those they are incurring in Kosovo. The alternative is to scale back expectations of both the pace and extent of political, economic, and societal change in Bosnia and concentrate instead on making sure that organized violence does not return to this country. So far, there is no indication that anyone is willing to pay the price of a more extensive engagement. In fact, the growing cost of the Kosovo engagement and increasing signs of retrenchment of the international presence in Bosnia point in the opposite direction. That suggests that the wiser course is to focus U.S. and allied engagement on the limited task of ensuring that force is no longer used to settle disputes in Bosnia. Since the overall cost of this more limited engagement will be far less than that required for the Kosovo model, it is likely to be far more sustainable at home and abroad over the longer term.

Relating Force to Diplomacy

The Clinton administration's Bosnia experience confirmed a key lesson about the relationship between force and diplomacy that it had learned from its earlier involvement in Haiti during the summer of 1994. In what Secretary Perry at the time referred to as "a textbook example of coercive diplomacy," the United States had sent a diplomatic mission to Haiti to convince the military leaders who had seized power from Haiti's first democratically elected president two years earlier to step down and hand control of the Haitian military and police over to a U.S.-led multinational force.[23] This diplomatic mission was backed by a very real and credible

23. Transcript of "Newsmaker Interview with Secretary Perry," on *MacNeil/Lehrer NewsHour*, September 19, 1994, p. 11. The actual textbook was written in 1971 by Alexander George, David Hall, and William Simons. For an updated and expanded version, see Alexander George and Williams Simons, *The Limits of Coercive Diplomacy*, 2d ed. (Boulder, Colo.: Westview Press, 1994).

threat of force: 20,000 U.S. troops aboard ships off the coast and en route in troop-transporting aircraft, all ready to launch a forceful invasion in a matter of hours. Once it was clear the invasion was actually under way, the Haitian military junta relented, accepting U.S. demands.

This success for coercive diplomacy was important in convincing Madeleine Albright, Anthony Lake, and others that a similar approach might work in Bosnia. By threatening decisive military action in case the parties refused to negotiate an end to the war, the endgame strategy drew on the concept. Unlike the case in Haiti, however, the situation in Bosnia actually required a full-scale demonstration of the use of force—in the form of NATO's two-week bombing campaign—to underscore the seriousness of that threat. Nevertheless, the strategy's success in bringing about a diplomatic solution convinced many in and outside the Clinton administration that the threat of force, especially of air power, was a useful tool for achieving diplomatic ends. So much so that the administration would rely on the strategy twice more: in Iraq, in order to convince Saddam Hussein to allow UN inspectors access to weapons sites; and in Kosovo, in order to persuade Milosevic to sign on to a peace plan for the region.[24] In both instances, coercive diplomacy failed to achieve the desired objective short of the actual use of force.

The issue in Iraq concerned Saddam Hussein's challenge to the right of inspectors of the UN Special Commission (UNSCOM) to conduct their business in a way that would fulfill their mandate—which was to ensure the elimination of Iraq's weapons of mass destruction and capability to launch missiles, and to monitor weapons productions sites to prevent new production. In early 1998, the United States (backed by Great Britain but not by other permanent members of the Security Council) threatened to use force unless Baghdad consented to give UNSCOM "free, full and unfettered" access to all sites in Iraq, including presidential palaces.[25] A last-minute deal worked out between Iraq and UN Secretary General Kofi

---

24. Since the use of force in Bosnia, the Clinton administration has threatened or actually employed force in two additional instances. In 1996, it sent two aircraft carriers to the Taiwan Straits as a deterrent threat to China, emphasizing that Chinese missile tests targeted around Taiwan posed a grave threat to peace. In 1998, it launched cruise missile attacks against a suspected chemical weapons facility in Sudan and terrorist training sites in Afghanistan in retaliation for the bombings of American embassies in Kenya and Ethiopia. Neither use of force, however, involved an exercise of coercive diplomacy.

25. "Remarks by the President on Iraq to Pentagon Personnel" (White House, Office of the Press Secretary, February 17, 1998), p. 3.

Annan temporarily averted a military confrontation.[26] But that deal, too, was soon violated by Iraq, leaving the Clinton administration little choice but once again to threaten and then use force. In mid-December 1998, the United States launched Operation Desert Fox, which, in President Clinton's words, was "designed to degrade Saddam's capacity to develop and deliver weapons of mass destruction, and to degrade his ability to threaten his neighbors."[27] The four-day operation damaged weapons development and production facilities, disrupted the security apparatus protecting weapons programs, and degraded Iraq's conventional military capability.[28] However, the UNSCOM inspectors who were withdrawn prior to the air strikes were not allowed back in, leaving the Clinton administration only with the threat of further military action and with the hope of an eventual change of regime in Baghdad to contain Iraq's ambitions. In this instance, force was unable to compensate for the failure of coercive diplomacy.

Coercive diplomacy was also the preferred strategy for the Kosovo crisis.[29] The Clinton administration first employed the threat of air strikes in the early fall of 1998 to buttress a UN Security Council demand for a cessation of Serb attacks against the predominantly ethnic Albanian population and the withdrawal of some military and police forces from the territory. Although Milosevic acceded in principle to these demands in October following talks with Richard Holbrooke, in practice he soon violated every provision of the agreement. In early 1999, the administration once again resorted to coercive diplomacy when it presented the Serbs and Kosovar Albanians with a detailed plan to resolve their differences. They were given two weeks to accept the plan's terms or else face military consequences: air strikes in the case of the Serbs and abandonment in the case

26. In a nod to coercive diplomacy, Annan made clear that the deal was made possible by the threat of force. "Diplomacy can be effective, but it helps to have a military presence in the region," he emphasized. "You can do a lot with diplomacy, but with diplomacy backed up by force you can get a lot more done." See transcript of "Press Conference by Secretary General Kofi Annan at United Nations Headquarters," UN Press Release, SG/SM/6470 (New York: United Nations, February 24, 1998), p. 2.

27. "Address by the President to the Nation on Iraq Air Strike" (White House, Office of the Press Secretary, December 16, 1998), p. 3.

28. "Remarks by Samuel R. Berger at the National Press Club" (White House, Office of the Press Secretary, December 23, 1998), p. 2.

29. For a more detailed examination, see Ivo H. Daalder and Michael E. O'Hanlon, *Winning Ugly: NATO's War to Save Kosovo* (Brookings, forthcoming).

of the Kosovars.[30] This time, coercive diplomacy failed—as did the attempt to demonstrate NATO's resolve by launching limited air strikes against Serbia following Belgrade's refusal to sign on to the plan. Instead, the Serbs escalated their campaign of the forced expulsion of ethnic Albanians that had already been underway. In response, the United States and its NATO allies were forced to abandon coercive diplomacy and embark instead on a major military operation.[31] Despite its initial failure to prevent the Serb onslaught against Kosovo's civilian population, the war ended successfully when Milosevic agreed to withdraw all Serb forces from the area and accepted the deployment of a 50,000-strong NATO force. As a result, the nearly one million refugees created by the conflict returned to Kosovo to rebuild their shattered lives in peace and safety.

Haiti, Bosnia, Iraq, and Kosovo show both the promise and the limits of coercive diplomacy. The promise lies in effecting a diplomatic outcome without having to incur the cost of using force—as proved to be possible in Haiti. Whether diplomacy in Bosnia could have succeeded without the actual use of force—by Croatia on the ground and NATO from the air— is impossible to know. But it seems clear that the actual use of force provided a much firmer basis for conducting diplomacy than would have been the case if force had not been used.

Iraq and Kosovo demonstrate the limits of coercive diplomacy, at least as applied by the Clinton administration in these two cases. Both instances were characterized by the absence of two critical requirements for success: first, a threat of military action that is credible in the eyes of the intended target; and second, a military strategy that demonstrates how a clearly defined objective can be achieved decisively if force is to be used. The threat of air strikes lacked credibility in the eyes of the Iraqi and Serb leaders, in part because neither cared much about the physical destruction or human suffering that force could inflict on their countries. Their credibility was further undermined by a lack of follow-through on earlier threats

30. "Secretary of State Madeleine K. Albright Remarks and Q&A Session at the U.S. Institute of Peace" (Department of State, Office of the Spokesman, February 4, 1999), p. 3.

31. The notion that the Kosovo war constituted a form of coercive diplomacy—as propounded by NATO's supreme allied commander, General Wesley Clark, among others—is fallacious. Just because the war excluded the use of ground forces and aimed (at least initially) to coerce Milosevic to accept the terms of the peace plan does not mean it was not a war. For Clark's statement, see "Clark Looks Back on Kosovo Conflict," *Defense Week*, August 23, 1999, p. 7.

of military action. In the case of Iraq, Baghdad's open defiance of the UN inspection regime dated back to at least November 1997; yet it took thirteen months to make good on the threat to use force first made explicit at that time. In Kosovo, the Serb crackdown that commenced in March 1998 was not met by a military response nor by a repeat of the threat that Presidents George Bush and Bill Clinton had issued years earlier to deter Serb military action in the province.[32] Periodic threats of air strikes thereafter also proved to be without substance. Even the clear and unambiguous violation of the October agreement produced yet more diplomacy and more threats rather than military action. In short, the U.S. reputation for following through on its threats to use force was severely weakened over time, undermining both their credibility and usefulness in backing up diplomacy.

Second, in both Iraq and Kosovo the threat of force was not tied to a military strategy that assured success if force had to be used. Instead, the objective was left vague; the degradation of military capabilities is not something that is easily measured, even if success can be readily claimed. Without a clear objective, the actual use of force becomes problematic, leading to calls either for its early termination or for further escalation. In the case of Iraq, the bombing ended in four days, even though there were many voices calling for continuing the campaign to force Saddam from power. In Kosovo, the campaign finally succeeded, but only after NATO defined its goals in unambiguous terms: Serbs out, NATO in, and refugees back. Even then, success required that Washington make clear that it intended to prevail at any cost, including by using ground troops if necessary.

Coercive diplomacy is an important and often useful tool for dealing with difficult and important foreign policy problems. As the cases of Haiti and Bosnia show, it can be successful. However, coercive diplomacy is

---

32. In December 1992, President Bush warned Milosevic that "in the event of conflict in Kosovo caused by Serbian action, the United States will be prepared to employ military force against the Serbs in Kosovo and in Serbia proper." Quoted in David Binder, "Bush Warns Serbs Not to Widen War," *New York Times*, December 28, 1992, p. A6. The threat was reiterated early in the Clinton administration. Yet when the crackdown occurred in 1998, the administration only noted that it had "a broad range of options available to us and we do not rule anything out, but we are not going to speculate now about what the appropriate response would be to the circumstances as they evolve." See "Press Briefing of Madeleine K. Albright and Lamberto Dini" (Rome: Department of State, Office of the Spokesman, March 7, 1998), p. 3.

neither a substitute for diplomacy nor an alternative to using force. It requires a capacity and willingness to do both. Most importantly, coercive diplomacy is unlikely to succeed unless it is backed by a credible and achievable strategy for employing force decisively to achieve clearly defined objectives.

A Europe Undivided, Peaceful, and Democratic

The war in Bosnia had profound implications for the Clinton administration's Europe policy. So long as the war festered, it proved impossible to exploit the opportunities created by the collapse of communism, the unification of Germany, and the dissolution of both the Soviet empire in eastern Europe and the Soviet Union itself to foster a more stable and secure European order. As early as January 1994, President Clinton had laid out both a vision for such a new order and a strategy for achieving it.[33] The vision was one of integrating the former communist half into the rest of Europe; of building a Europe that was undivided, peaceful, and democratic. The strategy for achieving it combined cooperating on military matters, building prosperous market economies, and developing strong democracies. The Partnership for Peace, launched at the 1994 Brussels Summit, and the prospect of membership in both NATO and the European Union were seen as the central tools for making the strategy work.

Bosnia proved to be a major stumbling block for realizing the administration's vision for Europe. The failure to end the war—or even to forge an agreed allied strategy—dominated all aspects of Europe and alliance policy, including the very NATO summit meeting where President Clinton launched his Europe initiative. As long as the war continued, NATO remained divided, further dimming any prospect for using the alliance to help integrate the other parts of Europe. It was this realization that led Clinton's top advisers in November 1994 to recommend that efforts to resolve Bosnia ought to take a back seat to efforts to bolster alliance unity.[34] America's strategic interests required a strong, united NATO; compared to that, Bosnia was a distinctly secondary issue. At a ministerial meeting of the North Atlantic Council in early December, Secretary Christopher consciously tried to delink Bosnia from NATO: "The crisis in Bosnia is

33. "Remarks by the President to Multinational Audience of Future Leaders of Europe" (Brussels: White House, Office of the Press Secretary, January 9, 1994).
34. See the discussion above, pp. 33–35.

about Bosnia and the former Yugoslavia; it does not diminish NATO's enduring importance. . . . [It] does not diminish our responsibility to build a comprehensive European security architecture that consolidates stability, addresses today's conflicts, and prevents others from happening in the future. On the contrary, the tragedy in the former Yugoslavia underscores the urgency of that task."[35]

Christopher and others would soon realize that the effort to delink Bosnia from NATO's future—indeed, from Europe's stability—was futile. If Bosnia, as Richard Holbrooke argued in early 1995, was "the greatest collective security failure of the West since the 1930s,"[36] its resolution was central to developing a new sense of purpose for the alliance. Christopher later conceded that the administration's Europe policy stood or fell on Bosnia, thus providing added impetus to the search for an end to the war.[37] Undoubtedly, success in Dayton did have this intended effect. It did much to restore NATO's credibility, particularly given the alliance's central role in the military efforts that both preceded and followed the negotiation of the peace accords in late 1995.

Dayton opened the door to NATO's transformation from a collective defense organization focused on defending against a threat to allied territory from the East to an instrument for extending the stability and security its members had long enjoyed to other parts of Europe. The means to that end involved two commitments: first, to open the membership door to any European country that both met the criteria for membership and desired to join; and, second, to use its military capabilities to back up efforts to resolve conflicts throughout Europe and help implement peace agreements that emerge as a result.[38] The first commitment became a reality in 1997, when the Czech Republic, Hungary, and Poland were invited to join NATO, which they did in March 1999. The second commitment was implemented first in Bosnia and subsequently in Kosovo, together making NATO the major military presence in that part of Europe.

---

35. Warren Christopher, "A Time of Historic Challenge for NATO" (Brussels: North Atlantic Council, December 1, 1994). Reprinted in Warren Christopher, *In the Stream of History: Shaping Foreign Policy for a New Era* (Stanford University Press, 1998), p. 232.

36. Richard Holbrooke, "America, A European Power," *Foreign Affairs*, vol. 74 (March/April 1995), p. 40.

37. Christopher, *In the Stream of History*, p. 230.

38. Ivo H. Daalder, *NATO at 50: The Summit & Beyond*, Brookings Policy Brief 48 (April 1999).

* * *

In the end, the United States made the right decision in becoming involved in Bosnia and it did so in the right way. If the conflict in this war-ravaged country was a cancer threatening to metastasize and envelop not only the Clinton presidency but also American foreign policy on a broad scale, then the decision to take the lead in ending the war was at once the most radical and the most successful way to ensure that the cancer was removed. Most immediately, the American intervention ended Europe's most bloody conflict since the end of World War II. For more than three years, the people of Bosnia had suffered unspeakable horrors and crimes. Dayton put an end to that.

Equally significant is the fact that at the cusp of a new century the project of building a Europe that is undivided, peaceful, and democratic is closer to being realized than at any time before. The significant effort that went into ending the war in Bosnia opened up new opportunities to move this crucial project forward. NATO accepted as a new and critical mission the need to extend security and stability to all parts of Europe. Its membership doors have been opened to all that meet the necessary criteria and desire to join, and allied troops are now deployed to areas far beyond their territory to enforce the peace. There now exists a new consensus among NATO's current and aspirant members on how Europe's stability and security must be assured. The road to such an undivided, peaceful, and democratic continent remains full of obstacles—as the war in Kosovo and continued uncertainty about Russia's political and economic future readily underscore. But Dayton proved that it is a road well worth traveling.

Index